What Is Theology?

John D. Caputo, *series editor*

PERSPECTIVES IN
CONTINENTAL
PHILOSOPHY

ADAM KOTSKO

What Is Theology?
Christian Thought
and Contemporary Life

FORDHAM UNIVERSITY PRESS
New York ▪ 2021

Visit us online at www.fordhampress.com.

Library of Congress Cataloging-in-Publication Data

Names: Kotsko, Adam, author.
Title: What is theology? : Christian thought and contemporary life / Adam Kotsko.
Description: New York : Fordham University Press, 2021. | Series: Perspectives in continental philosophy | Includes bibliographical references and index.
Identifiers: LCCN 2021027353 | ISBN 9780823297818 (hardback) | ISBN 9780823297825 (paperback) | ISBN 9780823297832 (epub)
Subjects: LCSH: Theology.
Classification: LCC BR118 .K685 2021 | DDC 230—dc23
LC record available at https://lccn.loc.gov/2021027353

Printed in the United States of America

23 22 21   5 4 3 2 1

First edition

In memory of Ted Jennings

Contents

PART III: THEOLOGY AND THE GENEALOGY OF THE MODERN WORLD

Preface

The materials that make up this book cover a period of fifteen years, but the work of assembling this manuscript—collecting and revising older pieces and drafting the new material that makes up the majority of the text—took place in the summer of 2020. Those who lived through those devastating and tumultuous months, which in the United States were marked by a global pandemic, the vast wave of Black Lives Matter protests, and the malicious and inept government response to both, might envy me the opportunity to direct my attention away from the chaos engulfing us and meditate on things eternal. That is how Anselm presents the theological task, for instance, when he opens his famous *Proslogion* with these calming and welcoming words:

> Come now, insignificant man, fly for a moment from your affairs, escape for a little while from the tumult of your thoughts. Put aside now your weighty cares and leave your wearisome toils. Abandon yourself for a little to God and rest for a little in Him. Enter into the inner chamber of your soul, shut out everything save God and what can be of help in your quest for Him and having locked the door seek him out.[1]

There is something deeply appealing in Anselm's approach, but it is not one that is available to me, because this book is not about God. It is about theology. That means that it is about human systems of thought that, while claiming to be responding in some way to the divine, are always also responding to human questions. In the words of my late mentor and friend

Ted Jennings, "Theology is an entirely secular, profane human discipline,"[2] "an inquiry into the meaning of human life pursued by fallible human beings for whom the meaning of their own lives and that of their neighbors is at stake."[3]

As a human discourse, theology is also necessarily a critical discourse. Socrates famously claimed that philosophy begins in wonder, but theology finds its starting point in dissatisfaction, even irritation. As Jennings observes, "Students in college or seminary who commence upon the tasks of theological reflection frequently do so out of a sense of the inadequacy of the life of the church out of which they come."[4] That was certainly the case for me. While many factors contributed to my decision to study theology rather than literature or philosophy, in retrospect I chose to pursue theology out of a sense that Christianity was in the process of ruining my life and the lives of those around me and would continue to do so until I figured out how it was doing so and how to make it stop. Others may have gone into theology for less desperate reasons, but no one chooses to do theology because they are certain and satisfied in their religious beliefs. In my experience, such people avoid theological reflection like the plague—and so I leave them to their own devices, since, in any case, "there is often better theological reflection occurring over beer in some pubs than in many churches or schools of theology."[5]

This book represents a series of approaches to theology as a critical human discourse, in light of an ever-expanding awareness of the degree to which Christianity is ruining all our lives. The introductory essay, "What Is Theology?," explores the complex and ever-shifting relationship between theology and philosophy from the perspective of the emergent discipline known as political theology, thereby establishing a basic framework within which the subsequent essays can be understood as contributing to a shared project. There is admittedly an element of artificiality in the gesture of beginning the collection with this essay, since—as often happens with methodological reflections—it was actually the last piece to be written. Yet in reviewing my past writings to determine which pieces might be suitable for the present collection, I could not help but recall a conversation with Giorgio Agamben in which he revealed that "when he returns to his earliest texts, he always finds that his key concepts were somehow present—'but I didn't know it at the time.'"[6] The further removed in time, of course, the more distant the terminology and approach are from that laid out in the introduction, but all the essays I ultimately chose to include here reflect, each in its own way, the same basic style of thought and set of concerns that I have carried forward into my most recent writings.

The main body of the text is divided into three parts, with three essays each. The grouping is broadly chronological in the sense that most of the essays in Part I are earlier than those in Part II, most of which are in turn earlier than those in Part III. Yet it should not be taken as indicating any kind of necessary development or continuous argument. Although I was tempted to revise the older essays in a way that would render the connections among them more immediately evident—in particular their connection to the framework laid out in the introductory essay—I ultimately limited myself to smaller clarifications and corrections, along with some changes to the titles and section headings.[7] This minimal approach is meant to maintain the fundamental character of these essays in light of the fact that they were previously published and to illustrate that the approach to theology I advocate here can take a variety of forms in practice. More broadly, I have sought to make each essay, even those that were written within a relatively short span of time, as self-contained as possible. Hence, although I have arranged them with the intent that they will have a par-ticular cumulative effect when read in order, readers should feel free to skip around based on their own interests and inclinations.

The three parts focus, in turn, on three aspects of the distinctive ap-proach to theology that this collection aims to explore. The first part, "The-ology beyond the Limits of Religion Alone," consists of a series of attempts at constructive theology outside the institutional confines of "religion"; the second, "Theology under Philosophical Critique," consists of a series of at-tempts to make sense of theological materials from a philosophical per-spective; and the third, "Theology and the Genealogy of the Modern World," consists of a series of genealogical investigations of the subterra-nean impact of theology on the secular world under the heading of politi-cal theology. Given that all three of these tasks are intimately interconnected, there is necessarily some overlap, such that two of the essays in Part I draw extensively on philosophy, for instance, and several of the essays in Parts I or II could be construed as genealogical in some way.

This overlap is true above all in the first essay of Part I, "Bonhoeffer on Continuity and Crisis: From Objective Spirit to Religionless Christianity." There I argue that Bonhoeffer's entire theological project, from his earliest publications to the *Letters and Papers from Prison*, is marked by an attempt to come to terms with the fact that the church is a social institution like any other. These reflections begin from the Hegelian concept of "objective spirit," which designates the impersonal cultural deposit that forms a nec-essary part of any social group. Over the course of his career, Bonhoeffer becomes increasingly convinced that the "objective spirit" of the Christian church has become an active obstacle to Christian discipleship, above all in its embrace of an otherworldly and individualistic concept of "religion." His final writings call for a "religionless Christianity" that would radically reconfigure the place of the church in a modern world that has no further need of God. While lacking the explicit conceptual framework that informs my more recent work, this essay is nonetheless foundational in that it presents Bonhoeffer as a model for the approach to theology that I am advocating. Indeed, my reading of Bonhoeffer even anticipates the structure of this book, insofar as it presents him as developing a constructive position that grows out of serious critical engagement with philosophy and a bracing honesty about the unintended and undesirable consequences of historic Christianity.

The second essay in Part I, "Resurrection without Religion," attempts to apply Bonhoeffer's "religionless" theological method to the doctrine of the resurrection of the dead. Through a careful sifting of the biblical evidence, this essay argues that the resurrection of the dead is less a miraculous event promised for the future than a warrant for living a life of radical community and radical fearlessness in the present. Rounding out Part I is "Toward a Materialist Theology: Slavoj Žižek on Thinking God beyond the Master Signifier," which explores and expands on the work of Žižek, who, like Bonhoeffer, attempts to find a new future for Christian theology after the "death of God." My investigation focuses on the ways that the theological tradition has presented God as a tautological and unquestionable "master signifier" that holds the world together. Reading Augustine and Pseudo-Dionysus through the lens of Žižek's work on theology, I claim, allows us to construct a new concept of God, not as the unchanging foundation for the world as we know it, but as the principle of endless transformation.

The essays in Part II all center on an encounter between theology and philosophy, but unlike Part I they each adopt a philosophical perspective. The first essay, "The Failed Divine Performative: Reading Judith Butler's Critique of Theology with Anselm's *On the Fall of the Devil*," argues that Butler consistently uses the term "theology" to designate any discourse—including the apparently atheistic thought of Lacan—that erects a transcendent standard that sets human subjects up for perpetual failure. After clarifying her understanding of "theology" through a close reading of her works up through *The Psychic Life of Power*, I stage a dialogue between Butler and Anselm, finding that her critique does apply to the medieval theologian's account of the fall of the devil, but does not exhaust the potential of Anselm's thought. The second essay, "Translation, Hospitality, and Supersession: Lamin Sanneh and Jacques Derrida on the Future of Christianity," is a comparison of a leading theorist of the phenomenon of "global

Christianity" and a leading European philosopher. Playing Sanneh's focus on the "translatability" of Christianity off of Derrida's examination of hospitality as central to the Abrahamic traditions, it argues that both thinkers fall into supersessionist patterns of thought. The final essay of this section, "Agamben the Theologian," explores the Italian philosopher's unique approach to theology, arguing that he downplays the distinctiveness of theological materials but at the same time seems to require theological concepts to achieve his highest goals.

Part III turns to the task of political theology. The first essay, "The Problem of Evil and the Problem of Legitimacy," attempts to expand the definition of political theology beyond the traditional focus on the homology between divine and human sovereignty and the question of secularization by placing it in the context of the Hebrew biblical tradition. There God and the earthly ruler, far from constituting an easy parallel, are bitter rivals, as the God of a marginal and dispersed nation struggles to assert his control over all the world. Within this framework, we can see that the more foundational homology for political theology is that between the problem of evil and the problem of legitimacy, which both attempt to shore up systems of authority in the face of events that threaten to discredit them.

The remainder of Part III puts this concept of political theology to work to explore the theological roots of the modern concept of race. These final two essays, even more than the others, are true essays in the etymological sense of a "try" or "attempt." They should be read not as definitive statements but as provisional reports on ongoing research. "Modernity's Original Sin: Toward a Theological Genealogy of Race" approaches the question of race from the perspective of individual racialized subjects, who are always treated as though they are to blame for the irremediable fact of their racial descent. Drawing on key texts in contemporary Black Studies, I argue that the intertwined doctrines of original sin and demonology gave Christians long centuries of practice in paradoxically holding God's creatures morally responsible for the conditions of their birth and that the figure of the Jew provided the model for a more intensified version of original sin that applies only to particular human subgroups. In "The Trinitarian Century: God, Governance, and Race," I come at the same issue from the perspective of the modern system of racialization, which has proved to be a tragically durable model of global governance in the colonial and postcolonial eras. Starting from Giorgio Agamben's contention that the doctrine of the Trinity is not primarily about the mystery of God's inner life but about the divine governance of the world, I show how God's governance in the Hebrew biblical tradition always required two distinct modes of agency (direct and indirect), which map out onto two human groups

(Jew and Gentile) with two different moral valences (faithful and wicked). After tracing the shift Christianity introduces into these complex dynamics, I argue, in dialogue with Jared Hickman's pathbreaking work *Black Prometheus*, that the modern racialized world-system represents a destructive new variation on the trinitarian theme.

Clearly this collection of essays cannot claim to constitute an exhaustive account of the meaning and promise of theology. The figures and topics chosen reflect the vagaries of my own intellectual trajectory, meaning that many relevant thinkers are omitted or dealt with only in passing and many important issues—such as gender and sexuality—appear primarily in supporting roles. Beyond that, there are occasional contradictions among the essays, reflecting developments in my own thought. For instance, the Bonhoeffer and resurrection essays reflect a much more optimistic view of Christian community than the later genealogical essays, and the reading of Agamben's *Kingdom and the Glory* is much less critical in "The Problem of Evil and the Problem of Legitimacy" than in "The Trinitarian Century." And even when there is no explicit counterpoint in the present volume, some essays reflect themes and figures that I have largely left aside in the intervening years.

The biggest gap between the earlier and later essays, however, is the growing centrality of the question of race—a development in my thought that began with *The Prince of This World* and that has led to an ever deeper engagement with the field of Black Studies. These investigations explain another potentially surprising aspect of this collection, namely the central role of Sylvia Wynter, above all in the title essay, where the Jamaican playwright, novelist, and critic is perhaps unexpectedly discussed alongside such canonical figures as Plato and Augustine. I have found Wynter to be an increasingly crucial interlocutor because her excavation of the foundations of modernity resonates deeply with my conception of the task of political theology at the same time that her hope for a true secularism and a true transcultural scientific knowledge represents a continual challenge to my insistence on the irreducibility of the theological legacy.

Perhaps the most idiosyncratic feature of this collection is that the essays chart a somewhat counterintuitive path from constructive theological work to more critical and genealogical approaches. Common sense would seem to dictate the opposite approach, moving from criticism to a positive alternative. Why the reversal? From a certain perspective, this apparently inverted course could be seen as nothing more than a reflection of the course of my own career—for instance, the fact that I have done most of my teaching in an interdisciplinary Great Books program rather than a seminary or department of theology. Yet I believe that the shift from construction to critique does represent a deeper necessity, insofar as every critique that aspires to be more than a purely negative criticism is motivated by a certain hope, or in other words, by the anticipation, however vague, of what a positive alternative might look like. Reviewing my earliest publications, I am struck by my fervent hope that theological reflection could point the way toward a new conception of human community that breaks with the individualism and self-satisfaction of contemporary Christianity in order to engage authentically with the world and all its most urgent problems. To do that kind of work with honesty and integrity, however, I recognized the need to grapple with the negative effects of Christianity—not dismissing them as betrayals or mistakes, but taking them seriously as plausible outgrowths of the Christian message.

After my initial burst of constructive theological reflection, therefore, I have largely followed the path of critique and genealogy and plan to continue primarily in that vein for the foreseeable future. Yet as every essay in this collection shows in some way, I still manage to cling to my hope against hope that theological reflection can lead us to a new and more livable form of human community. If we wish to reimagine theology as a liberatory practice, however, we must allow ourselves to admit how many times it has been—not been mistaken for, not been abused as, but *really been*—a tool of domination, destruction, and death. Hence I hope that this volume can stand as a challenge and a provocation to a theological establishment that has allowed sentimental moralism, wishful thinking, and institutional self-regard to take the place of real theological work. At the same time, I hope it can equally stand as a challenge and a provocation to those—among whom I can sometimes count myself—who wish that they could wash their hands of theology once and for all. Theology names an irreducible necessity of human thought and community, one that too many people of good will have dismissed as irrelevant or somehow inherently oppressive, effectively ceding the power of theology to the liars, fools, and sadists who have transformed our world into a living nightmare. They have succeeded where we have mostly failed because they recognize intuitively what the work of genealogy never fails to show us: theology is not a scholarly game or an edifying spiritual discipline, but a world-shaping force of great power. Lives are at stake when we do theology—and if we don't do it, someone else will.

What Is Theology?

Introduction
What Is Theology?

What is conventionally called the Western tradition has been marked by a rivalry between two discourses that aspire to the widest possible scope: philosophy and Christian theology. The relationship between the two has taken very different forms at different historical moments. When Christian theology was first emerging as a systematic discipline, philosophy provided both a model and a provocation. During the medieval period, by contrast, Christian theology confidently declared itself the "queen of the sciences" and relegated philosophy to the status of a "handmaid." And in early modernity, as philosophy once again asserted its priority in a secular scientific age, many philosophers tried to legitimate their innovations by presenting them as expressions of the deepest truths of Christianity.

By most accounts, the struggle between these two purported "theories of everything" has fallen by the wayside in the contemporary world. Secularism has rendered Christian theology an apparently provincial and anachronistic concern, while the natural sciences and economics are now widely regarded as the most promising candidates for the kind of holistic account of the natural and social world to which philosophy long aspired. To the extent that these two great rivals have a role to play in contemporary intellectual life, it is much diminished. Theology, when it is not reduced to a simple punching bag in secular rhetoric, survives as a way of articulating the self-understanding of particular religious groups. Philosophy plays a slightly more glamorous role as either a methodological propaedeutic for the humanities and theoretical social sciences (in its "continental" vein) or else as a largely gratuitous handmaid to the sciences (in its "analytic" variant).

In this Introduction, however, I want to argue that rethinking this seemingly outdated rivalry between two hugely ambitious modes of thought can provide unexpected resources for reimagining a livable future in the modern world that the West has created. I do not want to be misunderstood here. I do not intend to claim that if we simply redoubled our efforts to find the most "correct" philosophy or the most "authentic" version of Christian theology, all would be well. I do not deny the benefits and even necessity of continued creative work in philosophy and theology, but for the purposes of this Introduction, I am only indirectly concerned with their contemporary continuations. My focus is on the ways that the encounter between philosophy and theology in the premodern period set the most fundamental parameters of Western thought in a way that has been carried over into modernity and continues to structure—and thwart—our attempts to conceive a better world.

My goal is ultimately to show the contingency of the West's philosophy-theology system, but I will also need to account for the apparent necessity or self-evidence of the pairing. To the latter end, I will be offering a kind of typology of the two disciplines, one that starts from each discourse's own self-understanding. Of course no typology—including the many classic typologies that dotted the theological landscape in the twentieth century (e.g., Aulen's *Christus Victor*, Niebuhr's *Christ and Culture*, Nygren's *Eros and Agape*, Dulles's *Models of the Church*)—can claim to be fully exhaustive or definitive. A successful typology is one whose productivity for thought outweighs the unavoidable costs of simplification and omission. In order to ground my typology more concretely—and leaven it, as it were, with contingency—I will be focusing on two towering figures in the Western tradition, Plato and Augustine, who are at once exemplary of their respective fields and yet undeniably idiosyncratic thinkers. In the case of Augustine in particular, it is easy to imagine the Latin Christian tradition taking a completely different direction if the "luck of the draw" had enshrined another thinker as foundational. More than that, though, I am drawn to Plato and Augustine because their remarkable attention to the political allows them to stand as models for the deadlocks of their respective fields when it comes to the question of political change.

I hope that by this point it is clear that I am not approaching the relationship between philosophy and theology from either a philosophical or a theological perspective. Instead, I will be adopting a third vantage point, one that has been designated as "political theology." At first glance, the juxtaposition of these two terms may evoke ideas of a politically engaged theology or a theologization of politics that treats it as a kind of religion. In my understanding of political theology, by contrast, the name serves fundamentally as an emblem of the field's rejection of the modern secular truism that politics and theology are supposed to be kept rigorously separate. From a secular perspective, religion is a purely private affair, and citizens should ideally keep their theological beliefs (if any) to themselves when engaging in public political discourse. On those unfortunate occasions when theology manages to insinuate itself into the political realm, mainstream liberal discourse presents it as an outburst of purely nihilistic violence (Islamic extremism), a corruption of religion (right-wing evangelicalism), or, at best, a quixotic effort doomed to failure (as in many accounts of Latin American liberation theology). By contrast, political theology asserts that politics and theology are inextricably intertwined, always and everywhere—hence the political relevance of my apparently abstract and antiquarian investigation here.

Secular modernity may claim to have separated the political and the theological, but that in itself is at once a political and a theological claim. It is a political claim because it addresses the distribution of power in society (in this case, between state and religious institutions), and it is a theological claim because it lays down a theological standard for what is to be regarded as an acceptable religion within the modern secular regime (i.e., one that is content with its "private" role). The inescapably political and theological nature even of secular modernity shows us that political theology *does* concern itself with both politically engaged theologies and theologically informed politics—with the proviso that in neither case is there any other kind, because it is impossible to do one without the other. We can see why this is the case if we define theology broadly as any set of ultimate normative values and politics as the attempt to organize and regulate human life. The two pursuits necessarily belong together, because every set of normative values envisions a certain organization and regulation of life, and every organization and regulation of human life are informed by normative values.

While stated values and actual political practice are often at odds, political theology claims that in any given historical moment, political and theological systems tend to correspond, meaning that they assume the same overall "shape." To use the example that was foundational for political theology, a society that espouses absolute monarchy will tend to embrace a similarly absolute monotheism, and by contrast—drawing on my own political theological work on contemporary neoliberalism—a society that values individual choice and responsibility above all will tend to have dispersed and disorganized centers of power.[1]

Drawing an analogy with Thomas Kuhn's famous account of the history of science, I have designated the political theological configuration that prevails in any given place and time as a "paradigm."[2] The analogy holds in two ways. First, like Kuhn's scientific paradigms, a political theological paradigm unites theory and practice into a cohesive whole for a given segment of the scientific community, giving researchers a durable framework that designates certain kinds of experiments and results as the most relevant and valuable. Second, both scientific paradigms and their political theological counterparts are ultimately partial and unstable. For Kuhn, every scientific paradigm is one anomalous result away from being toppled, and in my view of political theology, every political theological paradigm is one serious disaster or sickening injustice away from meeting its demise.

This vulnerability stems from the fact that both political and theological systems claim to be not just descriptive, but prescriptive. It is not just that the king happens to be the person who commands the loyalty of the greatest number of armed men, but that he *deserves* to be king. It is not just that God happens to be the most powerful entity in the universe, but that he is *worthy* of our worship and obedience. In other words, every political theological paradigm is founded on a claim of the legitimacy of the current order, a claim that the political-theological system reflects the way that the world is and ought to be. In the normal run of things, most people living under a particular paradigm (or at least enough of those with the power to do anything about it) will find its claims to legitimacy convincing enough to go along with it. But no human system can account for every possible eventuality. An unforeseen disaster that catches the system unawares or—even worse—an unanticipated and seemingly perverse result of the system's own internal logic can shatter the system's legitimacy, opening the way for its reform or replacement.

At this point, we are in a position to say two things about the "theology" in political theology. The first is that political theology views every form of "theology" from a broadly secular perspective, in the sense that it brackets the question of divine inspiration and focuses on the human construction of theological systems. The second is that both Christian theology and philosophy—or indeed, any articulation of the two into a single coherent system—could be seen as a "theology" in political theology's broad sense of the term. This might count as an answer to my title question, but not a very interesting or informative one. If anything, it only raises the further question of why the term political *theology* was chosen in the first place, instead of a more neutral one such as political ontology.[3]

While I will be returning to that question in my conclusion, for now I would like to set it aside and point out that political theology's broad definition of "theology" fails to account for the observation with which I opened this Introduction, namely that the so-called Western tradition is characterized by not one but *two* competing comprehensive value systems (or "theologies" in the broad sense), only one of which self-identifies as theological. It may well be productive from certain perspectives to regard those two systems as somehow "the same thing." But such an approach certainly does not do justice to the fact that the two discourses have most often viewed each other not simply as two competing versions of the same basic pursuit (like Aristotelianism and Neoplatonism or Catholicism and Protestantism), but as qualitatively different in a way that remained decisive even in those cases where they were collaborators rather than outright rivals.

I begin my investigation by treating philosophy and theology in turn, based on a close reading of the exemplary figures of Plato and Augustine, before turning to an abstract and speculative account of the legacy of the rivalry between the two discourses in modernity. My guiding hypothesis is that the conflict and, at the same time, the uneasy cohabitation of these two master discourses reflect a political deadlock in the ancient and medieval world, which made it very difficult, at least for elite thinkers, to take seriously the possibility of systematic, rational social and political transformation. This deadlock led each discourse into a kind of political fatalism that came to seem increasingly self-evident—at least until the event of 1492 unleashed a radical and unavoidable transformation at both the political and theological levels. In critical dialogue with Sylvia Wynter's magisterial account of the structure and consequences of that inaugural event of modernity—an account that very intentionally keeps its distance from both philosophy and theology—I will argue that the traditional "division of labor" between the two master discourses of the West collapsed into a new dynamic that was not just politically impotent but actively harmful. Only by interrogating and reconfiguring the contemporary patterns of thought that, in unexpected and unacknowledged ways, grew out of the post-1492 reconfiguration of the philosophy-theology dyad can we begin to direct and control what Wynter, following Frantz Fanon, calls "sociogeny"—the production and reproduction of our shared social world.

Philosophy and the Perennial

It is by no means obvious at first glance that philosophy and theology should be at odds with each other. In fact, the Greek term *theologia* was first coined by Plato in Book II of the *Republic*.[4] The context is, fittingly enough from my political-theological perspective, the place of stories about the gods in the ideal political order. After recounting some of the most objectionable Greek myths, Socrates declares that "it's absolutely not fit to say that gods make war on gods and plot against them and fight them, since it's not even true" (378c). Such stories as we find in Homer and the other poets "are not to be allowed into the city, whether they've been made with or without deeper meanings. A young person isn't able to discern what's a deeper meaning and what's not, but what he takes in among his opinions when he's that age tends to become hard to rub off and impossible to change" (378d–e). Given the important role of stories about the gods in shaping the younger generation, Socrates's interlocutor concludes that it is important for any prospective city-founder to get a grasp of "the general outlines for talk about the gods [*theologias*]" (379a). This newly established science of the divine turns out to consist of claims that few Christian theologians would disagree with—above all the idea that "the god is good in his very being" (379b), meaning that "while no one else should be given the credit for the good things, some other causes need to be sought for the bad ones, but not the god" (379c).

Theology, in Plato's inaugural usage, is therefore a subfield of philosophy that aims to provide an account of the gods that conforms to reason and reinforces a rational social order. The rivalry here is not between philosophy and theology, but between a philosophically purified theology and the mythical narratives of the poets (above all Hesiod and Homer, but also including lyric poets and tragedians; 379a). Plato was hardly the first to notice the often shocking amorality of the Greek gods, which prompted some readers to search for allegorical or symbolic truths behind the surface of the narratives (the "deeper meanings" that Socrates mentions). This quest for more acceptable interpretations of the poetic texts was not a purely academic enterprise, but an attempt to legitimize the absolutely pervasive role of mythic poetry in Greek public life. The memorization of the Homeric poems was central to education—hence the concern with the formation of young minds. The performance of Homer's epics by skilled rhapsodes was both a common entertainment and, during the Panathenaic festival, a ritual competition that conferred great prestige on the winners. At that and other festivals, various myths were reenacted, commemorated via sacrifice, or both, and it is well known that the performance of tragedies, with their mythic plots, grew out of religious rituals. Athens justified its imperial ambitions within the Greek world by claiming the blessing of the goddess Athena, whom Aeschylus presents as laying the groundwork for the distinctive democratic system of Athens in *The Eumenides*—the final play in a trilogy that documents the aftermath of the events related in Homer's *Iliad*. When Socrates bans poets from his ideal city, then, he is not thinking of texts that one might happen to read or not, but of literary monuments that provided the framework for political order and common life. Where modern readers might object to censorship, Plato's contemporaries would be more likely to ask how a city without poets would be recognizable as a city at all.

The lack of poets is of course only one of the many objections one could lodge against Plato's hypothetical city. As the dialogue unfolds, the proposed social reform becomes more and more radical, as Socrates and his interlocutors gradually conclude that (at least among the ruling classes) not only mythic poetry and its attendant rituals, but family life, gender distinctions, and even the personal choice of sexual partners have no place in a city governed by the dictates of pure reason. Many critics—starting with Plato's own pupil Aristotle—have asked, with some justification, whether the social structure laid out in the *Republic* is feasible or even desirable. From my perspective, though, the details are less important than the sheer fact that so many aspects of our social life, including seemingly self-evident institutions like marriage and family, are "up for grabs." Even if we cannot actualize the social order Plato describes, his claim that this strange city is somehow demanded by reason calls all our actual-existing social orders into question. That this is Plato's intention becomes clear when Socrates concedes that "since everything that comes into being is destructible, even an organization like this one won't endure for all time, but will come undone" (546a) and gives an account of the city's gradual dissolution over the course of generations. Step by step, the city devolves into a militaristic regime driven by honor, an oligarchic regime driven by wealth, and finally a democratic regime driven by unruly desires. This narrative of decline is surely not meant to be a historical account of the origin of actual political regimes, but expresses Plato's conviction that every actual-existing city is somehow a failure to live up to the demand his ideal city represents.

Plato presents this conviction as more than simply a personal preference on his (or Socrates's) part—anyone who took the time to think carefully about the matter would, he implies, come to a broadly similar conclusion. This pattern of thought occurs over and over again in Plato's work, perhaps most radically in his claim that the kind of philosophical knowledge he is after—which he most often designates as knowledge of the eternal Forms—is ultimately knowledge that we all already possessed even before we were born. The process of embodiment causes us to forget, but with proper philosophical education, we can regain it. And the raw material of that education is not the mythic poetry that formed the basis of Athenian education, but systematic reflection on our everyday speech. The procedure, especially in the earliest dialogues, consists in asking ourselves, whenever we encounter an abstract valorized category such as "goodness," "justice," "beauty," or "friendship," what it is that allows us to recognize our usage of those terms as appropriate or inappropriate. Though few of Socrates's interlocutors prove to be up to the task, the implication is that anyone who thinks rigorously about what they mean when they speak can attain some glimpse of the eternal Forms.

Here Plato is exemplary of the most fundamental aspiration of philosophy, which is to seek perennial truths that are, in principle, available to anyone with the time and inclination to think seriously. There are of course good reasons to doubt that philosophy does in fact provide access to such perennial knowledge in practice. Even Plato's harsh critique of Athens is deeply embedded in Greek culture, drawing almost exclusively on other Greek models (such as that of Sparta) when considering alternatives to Athenian institutions and practices and displaying a singular lack of interest in the question of whether philosophy could be carried out in a language other than Greek. Yet despite those cultural blinders, the aspiration remains—and the perpetual failure to attain the goal in all its fullness is implicit in the very name *philosophy*, which famously designates not wisdom itself, but the love of wisdom.

By the time Plato began writing, philosophy was already an active tradition in the Greek world. In contrast to Plato's focus on moral and political questions, many of these early Greek thinkers, customarily designated as the "pre-Socratics," focused primarily on understanding the structure of the natural world—what it was ultimately made of, how it came into being, and what caused the various events we see around us. In a tacit rebuke to the tradition of mythic poetry, where events mostly proceed from quarrels among anthropomorphized divinities, the pre-Socratic philosophers sought natural forms of causation that could be discerned through careful reasoning or (less often) direct observation. Once again, there is an aspiration toward perennial truth, independent of any particular cultural deposit.

Despite this apparently implacable critique, however, Greek philosophy never actually attempted a full break with the tradition of mythic poetry or the rituals with which it was so deeply intertwined. Indeed, the Platonic dialogues present Socrates as possessing an encyclopedic command of Homer's poetry and frequently show him participating in festivals and ritual occasions. The reason for this rapprochement can be found in the above-mentioned search for "deeper meanings" in the mythological heritage—a search that frequently uncovered seemingly perennial truths in symbolic garb. Often the quest for a "deeper meaning" must have been fairly straightforward, as many myths plainly dramatize recurring events like the changing of the seasons, and many gods are obviously anthropomorphized versions of natural forces or cultural institutions or values. Some myths prove more challenging to account for in these terms, of course, but broadly speaking, the mythological heritage can be made to fit with the philosophical search for perennial truths.

The Greeks were hardly alone in arriving at this kind of symbiotic relationship between philosophy on the one hand and the world of myth and ritual on the other. A similar pattern occurs in the cultural traditions of China and India, for instance, which suggests that such a dynamic was actually the norm in the ancient world. Even the philosophical version of "theology," which describes a God who sounds so similar to the deity of the three great monotheistic religions, does not seem always and everywhere to entail a polemical stance toward the many gods of myth. The tendency toward a philosophical monotheism is perfectly compatible with an acknowledgment that the many gods "exist" in some sense—perhaps as subordinate to the singular God, perhaps as a focused emanation of that God's power, perhaps as a mixture of both. Conceptually, this philosophical theology might claim to transcend myth and ritual, but practically speaking, the latter's centrality to public life remains secure.

Plato's procedure illustrates this fundamental compatibility between philosophy and myth. Even if Plato can fantasize about discarding the more questionable aspects of his cultural myths, he himself finds the language of myth indispensable as a way of pointing toward realities that exceed our linguistic categories or range of experience. The "Myth of Er," with which he concludes the *Republic*, is a case in point (614b–621d). In this myth, Socrates narrates the experience of a man named Er, who has been given the chance to witness the process by which souls that have died are assigned to new lives. The wisdom and suitability of their choice depend on the habits and character traits the souls cultivated during their last earthly life, and of course those souls who have devoted themselves to philosophy will be in the best position to choose rightly. In the middle of this mythical tale, Socrates pauses to observe that

> it looks like everything is at stake for a human being here, and for that reason each of us needs to pay the utmost attention, neglecting all other studies so that he may be a seeker and student of this study [philosophy], if there's anywhere it's possible for him to learn and find out what will make him capable and knowledgeable for distinguishing a worthwhile life from a worthless one, in order at all times and places to choose the life that's better from among those that are possible. (618c)

As Giorgio Agamben has pointed out in his commentary on the myth,[5] this exhortation to pursue philosophy in the present life seems to be what is really at stake here, as the process of selecting a new life after death is presented as arbitrary and unreliable, to say the least. And the fact that Plato chooses to end the work with this focus on the individual pursuit of philosophy reminds us that his elaboration of a hypothetical city is initially motivated by a desire to see the virtue of justice at a larger scale than that of an individual life and that his investigation continually returns to the question of personal justice.

More important than political reform—a hazardous and uncertain pursuit at best—is the reform of one's own life, which can be carried out under virtually any circumstances (or at least any circumstances of sufficient privilege). This preference for the personal over the political is perhaps understandable if we recognize that Plato's dialogues are set in the aftermath of the Peloponnesian War, a disastrously misjudged conflict that wound up, through a combination of hubris and sheer bad luck, shattering the hegemony Athens had once enjoyed—and of course he was writing in the wake of the Athenians' execution of Socrates. Plato has been criticized for his distrust of democracy, but in his context, one can perhaps see how he could come to the conclusion that democracy was a failed experiment. However we judge Plato's politics, though, a survey of the history of philosophy shows that we are not dealing here with the idiosyncratic preferences of an individual thinker: Even if the search for perennial truth can motivate a radical critique of one's own society on an intellectual level, it tends in practice to embrace a kind of political quietism.

Theology and History

In ancient polytheistic societies, then, there is simply no reason for the kind of rivalry to arise between philosophy and theology that we see in the later Western tradition. In fact, the tendency toward something like monotheism in many forms of philosophy initially appears to be grounds for productive collaboration between philosophy and monotheistic religious traditions. Such was the case for Augustine, the North African bishop whose work would prove absolutely foundational for both the medieval Latin theological tradition and the Protestant reaction against it. In the *Confessions*,[6] he relates that the teachings of Platonism—most likely mediated through later Neoplatonic thinkers like Plotinus and Porphyry than through Plato himself—were a crucial step in his journey from the dualistic worldview of Manicheanism to orthodox Christianity, insofar as they helped him think of spirit and body as distinct realities that nonetheless formed part of a single system. So compatible did he find these aspects of Platonism with Christianity that he suspects that if he had first become thoroughly acquainted with Scripture and "had come later upon these books of the Platonists, they might have swept me away from the solid ground of piety" (7.20.26). Instead, turning from Plato to the Apostle Paul, he concludes that the Platonists, for all their wisdom, lack knowledge of what initially appears to be a miscellaneous and disordered list of Christian themes: "the face of [God's] love, the tears of confession, [God's] sacrifice, an afflicted spirit, a contrite and humbled heart, the salvation of [God's] people, the espoused city, the promise of the Holy Spirit, the chalice of our redemption" (7.21.27). As a result, addressing God as he does throughout the book, he claims that it must have been

> your will that I should come upon these books before I had made study of the Scriptures, that it might be impressed on my memory how they had affected me: so that, when later I should have become responsive to you through your Books with my wounds healed by the care of your fingers, I might be able to discern the difference that there is between presumption and confession, between those who see what the goal is but do not see the way, and [those who see] the Way which leads to the country of blessedness, which we were meant not only to know but to dwell in. (7.20.26)

In other words, the Platonists were close to orthodox Christianity—but this affinity is seen not as the basis for dialogue, but as a terrible temptation.

At first glance, Augustine's critique of Platonists seems very strange. On the one hand, he essentially blames them for not being Christians, which seems like an arbitrary critique of a movement founded by a thinker who lived centuries before Christ. On the other hand, he paints them as somehow presumptuous or prideful in their claims to knowledge, even while acknowledging that they are in fact correct. From a commonsense perspective, each line of attack can appear as a non sequitur: What does a person's religious affiliation or moral standing have to do with the correctness of their opinion on some particular issue? For Augustine, though, these paired critiques are not only absolutely decisive, but—as shown by the way he interweaves both concerns in his lists of what is missing from the Platonists—deeply connected. And in fact, this twofold standard is ultimately the one to which he holds himself. Later in the *Confessions*, he relates that even long after he has accepted that Christianity's account of human existence is the most satisfying one available and the answer to all the questions he has had his entire life, he struggles to "convert" in the sense of making an act of submission to God. That final step occurs only when, weeping in bitter despair at his inability to turn to God, he hears a child's voice repeating, "Take and read, take and read," opens a nearby Bible at random, and is shocked to find that the book opens to passages that feel like they were written with his situation in mind. After reading two such serendipitous passages, he reports, "I had no wish to read further, and no need. For in that instant, with the very ending of the sentence, it was as though a light of utter confidence shone in all my heart, and all the darkness of uncertainty vanished away" (8.12.29). This final act of conversion, Augustine concludes, was not a result of his own act of will, but was purely God's gift of grace. Or as he puts it, once again in the direct address to God that permeates a work that is at once an autobiography and a prayer: "For You converted me to Yourself" (8.12.30).

What is missing from the Platonists, then, is not any particular piece of information or any specific opinion, but an encounter with God. Such an encounter, Augustine's own experience teaches him, cannot be brought about by one's own efforts, intellectual or otherwise. When God comes to us, we experience God as coming from the outside, at a discrete moment in our lives. Platonists may say things about the entity they call "God" that are compatible with Christian doctrine, but the Christian model of encounter and conversion is qualitatively different from the Platonic model of recovering perennial knowledge that we somehow knew all along.

This is the origin of the conflict between philosophy and theology—not the internal evolution of philosophical thought (for instance, toward something like monotheism in contrast to a broader cultural polytheism), but the encounter of Greek thought with a new and qualitatively different conception of God that ultimately originates from the Hebrew biblical tradition. We should be clear here that the very fact of a cross-cultural encounter did not make conflict inevitable. As Jan Assmann has pointed out, polytheistic traditions have historically been quite adept at "translating" among various pantheons and myth traditions.[7] And there have been many attempts to "translate" the tales and rituals found in the Hebrew Bible and New Testament into terms compatible with Greek thought—for instance, to read the story of the Garden of Eden as a mythical representation of the perennial problem of the fall into embodiment.

Yet the fact remains the patriarchs of the Hebrew Bible do not ponder intellectually and come to the reasonable conclusion that there is a single God. God comes to them, unbidden and unannounced, to bestow promises and make demands. These are not one-off arbitrary events, but part of an intergenerational relationship between God and a particular family that grows into a particular nation. And when that nation finds itself reduced to slavery and oppression in the land of Egypt, God liberates them and crushes the oppressor—not symbolically, not as a way of illustrating some perennial truth, but *for real*. The foundational event of the Exodus defines a unique relationship between God and the Children of Israel, who are bound exclusively to God in a way that is essentially unprecedented in the ancient world. The introductory presentation of the Ten Commandments neatly captures all these dynamics in a few words: "I am the LORD your God, who brought you out of the land of Egypt, out of the house of slavery; you shall have no other gods before me" (Exodus 20:2–3). No other God in the ancient world lays down laws in this way, and no other God demands this type of exclusive loyalty from all his followers.

Even if the philosophical tradition can reconcile itself to the content of the biblical tradition, then, it is incompatible at the level of form. The problem is not conceptual, since as we have seen, many Greek philosophers had come to the conclusion that there is ultimately one God. The problem is, we might say, political. At bottom, Hebrew monotheism is intrinsically, irreducibly polemical in its approach to other religious traditions. As Assmann says, what is really distinctive about Hebrew monotheism "is not the distinction between the One God and many gods but the distinction between truth and falsehood in religion, between the true god and false gods, true doctrine and false doctrine, knowledge and ignorance, belief and unbelief" (2). This monotheistic vision is not a natural evolution from polytheism, but an unprecedented breakthrough that calls for a novel means of transmission. Every culture with written language has mythical and ritual texts in some form, but in Assmann's telling, only monotheistic religions have *scripture* in the strong sense:

> This exclusive truth is something genuinely new, and its novel, exclusive and exclusionary character is clearly reflected in the manner in which it is communicated and codified. It claims to have been revealed to humankind once and for all, since no path of merely human fashioning could have led from the experiences accumulated over countless generations to this goal; and it has been deposited in a canon of sacred texts, since no cult or rite would have been capable of preserving this revealed truth down the ages. From the world-disclosing force of this truth, the new [monotheistic] religions draw the antagonistic energy that allows them to recognize and condemn falsehood, and to expound the truth in a normative edifice of guidelines, dogmas, behavioral precepts, and salvational doctrines. (3)

In practice, of course, "the unavoidable compromises that determine the everyday practice of religious life" wind up watering down this uncompromising demand—but its codification in Scripture means that the irreducible antagonism of monotheism is always waiting to break out again, even (or especially) against those who claim to be its faithful followers (3).

This exclusive demand for loyalty to a unique God who intervenes in history in concrete, particular ways is the foundation of what we in the West think of as "theology" in the proper sense (as opposed to the subdiscipline of philosophy that goes under that same name). The later monotheistic traditions obviously differ in the content of the historical events to which they bear witness—the incarnation, death, and resurrection of Jesus of Nazareth in the case of Christianity and the sequence of prophetic missions culminating in the revelation of the Qur'an through the Prophet Muhammad in the case of Islam—but their fundamental gesture remains the same on the level of form.

Nevertheless, there is something peculiar about Christianity relative to the other two monotheisms, because in neither of those other cases did the monotheistic demand issue in the elaboration of a baroque conceptual edifice like that of Christian theology. In Judaism, for instance, where the demand was first elaborated and has formed the basis for a cultural and religious identity that has maintained its distinctiveness to this very day, "theology," in the sense of detailed reflections on the nature of God and its consequences for our understanding of the created world, plays a very subordinate role in comparison to the specification and extrapolation of the behavior dictated by the Torah in all areas of life. Arguably it is only with the rise of the distinctive form of Jewish mysticism known as Kabbala in the late medieval period that Judaism developed a conceptual apparatus parallel to that of Christian theology. Similarly, in the Islamic tradition, the tradition of explicit theological reflection known as *kalam* has enjoyed much less prestige and importance than *sharia* legal thought or Qur'anic commentary. Only in Christianity has theology emerged as arguably *the* primary concern. This is so much the case that the term "theology" is often used as a synonym for "Christian theology," as though there were no other kind.

What accounts for the Christian obsession with theology? I would suggest that two factors are at work here. The first is that Christian claims about the divine status of Christ provoked very serious questions, and not only from the perspective of strict monotheism. In comparison, both Judaism and Islam simply had less conceptual work to do in order to make sense of their intuitions about God and his role in the world. We can see this even at the level of the creedal affirmations required by each religion: Judaism's *Shema* ("Hear, O Israel: The LORD is our God, the LORD alone," Deuteronomy 6:4) and Islam's "there is no god but God" are much more compact and straightforward than any Christian creed.

The second factor stems from Christianity's efforts to distinguish itself from Judaism, such that Christian practice was defined first of all as a rejection of Jewish ritual practices.[8] Whereas Christianity has of course developed its own ritual norms, the legacy of this initial antinomianism is still evident, for instance, in the fact that Christianity alone among world religions has no defining food taboo—or, perhaps more precisely, it has a taboo against food taboos. Paul and the authors of the Synoptic Gospels apparently anticipated that this rejection of religious ritual in the narrow sense would open the space for a more radical pursuit of love and justice.[9] Paul claims that escaping the narrow subjection to law will result in the enjoyment of the fruits of the Spirit, "love, joy, peace, patience, kindness, generosity, faithfulness, gentleness, and self-control," against which "there is no law" (Galatians 5:23). Perhaps more radically, Matthew 25 envisions a final judgment based solely on each person's behavior toward the weakest and most vulnerable, which will be rewarded or punished as though each deed (or omission) were directed at Jesus himself. Right belief is not a factor here, as both the redeemed and the condemned are surprised to learn of the standard by which they have been judged. Already within the New Testament writings themselves, however, one can see that the absence of a concrete lawlike norm has led to a religiously sanctioned cultural conformism (e.g., the "Household Codes" in Colossians, Ephesians, and 1 Peter) or even to an open-ended demand for "belief" in Jesus's claims to divinity, shorn of any substantial moral guidance (as in the Gospel of John).

The disproportionate emphasis on right belief or theology in Christianity thus correlates with a lesser emphasis on moral practice. The divergence between the two is arguably unexpected from the perspective of the prophetic monotheistic tradition, because, in Assmann's words, unlike "the pagan gods," who "stipulate that their priests be undefiled, their rites correctly performed, and their sacrifices plentiful, the god of the Bible is concerned solely or primarily with justice. This god is not served with fatty burnt offerings, but through righteousness and charity" (44). The demand for justice is not an ancillary or incidental concern for the monotheistic God, but is central to the case that God alone is worthy of loyalty or worship. Thus the distinction between true and false religion, far from being the arbitrary concern it appears to be from a secular perspective, has a concrete practical payoff: "The false religion can be recognized as such because it subjugates, denigrates, and enslaves" (45). As Assmann points out, this standard of judgment is hardly the last word on monotheistic belief, which in all three of its major forms does often demand in-group loyalty and conformity of belief in ways that have no clear connection to moral practice. In my view, though, the ways that Christianity chose to differentiate itself from Judaism has historically exacerbated the latter tendency and reduced the urgency of moral striving for the average Christian.

To summarize the discussion so far, then, we can say that theology is a conceptual and creative reflection on the implications of a concrete historical revelation of a God who demands exclusive loyalty and worship and who claims to be a God of justice. In the broadest sense, this definition would include pursuits not normally identified as strictly "theological," such as rabbinic commentary on the Torah, debates on *sharia* law, or even the elaboration of ecclesiastical law. I designate it by the narrower term "theology" not to privilege that kind of conceptual elaboration above other more practice-oriented modes of religious reflection, but in recognition of the outsize role that "theology" has played in the specifically Christian version of monotheism that has proven decisive for the Western tradition.

With this definition in hand, we can see that Augustine's theology represents a radicalization of the main features of a distinctively Christian monotheism. First of all, Augustine is absolutely insistent on the centrality of history for theological reflection. His masterwork, *City of God*, reflects the universal aspiration of Christianity in its articulation of all of human history (as far as it was known to him) through the lens of Christian revelation. In fact, he insists much more on the historical truth of the biblical tales than most of his predecessors had. Where previous theologians were happy to interpret the story of the Garden of Eden allegorically, Augustine insists that our first parents really did sin in a way that really did affect all of their descendants—meaning that every human being who has ever existed is caught up in a single, particular narrative of sin and redemption.

The implications that Augustine draws from this literal interpretation of Genesis reinforce the Christian tendency to de-emphasize moral striving in favor of belief. As is well known, he claims that Adam and Eve's sin damaged human nature in such a way that no one is capable of not sinning. Deprived of any ability to carry out the righteous actions demanded by the monotheistic God, we must rely solely on God's grace for our salvation (as he established in his debate with Pelagius). On the concrete level of practice, that means that we must participate in the sacramental rites of the church, which mediate God's grace to us apart from the moral worthiness of the participant or even the officiant (as he established in his debate with the Donatists). On the strict level of theology, though, we must rely ultimately on God's inscrutable will, which predestined each individual to salvation or perdition from the foundations of the world. The result is a paradoxical short circuit of the monotheistic correlation of right belief and justice. For Augustine, the revolutionary demand for justice is fulfilled by the admission that we are incapable of righteousness, and any claim to achieve or deserve anything out of our own merits (such as the Platonists' claim to knowledge on topics where Augustine concedes they do in fact possess knowledge) represents a damnable pride.

Here Augustine seems to redouble Plato's political quietism into an outright fatalism. And as in the case of Plato, we can understand how Augustine's context made such a conclusion plausible. Where Plato was dealing with the disastrous failure of democracy, Augustine lived in the Roman Empire, which had functioned for centuries as a military dictatorship. The only hope for more positive political outcomes was that a better emperor would temporarily prevail in the endless power struggle, and even that slim hope was called into question by the sack of Rome. Amid such constant, meaningless tumult, why not focus on one's eternal fate? Once again, though, even if Augustine's approach is in some ways more radical than those of other theologians, there is an undeniable tendency throughout the history of Christianity for salvation to trump political activism in a world that is passing away.

From Political Theology to Sociogeny

We are now in a position to lay out the basic terms of the two master discourses that define the Western conceptual space. As I stated above, I am not laying out a once-and-for-all definition of either discourse but instead a typology, which is necessarily partial and simplified but can, for that very reason, allow certain key features of each mode of thought to stand out more clearly than they otherwise would.

On the one hand, there is philosophy, which seeks after perennial truths that are knowable, in principle, by every human being with the time and inclination to think carefully. Despite their universal accessibility by the mind, however, these perennial truths can only ever be approximated in our material world. Hence the satisfactions of knowledge and contemplation come to take priority over the futile tedium of political reform. On the other hand, there is theology, which seeks to remain faithful to a concrete historical event that claims to encompass the meaning of all human history. Where philosophy consigns us to an indefinite approximation of an unattainable truth, theology witnesses a perpetual falling away from the full demands of divine truth, leading to repeated attempts to "reboot" to the purity of the founding moment. Yet in the last analysis, no one in this fallen world can truly live up to what has been revealed. Hence salvation is available only through adherence to the community that preserves the memory of the founding moment and dispenses the grace that God has made available.

Contemplation of perennial truth thus confronts salvation through loyalty to a once-and-for-all historical event. In practice, of course, the opposition is not so stark. Philosophers regularly investigate particular historical events or material empirical facts and take the texts of particular thinkers as uniquely authoritative, for instance, and theologians just as regularly use philosophical concepts to clarify their doctrines and attempt to formulate their arguments in terms that would be acceptable or at least comprehensible for those who have not yet pledged loyalty to the God revealed in history. What allows for this coexistence and overlap is a commitment to some form of universalism, even if from the philosophical perspective the theologian seeks it via a circuitous and counterintuitive route. More important, though, is the nature of the universality to which both discourses aspire, namely, a universality that somehow transcends our everyday experience of the world. Salvation is found not here, but with God, just as philosophical truth is found in (something like) the world of Forms. Moreover, these modes of transcendence can overlap, as when Scholastic philosophers hypothesized that universal categories existed eternally in the mind of God.

This basic structure of transcendence, Sylvia Wynter argues, existed in essentially every premodern culture, from medieval Christianity to Aztec sun worship, allowing each human group to imagine a world organized around them and their self-understanding. And in the event of 1492, all such structures of transcendence are, in principle, dealt a decisive blow, as European exploration and conquest undercuts such parochial worldviews and "brings in, for all humans, a new image of the earth and conception of the cosmos."[10] Columbus inaugurates, and Copernicus later confirms, a single undifferentiated world-space, occupied by all human beings in common—a space in which no transcendent endorsement or guarantee is available.

Within this space of global immanence, I would argue, the dyad of theology and philosophy continues to operate, but in a strangely distorted way. On the one hand, ostensibly "secular" events take on a theological charge, attracting partisans who treat them as revelatory of the fullness of truth and seek constantly to reactivate their revolutionary potential. Perhaps the most successful such theologization is the American cult of the Founders, whose supposedly unmatched probity and wisdom make them the ultimate arbiters of all contemporary political disputes. Like the revelatory event of classical theology, the Founding can never fail, only be failed. Similarly, later European revolutionaries almost always measured themselves by the unsurpassable standard of the French Revolution—most famously Lenin, who himself set in motion a revolutionary sequence that retains a revelatory quality, as many contemporary leftists continue to position themselves in terms of the imposing array of debates and counterfactuals that have grown up around the Bolshevik Revolution and its aftermath.

On the other hand, the perennial truth that philosophy once found in the transcendent realm of the intellect has been identified with the structure and laws of the material world itself. This type of perennial truth has reportedly been achieved most successfully (or at least most prestigiously) in the natural sciences, but it can also be found in a more tentative form in the social sciences, which purport to expose the "natural laws" of human politics and society. Just as in classical philosophy, this perennial knowledge cannot be fully exhausted in practice, but continual progress toward that lofty goal takes the place of an indefinite approximation of the unattainable transcendent norm. Yet even this purely secular and material knowledge can be "theologized" in the immanent space of modernity. Where medieval theologians could claim that philosophy's perennial truth is fundamentally compatible with the revealed truth of theology, contemporary quasi-theologians often legitimize their revelatory event precisely by claiming it enjoys privileged access to the perennial truth of science. Hence European culture, for instance, can claim to represent the highest human achievement precisely insofar as it "discovered" the natural sciences and the secular sphere—so that the supposedly universal heritage of all human beings, the truth of the natural and social worlds we share, becomes the unique province of a particular human group.

In short, when deprived of their shared transcendent reference point, the immanentized versions of philosophy and theology came to overlap and short-circuit in new and unanticipated ways. Obviously both continued to exist as distinct disciplines in modernity, and many individual theologians and philosophers have mounted radical critiques against the many crimes and hypocrisies of the West in the modern period. The more consequential legacy of the philosophy-theology dyad in modernity, however, is found in the deeper patterns of thought that emerged in the wake of the immanentization of the two great master discourses of the West. These patterns emerged as a kind of cultural common sense that has gone beyond the implicit quietism and fatalism of premodern philosophy and theology and degenerated into little more than clichéd apologetics for power.

Wynter's account of modernity—whose interdisciplinary or even omni-disciplinary approach places it outside the bounds of either traditional master discourse—is in many ways well-attuned to the kind of self-congratulatory short circuits of the particular and the universal that grew out of the immanentization of the philosophy-theology dyad. In her telling, the story of modernity becomes one of perpetual rearguard efforts to set up new cultural hierarchies with new transcendent guarantees and of an equally relentless shattering of those false idols through scientific knowledge. The most destructive of these misbegotten modern hierarchies was the concept of race, an "essentially Christian-heretical positing of the *non-homogeneity of the human species*" that "was to provide the basis for new metaphysical notions of order" (36), yet this botched attempt at transcendence was shattered, at least in principle, by Darwin (38).

And now, Wynter claims, the anticolonial movements represented by Fanon have called forth a new "poetics" of human self-fashioning, "one as directed at the winning of the autonomy of our cognition with respect to the social reality of which we are always already socialized subject-observers, as that first *poetics* had made possible that of our cognitive autonomy with respect to physical reality; and, after Darwin, with respect to organic reality" (49). The first step is to overcome the "misequation" of membership in a particular human group (i.e., white bourgeois Europeans) with humanity as such, which "functions strategically to absolutize the behavioral norms encoded in our present culture-specific conception of being human, allowing it to be posited *as if* it were the universal of the human species" (43). This will allow us to center our analysis on "the *concrete individual* human subject," particularly as represented by Black people, who are regarded as the lowliest and most unworthy in the current system (47). Only then will it become possible "for us to have knowledge of our social reality *outside* the limits of our specific culture's self-understanding" (48), which will allow us to achieve true social and political autonomy for all human beings.

As later essays in this collection show, I embrace much of Wynter's account of modernity, including the theological roots of the concept of race, and more than that, I share her ultimate goal. I believe, though, that my account of the legacy of the rivalry between theology and philosophy for modernity can helpfully supplement Wynter's in an area where many critics have called it into question—namely, the privilege she grants to secularism and science.[11] Here she appears to accept that secularity is a European invention or discovery, one that began to emerge prior to Columbus in the rise of humanism and the secular state. This "epochal shift" introduced "an increasingly secularized, that is, degodded, mode of 'subjective understanding,'" which gave rise to modern states whose "global expansion . . . would bring into being our present single world order and single world history" (13). She is clear that this is a shift away from the theological toward the secular, or in her words, a replacement of "the eternal salvation of the Augustinian *civitas dei*" (13) with "the new *this-worldly* goal of the growth, expansion, and political stability of each European state in competitive rivalry with its fellow European states," which represents a "rational redemption, through the state as intermediary" (14). This achievement, Wynter believes, must be granted "an ecumenically valid meaning" for all people (14).

As her account develops, it is clear that Wynter displaces Eurocentrism, above all by privileging the Black perspective as the means to attain, at long last, a true secularism. Yet she does arguably theologize secularism in my terms, turning the European discovery of a "degodded" world into a revelatory event that, in principle, already shows us what needs to be achieved. And part of this theologization (in my sense) is her acceptance of the habitual secular scapegoating of supposedly anachronistic avatars of theology (in the more narrow sense) for the failures of secularism itself.[12] I have already quoted her characterization of the concept of race as "essentially Christian-heretical" (36), for instance, and her account of Columbus attempts, unconvincingly, to separate out his (progressive, promising) secular, state-oriented goals from his (anachronistic, retrograde) apocalyptic Christian beliefs. Here theology, in the broader sense of the premodern baggage of a spurious transcendence, ironically plays the role of what is perpetually causing us to betray the founding insights of a theologized secularism—so that even Fanon can ultimately be presented as providing a means to the end of fully actualizing the discovery of the secular in early modern Europe.

Political theology points the way beyond this sterile binary between the secular and the religious. It originates in Carl Schmitt's reactionary rejection of secularism and his attempt to find some principle of legitimacy for modernity by reestablishing a connection with the theological heritage of the West. Schmitt's own agenda—which posited that a dictatorship was necessary to restore order amid the nihilism of the secular world—was discredited by his affiliation with National Socialism, but his methodology found a home on the political left, where it served as a continual provocation against the presumption and complacency of secular modernity. Again and again, secularism's claim to represent a universal norm or aspiration has been undercut by political-theological genealogies that have traced an ever-increasing number of modern political concepts and institutions (e.g., sovereignty, economy, race) to medieval Christian roots.

In some cases, these studies appear to be seeking, like Wynter, to discard the remaining unrecognized theological baggage in order to attain, at long last, a "true" secularism. From this perspective, political theology would be primarily a diagnostic tool, aiming ultimately to free us from theology altogether. Although the findings of such studies are doubtless valuable, I contend that the goal of finding a "true" secularism beyond theology is simplistic and self-defeating, insofar as it plays into the paradoxical theologization of the secular itself. Within such a framework, we may think that we are progressing endlessly toward the goal of full secularism, but in reality we are, just like Augustine's sinners, continually failing to live up to the consequences of the breakthrough to modernity. In our very pursuit of the perennial truths once promised by philosophy, we are ironically enshrining secularism itself as a moment of revelation. And as such, we blind ourselves to the task of imagining a truly human world by our insistence that we already know, in principle, what that looks like and what it will take to get there—if only we could repent and be faithful!

More promising, in my view, are the modes of political theology that, whether implicitly or explicitly, challenge the terms of the modern philosophy-theology divide in a more thoroughgoing way. Such studies do include a philosophical moment in that they often discover what appear to be perennial features of human societies and their transformation. In my own account of political theology above, for instance, I present the vulnerability of every political-theological paradigm to overthrow as a perennial reality—and with all due humility, I must admit that it is very difficult for me to imagine a human-made social form that could escape such vulnerability. Yet to the extent that it is a perennial truth, it is not a norm or aspiration, but a *problem* that is universally insoluble. Similarly, political theology has focused overwhelmingly on one particular historical tradition, namely that of the Christian West, as somehow uniquely relevant or revelatory. Like the revelation of historical monotheism, this particular history does in fact have universal significance, but this is only insofar as the contingent event of 1492 has rendered its deadlocks and unexamined baggage in one way or another *everyone's problem*. In other words, the "revelation" of the Christian West is not a permanent historical deposit of meaning to which political theologians hope to return, but an ongoing disaster we seek urgently to escape.

This historical groundedness, it seems to me, is the primary reason to preserve the reference to "theology" in the name of political theology. Yet if we want to break from the futile quest for a "true" secularism, the reference to theology cannot remain purely diagnostic and critical. We must take the next step into creative, constructive, and speculative theological work. This will represent a kind of continuation of the theological tradition in the narrower sense, because theology, even in its doctrinal or confessional forms, has never been purely backward looking. No matter how much theologians try to pass themselves off as conduits for an unchanging tradition, it requires hard work and no small amount of creativity to bring the revelatory moment into the present and clarify how it is the answer, not only to the problems of yesterday, but to those we face right now.

Augustine is a case in point, as effectively all of his signature doctrines—original sin, predestination, the irrelevance of a minister's moral qualities—were his own theological innovations, in response to contemporary debates, under circumstances that none of his predecessors could have anticipated. Even though there are arguably precedents for some of his teachings, the unique synthesis of Christian doctrine and sacred history Augustine crafted in *City of God* was unprecedented in its scope and coherence. I personally view all of Augustine's innovations as destructive, both in themselves and in their later unintended consequences. Nevertheless, I believe that we political theologians should imitate his creativity and daring in constructing a new political-theological paradigm that can serve as an answer to the problem our history has become for us.

Taking this creative step may sound difficult, but the task of genealogical investigation demonstrates that it has been achieved countless times, in countless places, most often through the efforts of people who did not possess the towering genius of Plato, Augustine, Frantz Fanon, or Sylvia Wynter. In a sense, nothing could be more ordinary, historically speaking, than the development of a new political-theological paradigm. Yet a political-theological paradigm that was consciously constructed in full awareness of the results of political theology's genealogical investigations could itself represent a paradigm shift, if only because it would be forced into a unique kind of honesty. To be true to itself, it could not claim to represent either the final universal truth or the reactivation of an idealized history, but would have to take the responsibility of saying—in this irreducibly particular historical moment, with no guarantee or alibi—"Behold, I am doing a new thing!"

PART I

Theology beyond the Limits
of Religion Alone

Bonhoeffer on Continuity and Crisis
From Objective Spirit to Religionless Christianity

Serious difficulties confront any interpreter of the work of Dietrich Bonhoeffer. The first is the great diversity of genres represented: two deeply scholarly works, lectures and seminars, devotional and spiritual works, sermons, and posthumous fragments. The second is the fact that his untimely death meant that his theological project remained essentially unfinished, in the sense of being unsystematized. But from another perspective, this difficulty is Bonhoeffer's greatest strength. As Ernst Fiel says, "All [Bonhoeffer's] texts lead again and again to those last letters from prison which stimulated all the interest in Bonhoeffer and without which little notice would be paid today to the earliest writings."[1] The compressed and fragmentary comments in the posthumous *Letters and Papers from Prison* have proven very productive for later theologians who have taken them as the starting point for more sustained reflection, in a way that they might not have been had Bonhoeffer lived to attempt to answer his own piercing questions.

Yet even if the importance of the *Letters and Papers from Prison* is unquestioned, the proper way to interpret them in light of Bonhoeffer's other work is not. Fiel lists several approaches to his work, with every possible starting point, and he remarks that the "possibility of making an unambiguous interpretation is quite slim if one cannot determine whether one is dealing with a work marked by qualitative leaps or by a continuous unfolding of its development."[2] While not providing a conclusive answer to this question, he notes Eberhard Bethge's caution against periodizing Bonhoeffer's work and then sets out to provide a reading of Bonhoeffer's whole theology in terms of his understanding of the world. In addition to this secondary testimony, one could point to the fact that while many thinkers (such as Ludwig Wittgenstein, Martin Heidegger, and Karl Barth) come to understand their thought as having undergone a fundamental transformation, Bonhoeffer himself evinces no such self-understanding. Although in a letter to Bethge he writes that he believes his friend "would be surprised, and perhaps even worried, by [his] theological thoughts and the conclusions that they lead to,"[3] only a week prior, he had written, "I don't think I've every changed very much, except perhaps at the time of my first impressions abroad and under the first conscious influence of father's personality. It was then that I turned from phraseology to reality."[4] He can "see the dangers" of *The Cost of Discipleship*,[5] but he stands behind it in a much less ambiguous way than, for example, Heidegger comes to stand behind *Being and Time*. Fundamentally, this is because "one can never go back behind what one has worked out for oneself"[6]—even if corrections and later developments must be made, the fundamental insights of one's intense theological reflection cannot be discarded.

This essay will be a partial experiment in reading Bonhoeffer's theological work as a coherent whole. There are, of course, many works that find clues to the meaning of the *Letters and Papers* in his earlier work; for instance, John de Gruchy, in his introduction to his anthology of Bonhoeffer's works, says that the basic theological viewpoint of *Sanctorum Communio* "provides a key building block for what follows, and is influential to the end."[7] I contend that we must go further than that: The concepts developed in such detail in *Sanctorum Communio* and *Act and Being* continue to undergo further development in his later works. A shift in style from the dissertations to the later more spiritual works does not indicate a shift in fundamental concerns or in conceptual framework. In order to test this contention, I analyze the place of the Hegelian concept of objective spirit from *Sanctorum Communio*. With some reference to the works in between, I then shift to the *Letters and Papers from Prison* to indicate the ways in which Bonhoeffer is still attempting to develop a distinctly Christian concept of objective spirit. Finally, I conclude with some brief remarks on the ways in which we can understand *Sanctorum Communio* as already providing some of the resources necessary to answer the questions raised in *Letters and Papers from Prison*.

Objective Spirit in *Sanctorum Communio*

The concept of objective spirit is well suited to this kind of inquiry for several reasons. First, it is a technical academic concept that would be equally out of place in a spiritual meditation such as *The Cost of Discipleship* or in a reflective letter written to a friend, so that the recurrence of the term itself in the later works should not be expected. Second, it is not in itself a theological term, but rather one of the ideas from that branch of phenomenological thought that Bonhoeffer calls "sociology." Since the key to the uniqueness of his theological approach in *Communio Sanctorum* is his attempt to make sociological concepts "fruitful to theology,"[8] one can reasonably conclude that his distinctive theological conclusions can be found, not simply in the rather obvious assertion that the church is a social reality, but rather in the ways that he redeploys specific technical sociological terms. "Objective spirit" is one of the most important sociological terms in Bonhoeffer's lexicon. Indeed, a careful study of the critical edition reveals that the term appears even more frequently in the parts of the dissertation that were edited out of the final publication. From this I conclude that it was an especially formative idea as he was originally formulating his theological argument, even if he recognized that his extensive reflections on the concept would not have appealed to a broader audience. Finally, unlike many of the sociological concepts deployed throughout the work, he explicitly refers to "the difference between the idealist and the Christian concept of objective spirit."[9] Although he is always careful to distance himself from idealism, he clearly sees "objective spirit" as a sociological concept that is so fruitful for theology that it can be brought into the fold.

To understand the way that Bonhoeffer redeploys the concept of objective spirit, one must first understand its use in the work of Hegel. Bonhoeffer draws primarily on the third part of Hegel's *Encyclopedia*, the "Philosophy of Spirit,"[10] which devotes an entire section to the idea of objective spirit. For Hegel, "objective spirit is the absolute Idea, but only existing *in posse* [potentially]." The free subject approaches objective spirit as "an external and already subsisting objectivity," which consists of both "external things of nature" insofar as they appear in the human world and "the ties of relation between individual wills which are conscious of their own diversity and particularity." Since Hegel is thinking in the context of the Prussian state, for him objective spirit par excellence is the law, by which he means "not merely . . . the limited juristic law, but . . . the actual body of all the conditions of freedom."[11] He includes under this heading not only the explicit law (including property, contract, and the general concept of right and wrong), but also such institutions as the family, the state, and the administration of justice, and even the idea of universal history. All of these are materials that present themselves to the free subject as self-evident and preexisting, but which act to shape the subject's concrete exercise of freedom. Both the material and conceptual aspects of objective spirit are equally self-consistent and equally beyond the control of the particular subject, and both are provided ultimately by "the plan of Providence . . . , in short, . . . Reason in history."[12]

Bonhoeffer adopts the same basic structure for his Christian concept of objective spirit. In the discussion of objective spirit in his chapter "The Primal State and the Problem of Community," Bonhoeffer notes:

> Mostly without realizing it, people mean two different things when they speak of objective spirit: (1) objectified spirit as opposed to unformed spirit, and (2) social spirit as opposed to subjective spirit. Both meanings are based on the fact that where wills unite, a "structure" is created—that is, a third entity, previously unknown, independent of being willed or not willed by the persons who are uniting.

This concept is called a "discovery of the qualitative thinking that became dominant in romanticism and idealism"—not a speculative flight of fancy, but rather a genuine insight that provides the only means to grasp "concrete totality, which is not a matter of quantity."[13] A person who wants to enter an already existing community, even one as small as the bond between two people, finds that objective spirit is already in place, and the two who are already on the inside interact with each other only by means of objective spirit.

In Hegelian terms, Bonhoeffer describes objective spirit as the battleground between the past and the present moment, the site where the past turns to meet the future. In Bonhoeffer's scheme, some principle of stability existing over against particular persons in the struggle of temporality is necessary for community, since he has previously declared that *"the person ever and again arises and passes away in time. The person does not exist timelessly; a person is not static, but dynamic. The person exists always and only in ethical responsibility; the person is re-created again and again in the perpetual flux of life."* The person exists only in "the moment of being addressed," but for this address to take place, that is, for the person to be possible, there must be a means of communication between two persons.[14] The means of this communication is, of course, language, which "combines the *objective intention of meaning* with its attendant *subjective emotion*, ultimately enabling empirical objectification and consolidation by sound and writing."[15] Although it never takes on as thematic a role as those with (post)structuralist sympathies might hope, for Bonhoeffer, language is one of the most basic elements of objective spirit. Precisely as objective, it is "utterly ineradicable, whether by each individual or by all members together."[16] A community cannot dispense with its objective spirit without ceasing to exist, and the same objective spirit that provides the conditions for their free interaction also has a will of its own that restrains that interaction.[17]

When defining his Christian concept of the person, Bonhoeffer criticizes idealist philosophy as being incapable of developing such a concept. This is curious, since his chapter on the primal state, in which the concept of objective spirit is most thoroughly investigated, is essentially a summary of idealist philosophy's discoveries in this regard. However, between the primal state and the communion of saints stands the problem of original sin. If not for the fall, idealist philosophy would be correct, but as it stands, idealism fails because "it has no *voluntaristic* concept of God, nor a profound concept of sin."[18] Where Hegel sees the state as provided by Reason in history to maintain the conditions of freedom, Bonhoeffer sees a community that is irrevocably broken, among persons who originate "only in the absolute duality of God and humanity."[19] In the primal state, even conflictual human interaction would be productive, just as in Hegel the conflict of opposites results in a higher unity. But in a direct swipe at Hegel's optimism, Bonhoeffer declares that "since the fall has there been no concrete and productive conflict in the genuine sense."[20] Conflict still produces community, but it is the community of sinners, the community of those who are utterly alone.[21] In such a state of affairs, where human beings stand in radical judgment under and separation from God, an a priori assumption of the existence of Reason in history is unwarranted.

God enters into this situation of hopelessness in his revelation as Jesus Christ, and he creates the church, which is Christ existing as community. Even at this very early stage of his work, long before the process of disillusionment brought on by the German church's capitulation to Nazism, this definition of the church is not meant to be a piece of triumphalism. As Luca D'Isanto explains: "The proposition is meant to locate the place in which the divine reality, which showed itself in the life, death, and resurrection of Jesus of Nazareth, can still show itself today."[22] This is not merely a return to the primal state. The existence of sin has rendered the location of the church ambiguous, and all members of the church live both in the community of sin and the community of grace, both in Adam and in Christ. Unlike in Hegel, where the location of the community created by God (Reason in history) is self-evident, for Bonhoeffer, the community is hidden.

It is at this point that one can begin to discuss a specifically Christian concept of objective spirit. As a community, the church does have objective spirit, and Bonhoeffer emphasizes that this spirit cannot be identified with God's spirit.[23] The church's objective spirit guarantees a certain degree of continuity. Although the collective person of the church, having "the same structure as the individual person,"[24] is every bit as temporal as the individual person, Bonhoeffer confidently states that the "church of Jesus Christ that is actualized by the Holy Spirit is really the church here and now. The community of saints we have outlined is 'in the midst of us.'"[25] Still, the actions of the church are never simply the actions of God, as they would be if the objective spirit of the church were identical to the Holy Spirit—that, he says, "would amount to the Hegelian position,"[26] in which the status of the community would be a given. As human, the objective spirit of the church is subject to change and to influences from those who are outside the community, but as it is taken up by the Holy Spirit, it has a redemptive role to play:

> The historical impact of the Spirit of Christ is at work in the form of the objective spirit in spite of all the sinfulness, historical contingency, and fallibility of the church; likewise the Holy Spirit uses the objective spirit as a vehicle for its gathering and sustaining social activity in spite of all the sinfulness and imperfection of the individuals and of the whole.[27]

The remainder of the book is an account of the institutions of the objective spirit of the church, laid out broadly along the lines of Hegel's account of the objective spirit of the modern state in *Philosophy of Spirit*—for example, the juxtaposition of individual congregation and universal church is parallel to Hegel's juxtaposition of family and state, and his eschatology (such as it is) is parallel to Hegel's idea of universal history.

Bonhoeffer shows remarkable confidence in the ability of objective spirit, empowered by the Holy Spirit, to sustain the church in the face of its inadequate members. In a position that is remarkable given the essential place of preaching in the church, he even opens up the possibility that those "who, at least at that moment, do not belong to the *sanctorum communio*" can preach the word effectively: "The fact that this preacher uses, and must use, forms shaped by the objective spirit means that the Holy Spirit is able to use that person as an instrument of the Spirit's own work." This is because "objective spirit not only consists of forms that have become fixed, but, just as much consists of the living power of public opinion, which means, for example, theology, or a strong resolve to tackle some kind of practical project, etc."[28] This broad definition of objective spirit might lead one to believe that the church is infallible, but Bonhoeffer guards his ecclesiology from triumphalism:

> We believe in the church not as an ideal that is unattainable or yet to be fulfilled, but as a present reality. . . . And yet within its historical

development it never knows a state of fulfillment. It will remain impure as long as there is a history, and yet in this concrete form it is nevertheless God's church-community.[29]

The emphasis is not on the church's inherent righteousness—after all, "there is no sociological structure that is holy as such, and equally there is no structure that would cut off all avenues for the word"[30]—but rather on God's faithfulness to the church. Yet God's faithfulness does not erase the boundary between God and humanity, meaning that the objective spirit of the church is still "subject to the historical ambiguity of all profane communities."[31] It is this ambiguity that will prove to be the key factor in Bonhoeffer's later investigations into the Christian concept of objective spirit.

The Afterlife of Objective Spirit through the *Letters and Papers from Prison*

As previously noted, one should not expect to find the term "objective spirit" in the later work for which Bonhoeffer is most famous—indeed, even in the published version of *Sanctorum Communio* he began to pare away explicit references to this very academic term. Aside from considerations of audience, genre, and context, his steadily increasing polemic against idealism explains his reluctance to use terms associated with Hegel, to the point where *The Cost of Discipleship* seldom mentions the work of the Holy "Spirit." I contend, though, that the conceptual space denoted in *Sanctorum Communio* by the term "objective spirit" actually increases in importance over the course of Bonhoeffer's career. More than that, by the time of the *Letters and Papers from Prison*, it constitutes the central problem of his theology, a problem he was unable to solve before his death. A complete review of his works is inappropriate in this context, but a brief analysis of the place of objective spirit in *Christ the Center* and *The Cost of Discipleship* should suffice to illustrate Bonhoeffer's continued engagement with the concept even as it remains unnamed.

Christ the Center is a Christology that continually slips into ecclesiology. Bonhoeffer emphasizes the continued, concrete presence of Christ in the world: "One cannot avoid encounter with the person of Christ because he is alive."[32] By this he means not that every person has a Damascus Road experience, but rather that Christ continues to exist as word, as sacrament, and as community.[33] Clearly, here the basic theological insight of *Sanctorum Communio*, that the church is Christ existing as community, is at work, and his analysis of the structure of the person and the church in that work is reiterated here in many ways. He conceives Christ's existence *pro me* as an address, and that address necessitates the objective spirit of a human community in order to be intelligible: "The divine Logos enters the human logos." Just as in *Sanctorum Communio*, the divine Logos never becomes identified with the human logos it enters. It remains the case, however, that "truth happens only in community," and the historical, contingent nature of God's revelation in Christ means that it happens only in a specific, contingent community, namely the church.[34]

Thus, in a move that seems bizarre in the age of historical criticism, Bonhoeffer's section "The Historical Christ" declares that "the Christ who is preached is the historical Christ," and that means the Christ who has been preached by the Christian tradition. Not only is the "quest of the historical Jesus . . . a blind alley," but so also is the quest to find out simply what the Bible says about Jesus.[35] Instead of the methods of historical criticism, it is the objective spirit of the church, represented here in the orthodox Christology established by the Church Fathers, that keeps open the space for encounter with Christ by excluding heresy. An interesting thing happens here, however. The very heresies that are excluded prove to be continual temptations for later theologians—Docetism in particular is "as old as Christianity itself" and "still lives in the present."[36] Keeping in mind that for Bonhoeffer objective spirit is established simultaneously with the community and is indestructible once it is established, one can conclude that heresy itself is part of the objective spirit of the church-community. Whereas in *Sanctorum Communio*, we read only vague assertions of the ambiguity of objective spirit, here we have active obstacles to encounter with Christ included in the church's objective spirit.

In *The Cost of Discipleship*, Bonhoeffer presents an even greater paradox: Correct doctrine itself becomes an obstacle to encounter with Christ. He still acknowledges that the church is Christ existing as community and that, as such, "the Word of God is to be heard in the preaching which goes on in our church." Still, something has gone awry:

> The real trouble is that the pure Word of God has been overlaid with so much human ballast—burdensome rules and regulations, false hopes and consolations—that it has become extremely difficult to make a genuine decision for Christ. . . . It is not the fault of our critics that they find our preaching so hard to understand, so overburdened with ideas and expressions which are hopelessly out of touch with the mental climate in which they live.[37]

His chapter "Cheap Grace" details the many ways in which the true elements of Reformation doctrine have become stumbling blocks on the way to true discipleship. Here he seems to be on the verge of the antitraditionalism that has ravaged certain sectors of the contemporary American evangelical church—when Bonhoeffer referred to the "dangers" he perceived in the work, this was likely among them.[38] Yet just when a decisive break with his previous theology seems to be in evidence, just when it seems that the Christian community must be reestablished from scratch, he includes a chapter on the structure of the church that largely duplicates the materials and arguments found in *Sanctorum Communio*, albeit in less academic terms. The individual called by Christ is called into a community, and that community still has access to scripture and Luther, preaching and sacrament. The discipleship envisioned in this work stands in continuity with the historical church, and the essential difference from Christianity as it is usually practiced is a greater vigilance in avoiding self-serving interpretations of the gospel that allow the believer to explain away his or her complicity and inaction in the face of sin.

Up to this point, the continuation of the church has never seriously been called into question. *The Cost of Discipleship* raises the possibility that the world, despite all its good intentions and openness to the gospel message, will be discouraged and put off by the church's internecine struggles, but the specific reasons why this may occur are not explored at length. This situation changes in the *Letters and Papers from Prison*. Drawing on the terminology of post-Kantian religious theorists who sought to distinguish, alongside Kant's faculties (of pure reason, practical reason, and aesthetic judgment), a religious faculty that would account for human openness to the divine, he asserts:

> Our whole nineteen-hundred-year-old Christian preaching and theology rest on the "religious *a priori*" of mankind. "Christianity" has always been a form—perhaps the true form—of "religion." But if one day it becomes clear that this *a priori* does not exist at all . . . —and I think that that is already more or less the case . . . —what does that mean for "Christianity"?[39]

Again, as with heresy, we have something that has been with the church from the beginning, but instead of being a persistent temptation, "religion" is the foundation of the comprehensibility of Christian preaching—seemingly the very deepest level of the objective spirit itself. Even worse, if "religion" must be preserved in order for Christianity to continue, then there are serious questions about whether Christianity is worth saving: "There remain only a few 'last survivors of the age of chivalry', or a few intellectually dishonest people, on whom we can descend as 'religious'. Are they to be the chosen few?" Even Karl Barth, who first drew attention to the problem of "religion," failed in Bonhoeffer's eyes to answer the challenge adequately.[40] Clearly, though, Bonhoeffer still maintains his belief in God, and beyond that, he still believes in the church and makes extensive use of scripture. His basic theological grammar is still determined by his decisive insight that the church is Christ existing as community, so that immediately after saying that "God is beyond in the midst of our life," he adds as a natural conclusion, "The church stands, not at the boundaries where human powers give out, but in the middle of the village."[41] For Bonhoeffer, people will still enter into and participate in the church, because the church remains the place where God happens.

Bonhoeffer suggests that ridding the church of its reliance on "religion" is a chance to repeat Paul's liberating move of removing circumcision as a requirement for church membership.[42] By Bonhoeffer's account, in Paul's time, the exclusively Jewish nature of the emerging faith meant that circumcision had been implicitly required from the very beginning—that is, it was a self-evident part of the objective spirit of the church, and anyone wishing to enter into the church community would have to relate to that objective spirit. What Paul instituted was a decisive change in the objective spirit of the church in order to remain faithful to the church's mission to be God's community. Precisely because he was such a radical Jew, Paul was specially positioned to make this move—and similarly, precisely because he was such a conservative and such a traditionalist on matters of doctrine, Bonhoeffer is able to announce a radical rethinking of the place of the church in the world. At the same time that he attacks the main methods of Christian apologetic as "in the first place pointless, in the second place ignoble, and in the third place unchristian,"[43] he proceeds as though the idea of dispensing with the Bible, for example, had never occurred to him.

Shifts, even radical shifts, in the objective spirit of the church are legitimate because objective spirit is not finally the point. The church must have objective spirit in order to be identifiable across time and space.[44] The goal of God's work in the church, however, is not simply to create and maintain a particular cultural tradition, but rather to create a community that, like Christ, exists for others.[45] In his "Outline for a Book," Bonhoeffer suggests that in order to start existing for others, the church "should give away all its property to those in need."[46] The specific context of these remarks indicates that he means physical property, but one can easily extend this to conceptual property as well—just as the church should have no building to call its own, so also it should have no conceptual apparatus to call its own. In the last resort, "religion" is the attempt to win for Christianity a particular conceptual home within the kingdom of the modern world, which repeats the error of monasticism and of "cheap grace."[47] As Bonhoeffer notes in *Sanctorum Communio*, the church always exists within both the collective person of Adam and the collective person of Christ. Everything contained in the objective spirit of the church already belongs entirely to the world, and it is clear that Bonhoeffer regards "religion" primarily as the church's way of relating itself to the world. Now, however, a "world come of age" needs a church come of age; no matter what relations previously obtained, Christians are now called, in Richard Bube's words, "to recognize that we are fully responsible for what goes on in our lives and our world, not attempting to push off onto God those responsibilities which formerly were not ours but now are."[48] All that remains is to determine the specific forms Christianity must take in the new religionless world.

Bonhoeffer and the "World Come of Age"

Bonhoeffer provides few directives in his letters for the church in the situation of religionlessness. He alludes to the nonreligious interpretation of biblical concepts,[49] but the circumstances of his imprisonment prevented him from providing any concrete examples thereof. Most of the rest of his references to the activities of the church center on coming to recognize the extent of the problem. In reflecting on the possibilities open to the church, he sees only the attempted return to the Middle Ages, which would be intellectually dishonest, and the way "through repentance, through *ultimate honesty.*"[50] The Confessing Church, in his view, has partially succumbed to the temptation to return to the Middle Ages, but the real work of the church now is to ask, "Well then, what do we really believe?" He includes his own answers immediately after the question: belief in a God who is transcendent due to his being for others, the interpretation of the Bible along those lines, a reinterpretation of "cultus."[51] There is no question for Bonhoeffer that the church will remain identifiably Christian, and even Protestant.

There is some question, however, of whether Bonhoeffer is being somewhat naïve about the "world come of age." Kenneth Surin cites the scathing critiques of psychotherapists and existential philosophers as evidence that Bonhoeffer does not have an adequate critique of the world. If the church is truly going to evacuate the zone of "religion," he argues, then it will need an "immanent critique or deconstruction of this world," which for Surin is best provided by Adorno.[52] Barry Harvey is in basic agreement with Surin and argues that the very idea of the "world come of age" must be read ironically in our present postmodern context, in which the "eschaton has slipped its leash, and humankind is left standing, empty-handed and dumbfounded. . . . No *telos* beckons us."[53] Interestingly, however, the new situation Harvey sees within the cultural logic of late capitalism is essentially the same as Bonhoeffer's conception of the state of sin in *Sanctorum Communio*: a mass of isolated sinners, heading nowhere.[54] Similarly, Bonhoeffer's critique of the idea of "the mass" and other current sociological ideas show his healthy skepticism toward the modern world. It may be true that he claims in the letters to prefer the company of unreligious people, but it is also true that Christ preferred the company of sinners to that of Pharisees.

Bonhoeffer's work remains unsystematized and fragmentary, but his reflections in prison help to indicate the likely directions he would have taken in a hypothetical future systematization of the ideas that he had developed in his earlier theological work. If we read *Sanctorum Communio* and the *Letters and Papers from Prison* together, as part of the same basic theological project, Bonhoeffer's attempts to distance himself from idealism and from other forms of social theory appear within the frame of a worldly Christianity. Since the church is irreducibly in the world, the sociological structure of the church is already an "immanent critique or deconstruction of the world."[55] Beyond that, Bonhoeffer's work provides the groundwork for a concrete practice, something that is too often lacking in the constantly proliferating critiques of the modern world. Though some might be understandably disappointed that his untimely death left the church with an unfinished ethics, a liturgy without a community, and a model of biblical interpretation without any examples, the incompletion might work to the church's advantage. Perhaps the best way for Bonhoeffer himself to avoid the trap of a "positivism of revelation" was precisely by leaving a set of useful concepts and provocative questions for the church to grapple with in the process of working through modern problems. In the end, he may give the church more by giving less—an already assembled system can be adopted wholesale and just as easily discarded, but "one can never go back behind what one has worked out for oneself."[56]

Resurrection without Religion

The resurrection of the dead has often occupied an ambiguous place in Christian theology. On the one hand, the resurrection of Christ is regarded as the ultimate proof of his divinity, and belief in his resurrection is one of the most frequent litmus tests for what counts as true Christianity. On the other hand, the resurrection of the dead more generally can sometimes seem like an awkward footnote to Christian doctrine. It is a spectacular event associated with the end of time—but for all practical purposes, the tradition has been much more preoccupied with the fate of the individual's immortal soul.

Attempts to reconcile belief in the resurrection with belief in the immortality of the soul have generated considerable intellectual gymnastics. This perhaps indicates that the two doctrines are not a natural fit, and indeed many contemporary theologians of a more traditional bent have significantly de-emphasized the immortality of the soul in favor of the resurrection. Such approaches are often presented as a long-overdue return to the more originary truth of the gospel, but it cannot be denied that they also represent attempts to make Christian theology more relevant to an academic culture that is increasingly fascinated with the question of "the body."

Outside of academic circles, stances toward the resurrection have largely fallen into a familiar conservative-vs.-liberal pattern. Conservatives emphasize "literal" belief in the resurrection, even though this is surely one of the most inapt possible designators for such a singular event. Meanwhile, liberals have tended to explain it in ways that are in danger of explaining it away—for instance, by claiming that the resurrection accounts are a later development and of course the early communities simply had a firmly held belief that Christ was somehow still with them. The goal of such liberal approaches to the resurrection is to return the focus where it belongs: the moral edification to be derived from Christ's teachings.

In this essay, I propose an alternative approach to the resurrection of the dead, using the methodology I developed in my book *Politics of Redemption: The Social Logic of Redemption*.[1] I have called that methodology a social-relational one and—drawing on Bonhoeffer's prison writings as well as the work of Dorothee Soelle—a religionless one. It is religionless insofar as it does not start with the framework of a transcendent God and an immortal soul and does not assume that biblical or theological texts require such a framework in order to be meaningful. It is social-relational insofar as it pushes beyond the irreducible individualism of that traditional paradigm and focuses on ways that biblical or theological texts speak to the *social* structure of human existence. In order to uncover a social-relational logic in the text, however, it is necessary to take it as a whole. Dismissing certain elements as mythological accretions to be explained away imposes an outside framework onto the text that proves just as counterproductive as presupposing the metaphysical framework of the soul and its God.

My test case for this methodology was the vexed question of atonement theory, that is, of the various theological attempts to make sense of the nature and meaning of Christ's saving work. An investigation of the classical articulations of atonement theory showed that they all rely on a fundamental connectedness among human beings. This fundamentally social structure of humanity allows Adam to create a problem that propagates itself to all human beings and similarly allows Christ to solve that problem in a way that is (at least potentially or in principle) equally universal in scope.

The earliest extended discussion of the resurrection of the dead in the New Testament holds out the promise that this theme will be similarly productive when approached from a social-relational or religionless perspective. I am speaking here of 1 Corinthians 15, where Paul insists on a radical inseparability between Christ's resurrection and ours.[2] This inseparability is visible in the very phrase "resurrection *from the dead*" (*ek nekrōn*). It is easy to treat this phrase as a quasi-jargon term, such that "from the dead" is a King James–style way of saying something like "from the grave," but it is important to emphasize that the Greek term for "the dead" is plural here. A more expressive translation might say that Christ was raised "from among dead people" or "out of dead people." The "resurrection of the dead" isn't a general power that God possesses and has used in the particular case of Christ, but rather a universal event that Christ's resurrection kicks off. He is the "first fruits of those who have died" (15:20), and his action will have as universal an effect as Adam's propagation of death (15:21–22). If Paul envisions any from among the dead being excluded from the resurrection, he does not mention such a possibility here—and that is fitting, given that such a possibility would conflict with Paul's repeated assertions that death will be utterly defeated (15:26, 15:54–57).

Paul equally ignores the possibility of an immortal soul surviving the body, instead putting forth a more complex account of continuity-in-discontinuity. Responding to a hypothetical question about the kind of body in which the dead will be raised (15:35), he first turns to the analogy of a seed, which is not yet what it will become (15:37–38). Paul emphasizes the diversity among the types of bodies that God has created, including the various types of flesh (15:39) and the contrast between earthly and heavenly bodies (15:40–41). The contrast between the "seed" of the mortal human body and the "plant" of the resurrected body is just as stark: "It is sown in dishonor, it is raised in glory. It is sown in weakness, it is raised in power. It is sown an ensouled body [*sōma psychikon*], it is raised a spiritual body [*sōma pneumatikon*]" (15:42–44; translation altered). Paul repeats this contrast in terms of his first Adam/second Adam schema: "Thus it is written, 'The first man, Adam, became a living soul [*psuchēn zōsan*]'; the last Adam became a life-giving spirit [*pneuma zōopoioun*]" (15:45; translation altered). It is not clear exactly what Paul means by "soul" here, but he cannot possibly be putting forth the traditional "religious" view of the immortal soul if the soul is aligned with the mortal body that is overcome through the resurrection.[3]

While Paul's account of the resurrection of Christ begins with an attempt to shore up the authority of the gospel message and those appointed to preach it (15:3–11), it almost immediately opens out onto broader reflections on the death-defeating, life-giving consequences of Christ's resurrection for *all* the dead. It emphasizes themes of human solidarity, with no explicit attention to the metaphysical question of the immortal soul as a survival of individuality beyond bodily existence. While the end times play a significant role, the real payoff of the passage comes in the consequences of faith or trust in the resurrection for the community. This trust issues in a practice that anticipates the "life-giving spirit" that Christ has become as "first fruits of those who have died" (15:20).

The gospel accounts are at first glance significantly different from Paul's theological meditation. All four trace a similar narrative, with relatively limited explicit theological elaboration. First, a group of women come to the tomb in order to attend to the body, but they are informed by some type of messenger or messengers that Jesus is risen. Jesus then appears in person to gradually larger groups of people, but soon ascends into heaven, having promised some form of future presence or empowerment to his disciples. This presence or empowerment is sometimes but not always identified with the Holy Spirit.

The four narratives differ significantly in details—such as the precise identities of the women who first come to the tomb, the number and nature of the messengers, the events associated with each appearance—and explicating all those differences is beyond the scope of this essay. Instead, looking at each gospel account in turn according to the general scholarly consensus of their order of composition, I would like to focus on what one could call the structural differences among these narratives, the unique elements that make them more than trivial variations on a theme. As I try to show, these structural differences, far from representing serious contradictions, actually allow each account to enrich in its own way the basic scheme found in Paul.

According to scholarly consensus, the oldest of the Gospel accounts of the resurrection is Mark.[4] Like the rest of Mark's narrative, his resurrection account moves very quickly, and the common thread throughout this account is disbelief in the absence of miraculous signs. The women arrive to find the stone rolled away (16:3), and see a young man sitting in the tomb (16:4). The young man tells them Jesus has been raised and orders them to tell the disciples, but they are afraid and do not do so. Jesus then appears directly to one of the women, Mary Magdalene, who finally obeys and tells the others, but they don't believe her (16:9–11). He subsequently appears to two others, and they tell the others, who don't believe *them* (16:12–13). Finally, he appears to the disciples all together, berates them for their lack of faith, and orders them to tell the whole world (16:14–16). Jesus promises them that signs will accompany their message: "By using my name they will cast out demons; they will speak in new tongues; they will pick up snakes in their hands, and if they drink any deadly thing, it will not hurt them; they will lay their hands on the sick, and they will recover" (16:15–18). He is then immediately taken up to heaven (16:19), at which point the disciples obey and begin preaching, "while the Lord worked with them and confirmed the message by the signs that accompanied it" (16:20).

The message here is clear: Those who expect others to trust that something extraordinary has happened should also have something extraordinary about them. At the same time, it is noteworthy that Jesus appears to be trying to keep his direct appearances to an absolute minimum, at first appearing only to one person, then to two, and finally—obviously annoyed—to his disciples as a group. Taken together with the famous theme of the "messianic secret," Mark presents us with a savior who very much wants to take people's mind off of *himself* as an individual. As soon as he jump-starts the movement by appearing to as small an inner circle as possible, he immediately ascends to heaven and begins helping them invisibly.

The signs that Jesus "worked with them" follow in this pattern of taking the focus off Jesus as a person—there is no sign of the cross, for instance, and no particular emphasis on baptism or other distinctively "Christian" rituals. Instead, they put forth the content of his message. Casting out demons has been a priority all along, in keeping with Mark's emphasis on the defeat of Satan. In addition, when one takes into account the ways that the demon-possessed (most notably the Gerasene demoniac of Mark 5) were cut off from human society, the ability to cast out demons and the ability to "speak new tongues" fit together as ways of expanding the circle of human fellowship. Similarly, certain types of highly symbolic invulnerabilities (to snakes and poison) highlight the disciples' fearlessness before death, while their healing abilities reflect the life-giving nature of the resurrection.

Matthew's account is significantly different, both in narrative details and in overall tone. Perhaps the most significant difference is that Jesus's resurrection is not the first one mentioned—instead, immediately upon his death, the evangelist claims that "the tombs were also opened, and many bodies of the saints who had fallen asleep were raised" (27:52). What's more, these resurrected saints "came out of the tombs and entered the holy city and appeared to many" (27:53). Thus the first consequence of Jesus's death was the resurrection *of other people*, an occurrence that contradicts Paul's claim that Jesus was the first fruits from among the dead, yet neatly captures the logic of his overall argument.

When we turn to the resurrection account proper, it is clear that Matthew's version of the story has considerably more bombast than Mark's, with the earthquake and the dramatic appearance of the angel who rolls the stone away (28:2–3). Notably, however, the core reality is the same: The women arrive to find Christ's body already gone. The moment of the resurrection itself is never depicted in either account. Matthew provides a more dramatic "reveal" than Mark, but the main event happened at some unknown time between his burial and the women's arrival, without the guards or anyone else noticing it. The women and disciples all bow down in worship, providing a clearer indication of Jesus' divine status than in Mark, but in contrast to the terrifying angel, Jesus's appearance goes unremarked. Furthermore, Matthew does not depict any post-resurrection miracles, not even the ascension into heaven. Nor does he promise that the disciples will be able to perform miraculous signs: He merely promises that he will be with them.

This notion of Jesus's presence is a theme common to Mark and Matthew. Notably absent here, however, is any explicit mention of the sending of the Holy Spirit in the sense familiar from the liturgical observation of Pentecost. Matthew associates the Holy Spirit with the commandment to baptize, yet in neither Matthew nor Mark (nor indeed Paul) is any particular connection drawn between Jesus's resurrection and the working or availability of the Holy Spirit. Instead, Jesus's presence—for which no specific mechanism is described—appears to play the empowering and emboldening role one normally associates with the Holy Spirit. Together with the fact that Paul depicts the post-resurrection body as a "life-giving spirit" (1 Corinthians 15:45), this perhaps indicates that there was not initially a strong contrast between the resurrected Christ and a separate entity known as the Holy Spirit.

Luke's most significant structural innovation is to add a two-level frame within which Jesus' post-resurrection appearances occur. The first level of the frame is the explication of Scripture, which includes within it a frame centered on the sharing of food. In the appearance to the two disciples on the road to Emmaus, he first explicates Scripture and then shares a meal (or at least begins to), while in his subsequent appearance to the main body of his disciples, he first shares a meal and then explicates Scripture. In both cases, Jesus continues with the theme of moving the emphasis away from himself.

I will begin with the inner frame of sharing a meal. With the Emmaus road disciples, his identity remains unknown until he breaks bread with them (24:30–31), an act that traditional interpreters have associated with the Eucharist. With the other disciples, by contrast, he eats a piece of fish in order to demonstrate that he is not a ghost (24:34–42). The tradition has tended to emphasize that the latter meal indicates that Jesus has been "literally" resurrected. If we take the two meals together, however, the "menu" is not that of the Eucharist, but rather of Jesus's most famous miracle: the feeding of the five thousand. If I am correct that this miracle is Luke's point of reference, then this account enacts a transition from Jesus as detached miracle worker (breaking the bread and promptly disappearing) to a *participant* in the miraculous feast (eating the piece of broken fish). In that perspective, the important thing about Jesus's "literal" resurrection isn't the way it demonstrates God's transcendent power, but rather its portrayal of Jesus as *one of us*—indeed he is paradoxically even more "one of us," in the sense of being less superhuman, than before he died. Like Mark and Matthew, Luke is sparing in attributing miraculous signs to the resurrected Jesus (aside from ascending to heaven), so that he is strangely less impressive after rising from the dead than before and in fact frequently appears to be just "some guy," as in the encounter on the road to Emmaus.

The frame of scriptural interpretation works similarly. The explication of prophecy on the road to Emmaus serves to demonstrate that Jesus really was the messiah, while his second hermeneutical exercise opens outward to include the disciples' mission: declaring "repentance and forgiveness of sins . . . to all nations, beginning from Jerusalem" (24:47). In contrast to the accounts of Mark and Matthew, the disciples will be empowered not by Jesus's own presence, but by another entity known as the Holy Spirit—a gap that is emphasized by the waiting period the disciples have to undergo after the ascension (24:49).

While the exact nature and status of the Holy Spirit is not explained in this account, it is clear that the shift in emphasis toward the Holy Spirit thus corresponds with a shift in agency toward the disciples rather than Jesus. The resurrection account at the beginning of Acts deepens this insight when the narrator claims that before being taken up to heaven, Jesus taught the apostles "through the Holy Spirit" (1:2). After a waiting period, the disciples then receive the Holy Spirit in a remarkable vision, which gives them the ability to speak foreign languages (2:1–4); later in Acts, the disciples perform all the signs promised in Mark (save immunity to poison) and more. Acts thus presents Jesus as *also* empowered by the Holy Spirit in his post-resurrection teachings, the same Holy Spirit that will empower his disciples to carry on his mission and to do signs that, in Acts, are arguably even more impressive than Jesus's own. The shift from Jesus's earthly ministry to the ministry of the Holy Spirit has the effect of turning Jesus into a kind of "first among equals."

The Gospel of John enacts the theme of displacing the interest from Jesus as a person in a unique way, through its use of Jesus's intimate relationships. John has Mary Magdalene come to the tomb alone to find the tomb rolled away (20:1), then stages an enigmatic race between Peter and the beloved disciple to be the first to see the empty tomb (20:2–10). The beloved disciple becomes the first to believe (20:8), while Mary is the first to see the resurrected Jesus. The presentation of this encounter is particularly intimate, as Jesus goes unrecognized until he calls Mary by name (20:16). Yet Jesus tells her "do not hold on to me" or "do not touch me" (*Mē mou haptou*) and instructs her to tell the other disciples (20:17). What is important is not her personal attachment to Jesus, but furthering his mission.

The same theme recurs in the discussion of the beloved disciple after Jesus's reconciliation with Peter in chapter 21, when Peter asks whether the beloved disciple will remain alive until the end (21:20–21). What is noteworthy here is that Jesus does not indulge Peter's curiosity, basically declaring it none of his business (21:22). This leads to rumor-mongering among the disciples (21:23), but though the evangelist seems to declare in conclusion that he is the beloved disciple, he too declines to respond directly to the rumor, instead simply pointing to his own trustworthiness in witnessing the events related (21:24). Yet again we can see that an excessive focus on Jesus as an individual—in this case, on the very special personal relationship that only the Gospel of John portrays—is inappropriate. Neither Jesus nor the beloved disciple dignifies Peter's curiosity or the disciples' rumor with a clear answer: the important thing is to follow Jesus, that is, to trust in the events related in the gospel and act accordingly.

John also introduces a new perspective on the Holy Spirit. Later on the same day, Jesus appears to his disciples (20:19). After wishing them peace, he "showed them his hands and his side" (20:20), and the disciples "rejoiced when they saw the Lord" (20:21). Breaking with Luke's narrative, Jesus "breathed on them," telling them, "Receive the Holy Spirit" (20:22) and entrusting them with the power to forgive sins (or not). This incident is interesting for several reasons. First, it posits an extremely close bond between Jesus and the Holy Spirit, playing on the fact that the Greek *pneuma* means both "spirit" and "breath." Second, it is worth noting that in the Gospel of John, the forgiveness of sins is not a significant part of Jesus's ministry—even in the case of the woman caught in adultery he merely refrains from condemning her (8:11), and the narrator is at pains to clarify that only Jesus's disciples baptized repentant sinners, not Jesus himself (4:2). As in Luke, this is something of a "hand-off": Jesus has fulfilled one part of a larger mission that the disciples must now continue in their own way.

Perhaps the best-known addition in John's Gospel is the story of "doubting Thomas," which like Jesus's meal of fish in Luke is often put forward as proof of the importance of a "literal" resurrection. The agenda of Thomas, however, is not to verify that Jesus really has a body, but that he is really the one who was crucified: "Unless I see the mark of the nails in his hands, and put my finger in the mark of the nails and my hand in his side, I will not believe" (20:25). When Jesus appears to him and invites him to perform his investigation (20:27), Thomas does not do so, instead immediately declaring Jesus to be Lord and God (20:28), just as the other apostles believed upon seeing Jesus's wounds. Jesus then declares, "Blessed are those who have not seen and yet have come to believe" (20:29), and the narrator declares that this sign—that is, Jesus's appearance with his wounds from crucifixion—was chosen out of many others in order that the reader "may come to believe" (20:31). The most important sign of Jesus, then, is the demonstration that he really was the same Jesus who was crucified, a theme that dovetails nicely with Paul's insistence on the solidarity of Christ with all those who have died.

After this brief investigation of the most important New Testament accounts, what can we say about the significance of the resurrection of the dead? It seems clear that the resurrection of the dead bears some relationship with eternal life, but the emphasis in Paul and even more so in the Gospels is on the availability of at least some anticipatory participation in that eternal life *here and now*. This participation is not premised on membership in a self-enclosed elite, but instead in a service that continually crosses boundaries—beyond the initial setting of Judaism, beyond the kinds of social divisions caused by differing languages and by demonic possession, and ultimately beyond the distinction between the living and the dead. Indeed, the resurrection even appears to actively confound this last boundary, as the resurrected Jesus still bears the marks of his death.

Trust in the resurrection allows us to live as those who no longer fear death, even as we must still await its ultimate defeat. The tradition has tended to associate this boldness specifically with the trinitarian person known as the Holy Spirit, but none of these New Testament accounts makes such a clear distinction between Jesus and the Spirit. Paul seems to identify the resurrected Christ as a "life-giving spirit," but the logic of his argument dictates that that is what we will also become. The gospel accounts, in turn, express different aspects of this basic dynamic. Mark and Matthew emphasize Jesus's presence and his continuing role in empowering his disciples. Drawing on the resources of the Greek language, John presents the "Spirit" as the "breath" of the same Jesus who has just proven that he is the crucified one who is now risen. Luke-Acts, meanwhile, puts forth the Holy Spirit as a broader reality in which Jesus and his disciples equally, though differently, participate. The Holy Spirit cannot be separated from Jesus because the Holy Spirit names the immediate consequence of trust in the resurrection, a general resurrection that Jesus has inaugurated. Hence some of these accounts can claim that the Holy Spirit somehow "is" Jesus, or even directly identify the function of the Holy Spirit with Jesus, without naming any separate entity. Yet what is the Holy Spirit if it isn't *simply* Jesus?

In a religionless approach, we can't presuppose either the metaphysical framework of the transcendent God and the immortal soul or the trinitarian orthodoxy that attempted to square the gospel message with that framework, and so we cannot say much about what the Holy Spirit is in itself, at least not with much confidence. All we can definitively say is that the Holy Spirit is *us*. I do not mean this in the Hegelian sense whereby Christ is resurrected as the *Geist* of the church as an institution. Instead, I mean to indicate that the Holy Spirit's only concrete existence, as portrayed in the gospels, is in the work of those who trust in the resurrection. This *us* is defined by its relationship to Jesus, but not limited by it. Indeed, it is just the opposite: Insofar as our relationship to Jesus empowers us to overcome the fear of death, it emboldens us to reach out to all we meet.

The *us* that the Holy Spirit is, allows us to anticipate the day when we will be able to say *us* in the broadest and most all-inclusive way. Jesus remains an indispensable point of reference, yet the gospel accounts leave us with the impression that, to paraphrase John the Baptist, "Jesus must become lesser, we must become greater." From a religionless perspective, we can see that Jesus did not come so that we could become Christians, but so that we could become *us*, in the most powerful sense of the word—an us that is constitutively open, continually transgressing every boundary, even and especially the boundary that sets it off from others.

This is the account of the resurrection that a religionless approach gives us access to. Yet some readers may be wondering whether this scheme really requires us to *reject* the traditional framework of the transcendent God and the immortal soul.[5] Might it not be safer to harvest the insights of a religionless approach and incorporate them into a more traditional view? For instance, one might say that although the emphasis is clearly on the resurrection of the *body*, nothing in these passages explicitly excludes the notion of an immortal soul that survives death. Yet how is the notion of a soul that can never die compatible with the crossing of the boundaries between life and death that we see in resurrection? Resurrection is certainly an overcoming of death, but it is far from an exclusion of it—after all, Jesus still carries the marks of his death on his resurrected body. And what sense can Jesus's—and, by extension, our—solidarity with the dead make if the dead are not really dead? Indeed, I would argue that the traditional concept of the soul, that hard core of individuality that is in the last analysis impervious to any influence aside from its own free will, is incompatible with anything but the most superficial kind of solidarity.

A potentially more serious question arises in connection with the necessity to reject the transcendent God: Who but a transcendent, all-powerful God could perform a miracle as profound as the resurrection? These accounts may emphasize the consequences of the resurrection for human agency, but don't they logically presuppose an act of God? To this I would reply that it does require an act of God, but not necessarily a *transcendent* God, nor a purely *miraculous* act of God. The notion of a miracle implies that God is somehow violating the laws of nature, yet Paul is able to present the resurrection through the naturalistic metaphor of planting seeds—and more generally, to portray the resurrection as God's ultimate goal for all of creation. The resurrection is certainly amazing and unanticipated from a human perspective, but to view it as the miraculous act of a transcendent God implies an inviolable boundary between God and creation, one that can only be crossed in one direction. Why should this one boundary remain pristine and unaffected amid the proliferation of transgressions the resurrection inaugurates?

One can also come at this question from another direction: How could one say all we have said about the resurrection and then maintain that the power of resurrection must be something God and God alone possesses? The resurrection is not the kind of power that can be "possessed," and in fact, one of its defining signs is breaking people free from "possession" by demons. The first fruits of the resurrection was Jesus, "who, though he was in the form of God, did not regard equality with God as something to be exploited [*harpagmon*]" (Philippians 2:6)—and what is a possession if not something seized in order to be exploited? Further, the agent of Jesus's resurrection is very often identified precisely as the Holy Spirit whose movement the resurrection inaugurates (e.g., Romans 1:4), in a strange time-warp logic that challenges any straightforward notion of agency.

The resurrection is undoubtedly divine, but it is an outgoing of the divine, with the goal of making us divine in just that outgoing way. We must never imagine that we possess the power of resurrection, lest we become something completely contrary to the *us* the resurrection seeks to make us. The way to prevent that is not, however, to keep the possession of the resurrection safely in the hands of a transcendent God, which would paradoxically enshrine possession as what is holiest and best. To become the *us* that the resurrection calls us to be, we must give up on possessing the resurrection, on possessing faith, on possessing the Holy Spirit, and above all, on possessing *us*—not because God actually possesses all those things in a way that excludes us, but because being *us* excludes any possession whatsoever.

Toward a Materialist Theology
Slavoj Žižek on Thinking God
beyond the Master Signifier

In 2008, I published a book titled *Žižek and Theology*.[1] In retrospect, it turned out to be a particularly fortuitous time to write a work on the theme of Žižek's use of theology. On the one hand, over the course of three books on Christianity, Žižek had arrived at a consistent view of the true meaning of Christian theology. On the other hand, he had just completed his self-declared "magnum opus," *The Parallax View*,[2] in which he consolidated his intellectual project in a new way. Accordingly, I chose to focus my work on an account of Žižek's intellectual development that highlighted the importance of his engagement with Christian theology as a kind of "hinge" between his earlier work and the more mature position reached in *The Parallax View*.

My goal in the present essay is to extend and deepen my account of the importance of theology in Žižek's work by responding to two persistent—and, in my view, completely justified—criticisms of *Žižek and Theology*. First, readers have criticized me for focusing too strictly on the interpretation of Žižek's work without applying his theological approach constructively. Second, they have rightly pointed out that my account of Žižek's development of "dialectical materialism" in *The Parallax View* did not seem to be as clearly connected to my previous argument as it could have been. Reflecting on these critiques, I have come to believe that they are closely related. In order to connect *The Parallax View*'s ontology and ethics—themselves interrelated—to theology, it was not sufficient to provide an expository account. Instead, I should have set the concepts to work theologically, or to put it differently, I should have set the concepts loose into theology. That is what I propose to do here, focusing on the relationship between dialectical materialism and the "death of God."

Theology and Dialectical Materialism

In *The Parallax View*, Žižek speaks of his project as a rehabilitation of "dialectical materialism," a goal that he associates both with the revival of Marxist movements and with the retrieval of the German Idealist attempt to develop the "System of Liberty."[3] Continually and variously applying his core concepts of the parallax gap and the death drive, he develops this project along several different axes, arguably the most innovative of which is his intervention into the field of cognitive science. Yet this self-proclaimed "magnum opus" also recapitulates and extends developments from earlier in his intellectual trajectory, including his focus on subjectivity as negativity, his insistence that a truly emancipatory politics must "tarry with the negative," and—perhaps distressingly for some secular readers—his engagement with Christian theology.

On the latter front, he devotes the entire second chapter to assembling "building-blocks for a materialist theology." There he follows a pattern that had already appeared in what I regard as the most fully realized of his three books on Christianity, *The Puppet and the Dwarf*,[4] and that is later repeated in his most recent work on theology, his contributions to *The Monstrosity of Christ*.[5] He begins with a kind of internal critique of a Christian thinker, in this case Kierkegaard. Although he finds a great deal to like about the thinker, Žižek is ultimately using him as a foil, showing how he falls short of the true radical core of the Christian message, namely Hegel's particular vision of the "death of God," which opens up the door to the only authentic atheism. Žižek then draws various ontological conclusions from this position, along with more or less explicit ethical consequences. In *The Puppet and the Dwarf*, the primary Christian interlocutor is G. K. Chesterton, and in *The Monstrosity of Christ* he continues to discuss Chesterton while adding Meister Eckhart to the mix. Though the details obviously change, the overall pattern is the same: the point of engaging with representatives of "actual existing" Christianity (even more or less marginal ones) is to set in relief Christianity's revelation of the "death of God," which itself is ultimately important not as a matter of religion or dogmatics but as a way of getting at the shape of the world we live in and the ethics that best responds to it.

The ontology toward which Žižek is pointing in all of these writings is, of course, his version of dialectical materialism. Yet this brand of materialism is also a theological one in some sense, or is at least developed out of a "materialist theology." In order to clarify what is going on here, I will not proceed by textual exegesis, but will instead take the risk of systematizing Žižek's work and bring together various patterns that my reading of Žižek has uncovered, using a dialectical form of argument to arrive at a dialectical materialism.

Let us begin with the ontology that is broadly characteristic of traditional Christianity. The two key components are God and creation, and they are related in two main ways. On the one hand, they are related negatively, as opposites: God is eternal while creation is temporal, God is infinite while creation is finite, etc. In short, we can derive the characteristics of God by taking what we know about creation and simply negating it. On the other hand, God founds and sustains creation, even going so far as to develop an economy of salvation when it falls into sin. The logic here is identical to that of the "master signifier" or "constitutive exception"—God founds creation while being exempt from all the limitations of creation. What's more, God reflects the tautologous character of the "master signifier," insofar as God is the point where the quest for explanation ends. The fact that we generally think of God in this way whether we believe in God or not can be seen in the debate over creationism. While creationists are forever claiming that the complexity of the world requires some transcendent explanation, it is relatively seldom that one hears the obvious retort that such a maneuver only exacerbates the problem: If the complexity of the universe requires explanation, surely the existence of a being who could create it is in need of *even more* explanation. The creationist's logic, which prevents this question from even arising, is ultimately tautologous. God doesn't exist because of some outside cause, God exists *because God exists*. And on the religious level as well, in the last resort, the answer to the question of why we should care what God thinks is *because he's God*. In sum, in the traditional Christian ontology, God is the constitutive exception to the created order, the one who negates it on every level and yet declares it "very good."

Materialism, in its most common or "vulgar" form, dispenses with God, leaving only the "very good" world. Yet for Žižek, the function of the master signifier remains very much in place, finding ever-new forms—ranging from the unalterable laws of Newtonian physics to the "historical necessity" that supposedly justified the crimes of Stalin. Particularly in the realm of evolutionary theory, the narrative of scientific progress is often thought to be one of overcoming theological prejudices, but from a Žižekian perspective, the conflict between Genesis and Darwin is a superficial one that masks a deeper complicity. Vulgar materialism wants to have a well-defined, self-consistent world, and for Žižek, the only way to achieve that is through some kind of constitutive exception. Hence this particular form of atheism nonetheless remains traditionally theological in form. And indeed, it is possible that the perceived conflict between faith and modern science may never have arisen if not for a certain stubbornness on the part of church officials, whose betrayal of the heritage of allegorical interpretation set up a fatal collision between the findings of empirical research and a flat-footed and unimaginative reading of Scripture. Healing that breach is in fact a major goal both of Pope Benedict XVI and of his Anglo-Catholic allies, the theologians of the Radical Orthodoxy school. Both argue that faith in God is necessary to found reason, and both miss the fact that modern scientific reason, at least as popularly understood, already has the "God" it needs in the form of a master signifier, whether that be the law of nature or even the notion of "the world" as such.

In a sense, then, vulgar materialism is always also theological materialism, even if its master signifier or "God" goes under different names. This is not simply a matter of "leftover" theological influences that must be purged—even if Richard Dawkins or Christopher Hitchens succeeded in convincing literally everyone on earth to abandon Christianity and indeed every historical religion, and even if all memory of the existence of the historical religions could somehow be erased, the essentially theological structure of vulgar materialism would remain.

The way forward is not to continue to negate "faith" in favor of "reason," but to take a step back and negate the very frame that allows us to distinguish between "faith" and "reason." Žižek believes that he has found that negation in Hegel's understanding of the significance of Christ's death on the cross. Where the orthodox doctrine of the Trinity attempted to ensure that there was some aspect of divinity that was not caught up in the Incarnation, Hegel claims that the Father's self-emptying of his divinity into Christ the Son is both complete and irreversible. On the cross, then, divinity empties out into the world in the form of the Holy Spirit, which is the bond of the Christian community. Žižek places considerable importance on the notion of the Holy Spirit as a new form of social bond that would escape the ideological structure founded on the master signifier, but for my present purposes, it is more important to focus on the Incarnation itself. I have pointed out that for traditional Christianity, God is the negation of the world, and if Christ really is fully divine, that means that he represents the entry of that negativity *into* the world. His death on the cross as "death of God" obviously marks the definitive end of God as exceptional foundation of the world. As a consequence, the very negation that God had cordoned off into a transcendent realm flows out into the world, shaking it to the core and opening up a wound that will never heal. This could sound like a mythopoetic elaboration, but it is important not to lose sight of the logical consequence of the "death of God"—it is not just that there is no longer a God, but there is also no more *world*.

When God dies, that means that the master signifier that gave the world its coherence is gone. Instead of the familiar picture of a solid world governed by inalienable laws, one is left with a shattered, inconsistent, internally conflictual world. As Žižek says, drawing on the Lacanian *pas-tout*, meaning non-all or non-whole: "For the materialist, the 'openness' goes all the way down, that is, necessity is not the underlying universal law that secretly regulates the chaotic interplay of appearances—it is the 'All' itself which is non-All, inconsistent, marked by an irreducible contingency."[6] Pushing Kierkegaard in a materialist direction, he goes on to claim that

> Kierkegaard's God is strictly correlative to the ontological openness of reality, to our relating to reality as unfinished, "in becoming." "God" is the name for the Absolute Other against which we can measure the thorough contingency of reality—as such, it cannot be conceived as any kind of Substance, as the Supreme Thing (that would again make him part of Reality, its true Ground).[7]

In other words, within the truly materialist frame, God is not the constraining figure we had to banish in order to get the world. Instead, God names the very contingency and inconsistency of the world as such.

At this point, an obvious objection arises: Once we've reached this point, why do we need to maintain the reference to theology? The answer is that the temptation to reinstall some kind of "big Other" is remarkably persistent even among those who are consciously trying to escape it, as the example of vulgar materialism makes clear. Preserving the reference to Christianity, or at least Hegel's version of it, is valuable insofar as we will always need to be reminded of the "death of God." Particular master signifiers "die" all the time, always to be replaced by something else, but for Žižek, Christianity gives us something unique: a master signifier that disavows itself. As Chesterton tells us and as Žižek never tires of repeating, the gospels present us with a God who himself becomes an atheist, a God who cries out "My God, my God, why have you forsaken me?" Within the frame of orthodox theology, it's difficult not to conclude that God the Father really *has* forsaken Christ, remaining transcendently uninvolved as he suffers and dies—even if the Father sweeps in on the third day to raise him to glory, the abandonment of the cross and the grave is all too real. Many contemporary theologians, most prominently Jürgen Moltmann, would claim that we need to think of the Father as suffering with Christ in order to avoid this monstrosity, but in the Hegelian frame, the solution is actually to make things worse. As Žižek says, "When Christ dies, what dies with him is the secret hope discernible in 'Father, why hast thou forsaken me?': the hope that there *is* a father who has abandoned me."[8] That hope is among the most durable features of human experience, and Žižek's retelling of the Christian mythos provides a way to crush it ever afresh.

Case Studies in Materialist Theology: Augustine and Pseudo-Dionysius

The picture so far seems rather grim, and so I expect some of my readers may be asking themselves why we should accept Žižek's vision of dialectical materialism. The answer, Žižek would reply, is that it is the only way to gain access to truth—albeit by first noting that we have no access to "truth" in the way we are accustomed to think of it, because there is no such thing. Although all of this sounds very abstract, Žižek believes that in principle it matches up with the picture of the world that is emerging at the frontiers of quantum physics and in cognitive science. In fact, Žižek is generally very optimistic about scientific inquiry, believing that it does give us some kind of account of the Real. This is possible not because he embraces a naïve notion of scientific objectivity or disinterestedness, but because he believes that the pursuit of knowledge can be an end in itself, enjoyed for its own sake. This enjoyment gives the scientist access to a truth unmediated by any master signifier, and so dialectical materialism is the unconscious practice of science at its best, even if the odds of practicing scientists embracing Žižek's philosophy seem slim.

I have already written elsewhere about my interest in the ethics that grows out of Žižek's dialectical materialism, which was in fact what first drew me to his work in a serious way.[9] In the remainder of this essay, I would like to turn to the question that I left largely unanswered in *Žižek and Theology*: What does Žižek's use of theology in his project mean for theology? I have tried to show what Žižek's version of a Hegelian "death of God" theology is doing for his own project, but what further use could be made of it? Žižek's own critique of orthodoxy in *The Monstrosity of Christ* points in an interesting direction, one that I would like to expand on here—namely, it points toward a way of thinking God outside of the framework of the "constitutive exception."

As I have already noted, traditional Christian theology has tended to think of God in terms of the "constitutive exception," and as Žižek points out, the development of the doctrine of the Trinity was motivated in part by a desire to reconcile belief in the full divinity of Christ with the conviction that God must be impassible or unchangeable, that is, to preserve "God-Father" as the one who "continues to pull the strings [and] is not really caught in the process" of divine kenosis or self-emptying.[10] My purpose here is not to critique the doctrine of the Trinity as such, whose development was of course overdetermined and whose "final" version has many features that continue to be productive of thought. Rather, I wish to suggest that the fact that the doctrine of the Trinity was so hard-won counts as prima facie evidence that the Hellenistic notion of an eternal impassible God (i.e., a God who acts as "constitutive exception" to the creative order) and the Christian narrative of God's kenosis in Christ do not fit together in an obvious way. Some theologians might claim that such a contradiction is unavoidable as we finite humans seek to know the infinite God, but I agree with Žižek's rejection of the notion of paradox, believing that, like its close cousin "mystery," it too often serves to indicate where a theologian gave up. Indeed, the notion of paradox often serves to shore up a concept of God as "constitutive exception," as when conservative theologians would have us believe that God disrupts our expectations sheerly for the sake of doing so. The counterintuitive has its place in theology as in all disciplines, but it must *lead somewhere*, or else it devolves into simple intellectual laziness.

In discussing the possibility of a thinking of God that escapes the logic of the "constitutive exception"—in other words, the possibility of a non-all or non-whole God—I would like to turn to two of the most influential texts of the Christian tradition: Augustine's *Confessions* and Pseudo-Dionysius the Areopagite's *Divine Names*.[11] My reason for taking this approach is a reflection of my own theological method—I prefer to be able to find some ground in the tradition if at all possible, both out of a fear of indulging in sheer speculation and out of a conviction that the Christian tradition is, if we read closely enough, consistently stranger than we expect it to be.

Augustine's *Confessions* provides a prime example of this strangeness. In his concluding commentary on the first creation account in Genesis, he devotes two full "books" of the text to the first two verses, spending much of Book 11 on a discussion of the nature of time and turning in Book 12 to the possible referents of the "heaven and earth" of Genesis 1:1. While acknowledging that the commonsense reading that refers them to the familiar sky and ground is plausible and has its own truth and utility, Augustine believes that it is more fitting to assume that the "heaven" of Genesis 1:1 refers to the "heaven of heavens," a purely intellectual realm characterized by closeness to God, and the "earth" refers to "a certain formlessness without anything to specify it" (12.3.3). Augustine is deeply perplexed by this formless matter:

Reason told me that if I wished to conceive of something that was formless in the true sense of the word, I should have to picture something deprived of any trace of form whatsoever, and this I was unable to do. For I could sooner believe that what had no form at all simply did not exist than imagine matter in an intermediate stage between form and non-existence, some formless thing that was next to being nothing at all. (12.6.6)

As Catherine Keller points out in *Face of the Deep*,[12] Augustine's attempt to pin down this formless matter leads him into interesting contradictions, which she mobilizes in her attempt to disprove the doctrine of the *creatio ex nihilo*. Perhaps the most interesting for my purposes is the path that he must follow in order to understand formless matter:

So my mind ceased to question my spirit, which was full of images of bodily forms which it changed and rearranged as it willed. I fixed my mind upon the bodies themselves, and looked deeper into the mutability by which they cease to be what they were and begin to be what they were not. (12.6.6)

This retreat from images exactly echoes his struggle, detailed at great length throughout the *Confessions*, to understand God as something other than a body, but in this case it leads him not to the perfect changelessness of God, but to changeability as such. Despite this apparent overlap, though, the fundamental difference between God and formless matter is clear: God is *above* form, while the primordial matter is *below* it.

A similar logic is at work in Pseudo-Dionysius's account of evil as deprivation of good.[13] The language that this mysterious author uses to describe evil can in many cases overlap with the language he uses to describe the God who is beyond being, as when he claims that evil "has a greater nonexistence and otherness from the Good than nonbeing has" (4.19)—like God, evil is beyond affirmation and negation. But again, the difference between the two is clear: God is above being, while evil is below it. Indeed, the Areopagite is unsparing in his denigration of evil: "It is a defect, a deficiency, a weakness, a disproportion, a sin. It is purposeless, ugly, lifeless, mindless, unreasonable, imperfect, unfounded, uncaused, indeterminate, unborn, inert, powerless, disordered" (4.32).

This insistence is interesting in itself: Could anyone fail to recognize that evil is, in fact, evil? Pseudo-Dionysius does refer to the metaphysical dualism that, in the form of the various Gnostic sects, would be a perpetual adversary to Christianity (4.21), but I would suggest that he is here reacting to the logic of his own text, which leads to a kind of overlap between his purely negative account of evil and his negative theology. That is not the only problem he faces with regard to evil, however. He must also deal with the problem that haunts all hierarchical ontologies: If evil is deprivation of being, then it becomes difficult to resist the temptation to declare beings that fall lower on the scale to be somehow inherently evil. Pseudo-Dionysius is much more consistent than Augustine in resisting this temptation, absolutely affirming the participation of even inert matter in the Good and declaring unequivocally that "the evil in souls does not owe its origin to matter but comes from disorder and error" (4.28). Even seemingly inherently evil beings such as demons are good insofar as they exist, but "are evil insofar as they have fallen away from the virtues proper to them" (4.34).

Evil beings are evil, then, not because they lack being—every particular being is lacking in the superabundance of God's being. Rather, they are evil because they have fallen from what they should be, which seems to mean their place in the ontological hierarchy that gives the created world its order and stability. Differences in degree within the hierarchy are appointed by God for the benefit of the world as a whole, whereas the differences caused by evil fall outside of God's plan and threaten the stability of the world.

Bringing together Augustine's reflections on formless matter and Pseudo-Dionysius's account of evil, we might say that evil is a change in form that goes against God's order, while good or divine action is a change in form that reinforces it. Both necessarily involve the moment of formlessness that Augustine detects in the transition between forms, and both can lead to good results—as Pseudo-Dionysius says, God's providence can make use of evil (4.33), a statement with which Augustine would surely agree. More broadly, it seems impossible to conceive of God as acting otherwise than by means of change, given that creation is inherently subject to change insofar as it is not divine. Even assuming that God's creation had remained in its initial state, as Augustine believes the "heaven of heavens" to have done, the very fact of being created would be a change, a fact that Augustine expresses mythopoetically in the (non)image of formless matter.

The only difference between evil change and good change, then, seems to be the initial reference to God as the guarantor of the world's order, that is, to God insofar as he serves as the constitutive exception of the world. Taking a step beyond Augustine and Pseudo-Dionysius's explicit intentions, if we remove God as master-signifier, we are left with changeability as such as simultaneously the foundation and the perpetual unfounding of the world—that is, essentially the same result that Žižek, following Hegel, claims for the incarnation and death of Christ. My point here is not simply to replicate Žižek's results from within the tradition, but instead to demonstrate a potential approach to the tradition for a materialist theology. Here I am extending Žižek's strategy of reading (normally marginal) figures in the history of theology as approaching dialectical materialism but falling short. By pushing this approach into even the most central figures of the tradition, I am claiming that we need to take seriously the possibility that when great minds such as Augustine and Pseudo-Dionysius attempt to think through the implications of Christianity with real rigor, they will, despite their cultural prejudices and philosophical leanings, necessarily end up at least laying the groundwork for an understanding of God as non-All.

A research agenda starting from that hypothesis would, for example, make the vast literature on evil as deprivation available in a new way—not as a direct presentation of "correct" views, of course, but as a tool to think with. More broadly, it would force us to reconceive what theology is and does. A materialist theology that rejected the authority of God as master signifier would necessarily be deprived of the institutional standing that currently founds the distinction between Christian theology and philosophy, a development that from my perspective would be all to the good. Instead of posing as the transmitters of the unchanging truths of God, either for or in opposition to a changing world, theologians would be disciplinarily situated as philosophers working from within a particular tradition, just as other philosophers work from within phenomenology or psychoanalysis. Standing in that tradition would no more predetermine their conclusions than Žižek's use of Lacan and Hegel predetermines his, as he reveals with particular candor in *The Indivisible Remainder*.[14] Instead of reflection on a body of doctrine, then, materialist theology would be an intellectual tradition that avows the double meaning of *tradere* as "to hand on" and "to betray"—a loyalty that finds its best expression in a rigorous infidelity.

PART II

Theology under Philosophical Critique

The Failed Divine Performative
Reading Judith Butler's Critique of Theology
with Anselm's On the Fall of the Devil

Of all the many examples of failed ideological interpellation, the fall of
the devil is undoubtedly the most extreme. Created to be the greatest of
all angels, Satan instead turns against God, becoming thereby the figure
of ultimate evil. Though it is legitimated through reference to a few ambiguous passages in Scripture, the story of the fall of the devil was created
virtually from scratch in the course of theological reflection in attempt to
account for the evil that already appears to be present before the fall of
Adam and Eve, represented by the tempting snake in the Garden of Eden.
In addition to this role as a "prequel" to the fall of humanity, the fall of the
devil came to serve as a way of thinking through the formal conditions of
a creature choosing to defy the divine intention.

This search for the conditions of possibility of rebellion against one's
creator resonates strongly with Judith Butler's account of ideological interpellation, which constitutes the subject but at the same time always necessarily "fails." In light of recent interest in Butler's work among scholars of
religion,[1] one might be tempted simply to offer a "Butlerian" reading of a
representative text on this theological theme. To skip directly to an appropriation of Butler for the purpose of understanding a theological text,
however, would be to ignore a major thread of Butler's development of the
notion of ideological interpellation and the allied concept of performativity: an uncompromising critique of what she calls "theological" patterns
of thought. Indeed, this critique is so pervasive that it is difficult to gauge
the precise stakes of her theory of interpellation unless one understands

what Butler means by "theology." In turn, a reading of a theological text in light of Butler's theory can serve as a test case to determine whether Butler's critique hits its target—or alternatively, whether theological texts might actually move in directions similar to Butler's own project.

For the purposes of this essay, I have chosen Anselm's *Fall of the Devil*[2] as my test case. Anselm's unquestioned influence on the history of theology allows me, at least provisionally, to take him as representative, not simply of the theological theme of the fall of the devil, but of the mainstream of Western Christian theological discourse. Before analyzing Anselm's text, however, I must achieve two interrelated goals: outlining Butler's theory of interpellation and clarifying her critique of "theology." My procedure, then, will be as follows. First, I examine what Butler means by "theology," focusing on her critique of Lacan in *Gender Trouble*.[3] I then elaborate Butler's closely related theories of performativity and interpellation as laid out in *Excitable Speech* and *The Psychic Life of Power*,[4] and in particular in her reading of Althusser's "Ideology and Ideological State Apparatuses"[5] in the latter work. Only after all this has been established do I attempt a Butlerian reading of Anselm, with an eye toward determining whether theological texts are always as "theological" as Butler seems to assume.

Butler's Theology

Butler refers to "theology" in nearly all of her books. These references are almost uniformly negative, but not in the sense of indicating an explicit polemic against theology or religion. She does take a Nietzschean critique of religion largely for granted, but the primary targets of her critique of "theology" are avowedly secular thinkers who take up positions that seem to Butler to function "theologically." What she means by this is perhaps best exemplified in her critiques of Jacques Lacan (which are echoed in her later critiques of Lacanians such as Slavoj Žižek and Mladen Dolar).[6] In one of her many discussions of Lacan in *Gender Trouble*, Butler makes a distinction between "the materialist and Lacanian (and post-Lacanian) positions" regarding sexual difference.[7] The materialist position, exemplified by Jacqueline Rose and Jane Gallop, "underscore[s] . . . the constructed status of sexual difference, the inherent instability of that construction, and the dual consequentiality of a prohibition that at once institutes a sexual identity and provides for the exposure of that construction's tenuous ground."[8] In this view, "the prohibition that constructs identity is inefficacious," so that "the paternal law ought to be understood not as a deterministic divine will, but as a perpetual bumbler." By contrast, in the Lacanian view (including Irigaray's post-Lacanian view), the "paternal

Law" as that which generates sexuation "bear[s] the mark of a monotheistic singularity."[9]

One is tempted, then, to say that for Butler, the Lacanian view *does* understand sexual difference as "a deterministic divine will," whereas a materialist view (i.e., Butler's own) emphasizes the constructed and fluid character of sexual difference. However, her account of the "monotheistic" nature of the Lacanian view is much more complex. Further on in *Gender Trouble*, Butler criticizes Lacan's conception of the Symbolic or paternal Law as constitutively unattainable, arguing against the plausibility of "an account of the Symbolic that requires a conformity to the Law that proves impossible to perform and that makes no room for the flexibility of the Law itself, its cultural reformulation in more plastic forms."[10] Such a view of the Symbolic leads to "a romanticization or, indeed, a *religious* idealization of 'failure,' humility and limitation before the Law, which makes the Lacanian narrative ideologically suspect."[11] Butler compares this concept of the law to "the tortured relationship between the God of the Old Testament and those humiliated servants who offer their obedience without reward," a comparison that for Butler is all the more telling in light of her perception that sexuality has taken the place of religion's "demand for love."[12]

Thus the "monotheistic" element of Lacan's thought consists in the idea of a law that is unilaterally imposed and nonnegotiable, but at the same time impossible to fulfill, leading Butler to wonder if the law aims only at enforcing the subject's feeling of "an enslavement to the God that it claims to be unable to overcome."[13] For Butler, therefore, "Lacanian theory must be understood as a kind of 'slave morality'" in the Nietzschean sense.[14] The task of the reader of Lacan is to look "for the theological impulse that motivates" the account of the unchanging paternal Law "as well as for the critique of theology that points beyond it." Most important, one must avoid the key move of "slave morality," namely, the disavowal of "the very generative powers it uses to construct the 'Law' as a permanent impossibility."[15]

The problem with "theology," then, isn't simply that it's an illusion, though it is clear that Butler's materialism commits her to the view that no extra-temporal absolute, either in the form of a personal God or an immutable law of all human culture, can actually exist. The problem is rather that the subject, by participating in and thereby maintaining this illusion, fails to recognize its own power. The Lacanian who resigns himself or herself to the inevitability of the Symbolic does not just decide not to waste energy on something impossible—in conceding the immutability of sexual difference, the Lacanian or "theological" subject lends his or her energy to the ongoing struggle *against* any reformulation of the Symbolic order. Yet despite this decisive rejection of a "theological" stance, it is not the case that "theology" is the sole object of Butler's critique. The third part of *Gender Trouble* is devoted to the argument that any attempt to ground gender in some kind of prelinguistic realm—including apparently quite "materialist" attempts—is always necessarily self-undermining insofar as it simply ends up repeating the patterns of the hegemonic norms of sexual difference.

With all this in mind, then, one can tentatively distinguish two types of error with regard to sexual difference in Butler's theory. On the one hand, there is what one could call the "vulgar materialist" error, which misrecognizes the appropriate field of battle, obfuscating the stakes of a political-cultural-linguistic struggle by misdirecting it toward a biological or otherwise prelinguistic ground. On the other hand, there is the "theological" error, which is correct insofar as it locates sexual difference on the level of culture and language, but goes astray in reifying a particular cultural construct (for instance, the paternal Law) and thereby attempting to put it above the fray—a move that necessarily generates, and is in turn reinforced by, feelings of failure and guilt.

With this concept of the "theological" in hand, we can now turn to Butler's theory of performativity as it is developed in *Excitable Speech*. The argument of *Excitable Speech* is closely related to that of *The Psychic Life of Power*, in particular to the reading of Althusser in the latter. In the introduction to *Excitable Speech*, Butler provides a capsule summary of this reading, arguing that "Althusser inadvertently assimilates social interpellation to the divine performative," resulting in a figuration of the "'voice' of ideology" as "almost impossible to refuse."[16] The "divine performative" and related notions, however, are developed in more detail in *Excitable Speech*, resulting in a kind of mutual co-implication—in order to fully understand either, one must start with the other. Given that this analysis is directed toward the reading of Anselm's *On the Fall of the Devil*, in which the account of the devil's "interpellation" presupposes the power of the divine performative to call the devil into being, I have chosen to begin with *Excitable Speech*, a choice that also has the benefit of clarifying the concrete political stakes of Butler's more abstract philosophical argument in *The Psychic Life of Power*.

As the above quotation illustrates, Butler makes reference to theology in connection with performativity in *Excitable Speech*, but it is not the only or even the primary mode in which she critiques various opposing theories of the performative. First of all, she frequently deals with Austin's distinction between *il*locutionary speech acts, where the effect happens immediately *in* the words, and *per*locutionary speech acts, where the effect happens *by means of* the words. Although she does not go so far as to say that they don't exist, she does find the notion of illocutionary speech acts deeply problematic insofar as it tends toward a "magical view of the performative,"[17] one which is automatically effective in any context whatsoever. For Butler, Catharine MacKinnon's theory of pornography as hate speech, which has found a certain amount of favor in court cases, amounts to such a "magical view." By contrast, Butler argues that "not all utterances that have the form of the performative, whether illocutionary or perlocutionary, actually work."[18] Consequently, Butler is "skeptical about the value of those accounts of hate speech that maintain its illocutionary status and thus conflate speech and conduct completely," preferring regulations that keep open "the gap between saying and doing" and acknowledge "that there is always a story to tell about how and why speech does the harm that it does."[19] Thus, to use a religious example that Butler does not, no act of hate speech, even the most unambiguously offensive, should be thought as doing harm *ex opere operato*, simply by being uttered.[20]

But the political stakes of Butler's argument in *Excitable Speech* go far beyond a simple policy recommendation. This is clear in her use of another word in addition to "theological" or "magical" to characterize misleading accounts of the performative: "sovereign." This word is so central to Butler's argument here that she titles the second chapter of the book "Sovereign Performatives." Before I turn to that chapter, however, it may be helpful to put my analysis of Butler's idea of "theology" to work, by addressing a passage in which Butler closely relates "theology" and "sovereignty." In the first chapter, Butler critiques notions of hate speech that privilege the prosecution of particular individuals as the best, or perhaps even sole, means of redressing the damage done by such speech. This approach depends on the installation of a monadic, "singular subject and act," which for Butler is a "clearly theological construction."[21] The first step in designating this construction "theological" is to claim that "the postulation of the subject as the causal origin of the performative act is understood to generate that which it names," on the model of God's creative "Let there be light."[22] As in the case of the Lacanian paternal law, the stakes of this "theological" turn move beyond the level of mere delusion to active dissimulation. That is, the installation of the subject covers over the history and citationality that actually render possible the damage of hate speech, and this particular dissimulation is itself a subspecies of the general dissimulation of the "subject-effect":

> If the function of the subject as fictive origin is to occlude the genealogy by which that subject is formed, the subject is also installed in order to assume the burden of responsibility for the very history that

subject dissimulates; the juridicalization of history, then, is achieved precisely through the search for subjects to prosecute who might be held accountable and, hence, temporarily resolve the problem of a fundamentally unprosecutable history.[23]

This analysis of the "theological" operation of the subject comes after a long analysis of the relationship between Austin's theory of performativity and Nietzsche's critique of the tendency to allow grammar to fool us into positing a doer who preexists the deed. Here Butler emphasizes that in Nietzsche's account, the "doer" is thought "primarily as a wrong-doer"[24] and relates that insight to the fact that "prosecuting hate speech . . . underscores the power of the *judiciary* to enact violence through speech."[25] And, indeed, Austin presupposes the "subject as sovereign" in his account and even uses a judge's sentence as a privileged example of performativity. By treating hate speech as the quasi-divine or "magical" performative of a sovereign subject, the courts effect a "displacement of [state] power onto the citizen and the citizenry, figured as sovereigns whose speech now carries a power that operates like state power to deprive other 'sovereigns' of fundamental rights and liberties."[26] Beyond that, it also opens up the possibility for the state to view the "sovereign" citizens' words as a violent threat to itself—a possibility that is realized in the Supreme Court decision that Butler so brilliantly analyzes later in the first chapter.

In the chapter "Sovereign Performatives," Butler generalizes the consequences of basing a theory of performativity on the presupposition of a sovereign subject. Specifically in the context of hate speech prosecution, Butler worries about "the peculiar *discursive power* given over to the state through the process of legal redress," namely, the power by which "*the state produces hate speech*"; that is to say, hate speech would not exist without the state's action of legally defining it in general and in particular cases.[27] Paradoxically, when the state produces hate speech through its juridical action, it produces it precisely *as* the act of a sovereign subject (the individual citizen), showing yet again that the subject-effect serves to occlude the subject's own historical origins. The idea of the sovereign subject is itself a "trope derived from state discourse," such that "figuring hate speech as an exercise of sovereign power implicitly performs a catachresis by which the one who is charged with breaking the law (the one who utters hate speech) is nevertheless invested with the sovereign power of law."[28]

In yet another turn of the screw, however, Butler follows Foucault in claiming that "power is no longer constrained within the sovereign form of the state," meaning that the exercise of law itself is no longer properly sovereign.[29] Illusions multiply:

This idealization of the speech act as sovereign action (whether positive or negative) appears linked with the idealization of sovereign state power or, rather, with the imagined and forceful voice of that power. It is as if the proper power of the state has been expropriated, delegated to its citizens, and the state then reemerges as a neutral instrument to which we seek recourse to protect us from other citizens, who have become revived emblems of a (lost) sovereign power.[30]

By presenting itself as a neutral arbiter of the political struggles represented by hate speech prosecutions, the state gains considerable leeway to intervene in those very struggles, most often in quite reactionary ways: "To give the task of adjudicating hate speech to the state is to give [the] task of misappropriat[ing hate speech] to the state."[31] Those who advocate a model of hate speech based on the performative act of a sovereign subject thereby end up reinforcing state power, a power of which Butler is, with good reason, deeply suspicious. Thus Butler repeats the basic structure of her critique of a "theological" view of sexual difference in her critique of sovereignty, adding the further complicating layer of the dialectical relationship between the state and the citizen. Here again, the primary target of her critique of "theology" is not so much contemporary religion as an ostensibly secular phenomenon—in this case, state authority.

Divine Interpellation

At this point, we are prepared to turn to Butler's reading of Althusser, who "inadvertently assimilates social interpellation to the divine performative."[32] This reading is found in the fourth chapter of *The Psychic Life of Power*, "Subjection Doth Make Subjects of Us All," which stands at a crucial turning point in the structure of the work as a whole, substantially completing the treatment of subjectification "in general" and opening the way for the consideration of melancholy and gender in the concluding two chapters. The project of *The Psychic Life of Power* is to bring together psychoanalysis and the Foucauldian theory of power, and it does so by examining a variety of texts that share a common structure. Each one, in its own particular way, locates the intersection of power and the psyche—of the "outside" and the "inside" of the individual—at the point of self-reflexivity, which is always figured as a religious or quasi-religious self-beratement. The guiding thread is provided by Nietzsche's analysis of "bad conscience" in *The Genealogy of Morals*, a text that is historically a common ancestor for both psychoanalysis and Foucault; Hegel's account of the "Unhappy Consciousness" appears to function primarily as a precursor to Nietzsche. Thus to a certain extent, the text itself retraces some of the same ground we have already covered. Hegel and Nietzsche correspond to Butler's critique of theology (which is of course explicitly based on Nietzsche in *Gender Trouble*), while Foucault corresponds to the application of that critique in a particular realm of state activity (prisons and hate speech, respectively). The reading of Althusser, then, should serve to complete the circle, presenting a vision of social life as completely saturated with what Butler has critiqued under the name of "theology."

Butler herself fiercely resists this vision, which leads to some interesting distortions in her reading of Althusser. The chief symptom is the general sense that she has somehow "caught" Althusser in something he did not intend to be doing. Butler proposes to reread Althusser's essay "to understand how interpellation is essentially figured through the religious example," so as to indicate the ways in which Althusser, like Hegel, Nietzsche, and Foucault, makes subject formation dependent on "a passionate pursuit of a recognition which, within the terms of the religious example, is inseparable from condemnation."[33] Here she follows her general principle of refusing to allow an example to be "merely" an example, and she defends this procedure as allowing "a symptomatic reading [note: this is Althusser's own term] that 'weakens' rigorous argument":

> I do not mean to suggest that the "truth" of Althusser's text can be discovered in how the figural disrupts "rigorous" conceptualization. . . . The concern here has a more specific textual aim, namely, to show how figures—examples and analogies—inform and extend conceptualizations, implicating the text in an ideological sanctification of religious authority which it can expose only by reenacting that authority.[34]

The problem here is not that Butler is making too much of the example, however, but rather too little—she is treating it precisely as "just" an example in the sense of a mere figure, when in actuality Althusser's references to religious ideology are grounded in his analysis of the situation of the Middle Ages, when the church was "the number-one Ideological State Apparatus."[35]

Although he proposes the school as the replacement for the church in the modern era, Althusser chooses instead to focus on Christian ideology (presumably because his readers are more accustomed to thinking of Christianity than of schools as a form of ideology), justifying this choice by his general principle that "the formal structure of all ideology is the same,"[36] or, as he often repeats, "ideology has no history."[37] Butler never quotes this principle in her reading of Althusser.[38] The lack of attention to this "unchanging" element in Althusser's theory is surprising given the strident "theological" critique to which she subjects Lacan in *Gender Trouble*, and one of Lacan's followers, Mladen Dolar, in this very chapter. We have already seen that Lacan's paternal Law, which is both nonnegotiable and impossible to fulfill, is "theological" in the Nietzschean sense of the word adopted by Butler. Dolar's critique of Althusser is characterized as "explicitly theological" due to its positing of a preexisting subject,[39] which again is based in the Nietzschean insight that was shown above to be at work in Butler's critique of the "sovereign" subject. Thus it seems to be out of step with Butler's general Nietzschean stance on "theology"—which up until now has proven to be remarkably consistent—to argue that Althusser's theory of interpellation is "religious" primarily (or even solely) because it uses explicitly religious examples.

What is missing here is any sense of the significance of Althusser's Marxism. For Butler, the use of religious examples serves to sacralize ideology, whereas for a Marxist such as Althusser, comparing bourgeois ideology to Christianity indicates that, like Christianity, bourgeois ideology is precisely an illusion. That is to say, Althusser himself is not being "theological" in his use of religious illustrations, but rather is showing—just as Hegel, Nietzsche, and Foucault do—that *bourgeois ideology* is "theological" in the precise sense that Butler uses the term. It may well be the case, however, that it is Althusser's Marxism—or rather, the unavailability of Althusser's Marxist stance to Butler—that leads Butler to the kind of reading she performs. Althusser claims that ideology is "endowed with a structure and a functioning such as to make it a non-historical reality, i.e., an *omni-historical* reality." He immediately specifies that this holds only under "what we can call history, in the sense in which the *Communist Manifesto* defines history as the history of class struggles, i.e., the history of class societies."[40] From the Marxist perspective, there is a classless society on the horizon, but if one cannot regard that as a viable possibility—as Butler presumably cannot—then Althusser is *effectively* saying that ideology is unchangeable and, more specifically, that ideology, even ostensibly secular bourgeois ideology, always bears features that correspond to what Butler finds undesirable about "theology." Beyond that, by implicitly positing that change in ideological structures is impossible without a radical and wholesale change in the means of production, Althusser is effectively cutting the ground out from under Butler's more piecemeal and cautious, though no less material, approach to ideological change.

Since my purpose here is to lay out Butler's theory of interpellation rather than to defend Althusser's theory from her critique, I am here going to read Butler's critique of Althusser somewhat "against the grain," based on the generally Butlerian principles discovered above. Bracketing for the moment Butler's antagonistic stance toward Althusser's references to religion, one can see that ironically, it is precisely the Christian references that provide Butler with the means to demonstrate the compatibility of Althusser's theory with her project in *The Psychic Life of Power*. Althusser makes some reference to psychoanalysis, but in general, he does not demonstrate a lively awareness of the inner life of the subject. This coheres with his project in the essay. All along, people had been accustomed to think of ideology as being primarily a matter of the inner life (individuals' opinions, prejudices, etc.). Althusser's innovation is to emphasize the "material existence" of ideology,[41] and so he consistently sidesteps questions of the subject's attitudes or inner convictions—even and especially in his analysis of Christianity—reducing the inner life to a secondary epiphenomenon.

Arguably, then, Althusser formally recapitulates on the level of ideology the tendency he critiques in the Marxist tradition. For Althusser, there has been a tendency to exaggerate the importance of the fact that the relations of production determine ideology "in the last instance" and to downplay the ways in which ideology functions precisely to keep those modes of production in place, that is, to downplay the "relative autonomy of the superstructure with respect to the base" and the "reciprocal action of the superstructure on the base."[42] What Butler's reading effectively achieves— even though Butler herself does not thematize this achievement—is to "correct" this tendency in Althusser by demonstrating the ways in which the "secondary" phenomena of the inner life of the subject serve to maintain the material institutions of ideology, or in other words, demonstrating the "relative autonomy of the subject with respect to ideology" and the "reciprocal action of the subject on ideology." Through setting aside Althusser's "deflationary" reading of Christianity and taking his examples literally, she is able to show how this "correction" is already implicitly at work in Althusser's text, even at the level of vocabulary, as in her analysis of Althusser's use of the verb *s'acquitter*.[43] The subject *really is* produced through a process of obfuscation relying on a paradoxical a priori guilt that precedes but also presupposes knowledge of the law (as in Althusser's famous example of the "hailing" by the police officer) and is exposed to the perpetual blackmail of choosing either obedience or non-being. Once the subject is established, however, it is not totally constrained to exercise its agency in the maintenance of the dominant ideology. By emphasizing— and arguably *over*emphasizing—the effectiveness of ideological interpellation in Althusser's theory, Butler sets in relief her own conviction of the ever-present possibility for subjects to overcome the blackmail of ideology by becoming "bad subjects" who demonstrate "a willingness *not* to be—a critical desubjectivation—in order to expose the law as less powerful than it seems."[44]

Thus for Butler, the "bad subject" does not simply dissolve into nothingness, but rather has the potential to affect the law in a way that upsets Althusser's Marxist scheme. Ideological change need not come about solely through a change in the "base," the mode of production. Rather, the very "secondary" epiphenomena that ideology generates in order to maintain itself contain the seeds, if not of ideology's thoroughgoing destruction, at least of genuine change. In the remaining chapters of *The Psychic Life of Power*, Butler looks at the specific resources for change that the dominant mode of ideological interpellation generates as necessary side effects (specifically mourning and rage), so as to open up the prospect for future forms of interpellation that would not be based on obfuscatory guilt. These hopes find more concrete development in her later works, where she tries to conceive a sociality that would be based on respect for vulnerability (in all its forms), rather than exploiting vulnerability in order to exact obedience.[45]

The Demonic Subject

The ground is now prepared for a Butlerian reading of Anselm's *On the Fall of the Devil*,[46] which is intended to serve as a test case for Butler's notion of "theology." Anselm's text is set up as a dialogue between a student and teacher on the vexed question of how the devil was able to rebel against God.[47] This difficult problem was largely self-imposed by the Western Christian tradition. Earlier tradition had proposed a narrative wherein the devil was initially a high-ranking angel who became jealous of God's favor toward humans and sought to sabotage them—a memorable and perfectly understandable narrative—but the theologians who followed in Augustine's wake were increasingly committed to the belief that the devil had rebelled from essentially the very moment of his creation. This schema has the perceived benefit of maximizing the devil's evil, both in intensity (making it a purely motiveless malignity) and in time (since he is evil for the longest time possible), but raises very serious questions about the devil's moral agency and God's apparent role in his fall. How can the devil be held responsible for a "choice" that happens in a condition of radical ignorance, when he has barely come into existence in the first place? Is God treating the devil fairly? Most disturbingly: Did God set the devil up to fall?

The text approaches these questions very indirectly, putting the most difficult objections to the post-Augustinian account of the devil's fall in the mouth of a student who is apparently afraid of the implications of the questions he is raising. Thankfully for him, the teacher—who represents the "official" position of Anselm himself—is there to set him on the right path. Thus, while the student does in a sense take the initiative of asking questions and sometimes even proposing theories (which the teacher invariably rejects), for the most part, he is fairly docile and eager to praise his teacher's brilliant solutions, a kind of "good subject" to stand in contrast to the extremely "bad subject" (i.e., the devil) whom they are discussing. I will not be foregrounding the student's role in the reading that follows, but one of the student's responses in particular seems to exemplify the stance of the "good subject": "Your argument neither accuses God nor excuses the devil [*accusat deum aut excusat diabolum*], but rather excuses God and accuses the devil [*sed omnino deum excusat et diabolum accusat*]" (§20; trans. altered).[48]

In order to avoid accusing God, the teacher lays out the principle that everything that exists comes from God, and everything that exists is good (§1). Based on this, the student points out that the gift of perseverance in a state of grace is good and therefore must proceed from God—and implicitly not from the subject's own free choice. Since the devil so dramatically lacked that gift, the only possible conclusion is that he must not have received it from God. This creates a conundrum based on a principle that Anselm shares with nearly every Christian theologian, namely, that merit or sin exists only where the subject's own free will is involved. If the devil never received this perseverance and could not have attained it on his own, then "he could not be justly damned if the fault was not his" (§2). Already, then, it is a matter of being able to attribute guilt, and the teacher's initial answer to this problem displays the same kind of "time-warp" character as the a priori guilt that plays such a central role in Butler's theory of interpellation. It is true, the teacher argues, that God did not "give" the devil perseverance, but only because the devil refused it, rendering ineffective the attempt to "give." The devil's "not accepting to hang on to what he abandoned is not because God did not give it, but God did not give it because he did not accept it. . . . The will to retain is not always prior to the will to abandon" (§3). In other words, the devil "preemptively" rejects God's gift, apparently without "receiving" it even to the minimal degree required to know what he is rejecting—like a petulant child who refuses even to hold out his hand to receive a birthday present.

This immature refusal is certainly not praiseworthy, but it is difficult to understand how it is morally blameworthy—especially in the case of a being who is only a single instant old. For the reader, questions of God's justice naturally arise here, but for Anselm, the real issue here is the devil's own obligation to behave in a just manner, which he defines as living in right relationship to God. And Anselm is constrained to say that the devil, in the very first moment of his creation, was in a state of original justice, since God created his will and pointed it in the right direction. If God did anything else, then he would have created the devil *as* an evil being, which would make God responsible for the devil's evil deeds—exactly the conclusion that the teacher and student are both at pains to avoid.

The gift of perseverance would have allowed the devil to maintain this initial state, but as we have seen, he refuses it from the first moment after he is created (cf. §16). But where could this contrary impulse of will have come from, if the devil's will and its initial orientation were both good in God's eyes? To solve this dilemma, Anselm splits divine will into two segments: a pre-rational will, which simply wills happiness, and the will toward justice or rectitude, which is a kind of meta-will that wills to subdue the creature's pre-rational will to God's demands (§12). What happened in the moment of the devil's fall is that the first will to happiness operated outside the bounds of the will to justice. By willing "to be happy to the degree that he knows it," he naturally "wills to be like God," who enjoys the height of happiness (§13). Indeed, Anselm says elsewhere that even if he did not explicitly will to be like God, he can formally be considered to have done so because "he willed something by his own will, as subject to no one. It is for God alone thus to will something by his own will such that he follows no higher will" (§4). But it is the very definition of will to have "no other cause by which it is forced or attracted, but [to be] its own efficient cause, so to speak, as well as its own effect [*sed ipsa sibi efficiens causa fuit, si dici potest, et effectum*]" (§27). The choice to fall away from God comes from the devil's own, definitionally self-causing will—and hence God's blamelessness for his fall is secured.

Yet a complication immediately arises, because it is by following the dictates of the pre-rational will that God gave him—and whose "direction," as it were, God set—that the devil runs afoul of God. Moreover, this pre-rational will to happiness is shared with the irrational animals and is in itself always formally blameless. We may regret what an animal does in its pursuit of happiness, but we do not generally regard it as morally blameworthy in the same way we regard destructive human actions as morally blameworthy. In itself, then, the pre-rational will can be neither just nor unjust. Only by receiving the will to justice can a rational being become morally accountable (§14). The devil, however, has not received this will, and so would seem to be formally blameless: "Before receiving justice, in fact, no one is just or unjust and, after having received it, no one becomes unjust unless he willingly abandons justice" (§18).

It is here that Anselm's argument takes a deeply Butlerian—or Althusserian—turn. As in the example of the "hailing" of the police officer, the devil is a priori unjust, parallel to Butler's account, where "to become a 'subject' is thus to have been presumed guilty, then tried and declared innocent."[49] Though Anselm all but admits that the devil should be regarded as formally innocent since he has not received the gifts that make a proper moral judgment possible, the devil is treated as guilty simply because God regards him as such, that is, as lacking justice that the devil ought to have (§19). For Althusser, the voice of Christian religious ideology works "by interpellating the individual, Peter, in order to make him a subject, free to obey or disobey the appeal, i.e. God's commandments"[50]— but as Butler points out, this is not a truly free choice, since choosing to be a "bad subject" is in a certain sense choosing not to be a subject at all.[51] Further strengthening the parallel with the scene of interpellation, Anselm depicts the devil as being in a state of radical ignorance of the consequences of his action (§21), though still responsible (§22), just as the modern subject of law is normally factually ignorant of most laws but still fully accountable for following all of them. In fact, knowledge of the possibility of punishment would only have increased his guilt if he had nonetheless sinned and tarnished his goodness if he had obeyed, since justice should be desired only out of love of justice, not out of fear (§23).

The good angels—like Althusser's "9 out of 10" subjects who respond appropriately to interpellation—were also in this state of ignorance about punishment, but obeyed nonetheless (§24). Therefore God confirms them in perseverance so that they can never fall, just as he closes off all possibility of the devil ever achieving the status he preemptively refused. Yet it appears that it is not simply by God's arbitrary decision to grant the good angels perpetual rectitude that they remain good ever after: "The good angel cannot now sin for this reason alone: that he knows the sin of the bad angel to have been followed by punishment, which inability does not deprive him of praise, but is the reward for having served justice" (§25). In terms of Butler's account of interpellation, then, it appears that the fate of Satan becomes a kind of warning that reinforces the blackmail of power, the choice between obedience and non-being. The parallel here is almost exact even on the verbal level, since for Anselm evil and injustice are, strictly speaking, nothing—so that, for instance, the devil's so-called will to injustice was actually a failure to will the justice that he should have willed (even before receiving the formal conditions of willing justice). A large part of the argument of this treatise is taken up with establishing the precise status of evil as privation and the ways that it can nonetheless have real effects. Following on the principle that everything that exists is from God and all that is from God is good, Anselm maintains that a bad will is not inherently evil, but remains good insofar as it exists (§8). Thus, if one understands the devil to be the 1 out of 10 who runs away from the police officer instead of turning when "hailed," it becomes clear that "bad subjects" are still interpellated, but they use the agency that interpellation grants them to turn against the voice of law. By the same token, the 9 out of 10 who do turn toward the police officer are still presumed guilty—a test precedes their confirmation as "good subjects."

To put this Butlerian reading of Anselm into schematic terms, then, one can say that in *On the Fall of the Devil*, we are dealing with a situation in which the rational being can only receive justice from God, but the very process of bringing about this justice necessarily presupposes the preexistence of a guilty moral agent, just as happens with the ideological interpellation of a moral subject. The situation is thus presented as one of free choice, but those who choose wrongly enter into a kind of limbo where they cannot properly be designated as moral agents at all. Thus it does appear that this theological text recapitulates the basic structure of Butler's concept of "theology." The subject is born out of guilt, and its installation creates a fictive structure that covers over its own origin. Even in this most extreme and formalized scene of interpellation, however, where the voice of ideology is quite literally God, the ones who insist on willing outside the parameters of the given order (i.e., "justice" or right relationship to God) do not face sheer annihilation, which confirms Butler's conviction that one must not take the blackmail of power overly literally.

In a sense, then, Anselm's text confirms Butler's refusal of the idea of a magical "divine performative." The divine performative that calls the devil into being has a concrete effect, but apparently not even God is in full control of the consequences of his performative acts. In fact, the "bad subjects" here have the opportunity to act in ways that influence the shape of the given order: in this case, causing the fall of humanity and triggering the Incarnation. In Nietzschean terms, the Incarnation is a highly problematic event that exponentially compounds the stranglehold of guilt or debt (*Schuld*) on the subject,[52] and it is not my intent here to argue or imply that Butler should somehow embrace the idea of Christ's Incarnation as a positive thing. There is one aspect of Anselm's text, however—and here Anselm is no longer a representative of the mainstream of Western Christian theology—that may resonate somewhat with Butler's hopes. In discussing the punishment of which the devil was and should have been ignorant before his fall, Anselm refers to the characteristically medieval idea that in the Kingdom of God, human beings would replace the fallen angels. Thus, because of the actions of this bad subject who demonstrated "a willingness *not* to be,"[53] a realm that was formerly populated only with abstract minds will now be filled with bodies—a notion that perhaps echoes Butler's call for a social order that would recognize our constitutive vulnerability rather than repressing and exploiting it. Even in this quite "theological" theological text, then, we find an implicit critique of "theology": both the formal conditions for agency and a small—but real—example of that agency's effects.

Translation, Hospitality, and Supersession
Lamin Sanneh and Jacques Derrida
on the Future of Christianity

From the very beginning, Christianity and colonial conquest went hand in hand. Christopher Columbus's fateful voyage was financed by Spain, whose recently "restored" Christian regime was arguably the most fanatical in Europe. And despite the tensions that arose between the missionaries and the conquistadores—as expressed, for instance, in Bartolomé de Las Casas's well-known protest against the mistreatment of the indigenous population of the New World—religion was one of the key means by which Western domination sought to legitimate itself. So closely intertwined were Christian mission and Western conquest that Homi Bhabha could refer to the project of "evangelical colonialism."[1]

Yet in what could appear to be a profound historical irony, it is precisely in the postcolonial world where Christianity has enjoyed its greatest success in recent decades, above all in Latin America and Africa. These trends have spurred the development of a new specialization within the realm of religious studies focused on "global Christianity," a wide-ranging field that includes extremely capacious studies synthesizing trends from essentially the entire world,[2] as well as ethnographic studies of Christian trends in particular countries, often focusing on Pentecostalism.[3] Although some studies suggest that the new wave of Christianity represents a form of cultural imperialism, others are strikingly optimistic about the prospects for Christianity in the Third World, and particularly in Africa. Other contemporary commentators outside the field of religious studies have expressed similar sentiments. Achille Mbembe—a resolutely secular thinker who has virtually nothing positive to say about the role of either Islam or premodern African tribal religions—sees Christianity's ascendancy in Africa as reflective of "the heretical genius at the root of the encounter between Africa and the world."[4] Far from contaminating or polluting African culture, Christianity in Mbembe's view has become a resource for cultural creativity.

Meanwhile, the West—with the notable exception of the US—has witnessed a sharp decline in Christian identification and practice. In Europe, this has led to a certain amount of soul-searching as to the cultural underpinnings of the project of European unification. If Europe is dedicated solely to supposedly universal secular values, then why did the integration of former Communist countries, which once belonged to a power bloc that threatened the West with nuclear annihilation, come about almost as a matter of course, while Turkey, an officially secular country and long-time NATO ally, could not be included? Some vestigial relationship to Christianity still appears to be decisive in European identity, and among continental philosophers, recent decades have witnessed a "religious turn" as a number of thinkers attempt to find new secular uses for Europe's Christian heritage. This trend embraces phenomenological studies of religious concepts and experiences; Marxists of various kinds seeking a new model for revolutionary subjectivity (above all in the figure of the Apostle Paul); political theologians seeking the theological roots of Christian concepts; and a variety of other thinkers pursuing diverse investigations.[5] What all seem to presuppose is the existence of an irreducible connection between Christianity and European culture, a link so fundamental that it can supposedly persist even in the face of mass abandonment of anything recognizable as Christian practice.

In this essay, I stage a dialogue between major representatives of the global Christianity and European "religious turn" discourses. From the field of global Christianity, I draw on the Senegalese theologian Lamin Sanneh, whose book *Translating the Message* argues that Christianity's strength lies in its translatability, that is, its ability to shape and be shaped by the cultures with which it comes in contact, of which European culture is only one among many.[6] Among the thinkers of the "religious turn," my focus is the work of Jacques Derrida, who was increasingly concerned in his later years to reactivate the "Abrahamic" tradition as a a challenge to contemporary culture. Central to this ambition is his account of hospitality, a value that Derrida takes to be foundational for the Abrahamic religions and that emerges as an effectively infinite demand that calls the identity of "host" and "guest" into radical question. Not only does this work provide an obvious point of contact with the question of Christian mission in the postcolonial world—indeed, one of his most extended meditations on hospitality deals with the highly idiosyncratic French missionary Louis Massignon[7]—but I argue that there is a profound structural homology between Sanneh's concept of translatability and Derrida's language of hospitality. My ultimate goal in this essay, however, is not simply to demonstrate an unexpected commonality between two apparently unrelated thinkers, but to trace that structural parallel back to a shared root—namely, Christian supersessionism, which shows forth most clearly in their one-sided treatment of Islam and which threatens to undermine both thinkers' worthy ethical goals.

Christianity as Translation

Sanneh's *Translating the Message* is in some ways a contrarian argument. Whereas much work in the field of mission studies maintains a "connection between mission and colonialism, confirming the view of mission as destructive of indigenous originality" (5), his goal is to shift the focus to "reception and appropriation in the field rather than on transmission and organization in the West" (9). In other words, while acknowledging the mixed and questionable motives of many missionaries, Sanneh shifts the focus to the African *reception* of the Christian message, a reception that was fundamentally determined by the decision on the part of virtually all Christian missionaries of this era to undertake the massive effort of translating the Bible into as many languages as possible. These translations made Africans active agents who reimagined Christianity in a new, distinctively African form. This explains the rapid expansion of Christianity in the era of decolonialization, a fact that is difficult to account for if Christianity was simply a tool of Western domination. As Sanneh puts it, "Missionary promotion of the vernacular, therefore, was tantamount to adopting indigenous cultural criteria for the message, a piece of radical indigenization more potent than the standard portrayal of mission as Western cultural imperialism" (3).

Far from confining his argument to Africa, however, Sanneh argues that translation has defined Christianity from the very beginning, because "the Christian Scripture had always been a translated Scripture" (9). Starting from the translation of a Jewish messianic movement into a Gentile religion, Sanneh supports his thesis with a tremendous range of historical examples, including the mission to the Slavs, the Reformation-era vernacular translations, and the cultural impact of the King James Bible, along with various episodes from modern missions to Africa, India, Japan, and elsewhere. So pervasive is this trend that Sanneh can claim that Christianity is essentially "a vernacular translation movement" (7). Although he recognizes that many see Christianity as primarily a system of belief, Sanneh argues that the impulse of translatability renders a static conception of Christianity impossible: "Even if in practice Christians wished to stop the translation process, claiming their form of it as final and exclusive, they have not been able to suppress it for all time and for others" (54).

The founding example of the mission to the Gentiles already indicates that much more is at stake than the literal act of translating the Scriptures—after all, the Greek translation of the Hebrew Bible existed long before the Christian movement. More broadly, Sanneh views translatability as affecting entire cultures, affirming and empowering them:

> Christian translation projects have helped to create an overarching series of cultural experiences, with hitherto obscure and marginal cultural systems being drawn into the general stream of universal history. Christian particularity has hinged on the particularity of culture and language, both essential components of translation. The resulting concrete cultural systems had their genesis in, or because of, the work of translation. (3)

Many of Sanneh's most compelling examples of this empowerment come from the African context, where missionary translators were often the first to introduce written forms of particular languages. Languages that previously had little purchase beyond the relatively small circle of a given tribe suddenly become a vehicle for divine revelation. In addition, the very insistence on translation into the local language places the missionary in a dependent position due to the nature of language acquisition itself, which requires the cooperation of native speakers in order to proceed. Due to the intrinsic bond between language and culture—which Sanneh claims, somewhat puzzlingly, is uniquely strong in premodern cultures (3)—the missionary becomes a servant of the local culture, cataloguing it in a way that often also revitalizes it.

Sanneh argues that this dynamic introduces a kind of reciprocity, but it is clear that in the last analysis, the receivers of the message maintain the upper hand, as the missionary cannot control how the locals will understand and adapt the gospel. In an image that is perhaps surprising in an author so intent on de-emphasizing imperial violence, Sanneh emphasizes the uncontrollability that comes along with translatability: "When one translates, it is like pulling the trigger of a loaded gun: the translator cannot recall the hurtling bullet" (60). Expanding on this analogy and perhaps pushing it in directions Sanneh does not intend, one could say that this bullet is definitely aimed at whatever imperial aspirations the missionaries bring with them—

no matter how chauvinistic or even racist an authentic missionary starts out, he or she will always wind up identifying with the local culture (131), on the model of the Apostle Paul becoming all things for all people.

At the the same time, the translation bullet euthanizes certain aspects of the local culture: "Cultural features that had been weakening by the time of the Christian encounter, either because of a lack of necessary stimulus or because of natural exhaustion, received the coup de grace" (58). If missionary translation (in the broad sense) always transforms Christianity, it also always transforms the local culture. Yet contrary to the romanticism of many Western observers who decry interference in non-Western cultures as by definition destructive, Sanneh believes this process is positive and healthy: "It may be that these new churches provide us with a unique opportunity to observe Africans, presented with a new challenge, adopting and directing it in time-tested channels, a process of change and assimilation that sheds new light on the question of origins in history, society, and ideas" (222). In other words, any given culture is at its best when it willingly takes on the challenge of development and change. Along these lines, Sanneh develops a less violent image, contrasting organic and neurological images of the nature of Christianity. In the organic model, Christianity is thought of "as a closed-circuit organism" for which change is necessarily disruptive and destructive (249). Missionary translation reveals a different, more fluid model:

> Translation is evidence that Christianity's neurological center is in flux, that its vocabulary is growing and changing, that historical experience has perspective-altering power, that the allotment of "neurons" continues because "neurogenesis" is a living process rather than a relic of evolution, that foreign influence lodges in the system like oxygen in the bloodstream, and that Christianity's "localization" in the frontal lobe of establishment Christianity has shifted to the central cortex of world Christianity where new and expanded tasks have stimulated tolerance and diversity in the religion. (250)

Using another biological contrast, Sanneh claims that foreign influences should be understood not on the model of infection and disease, a model that underwrites the attempt to root out syncretism and heresy, but as a kind of biodiversity that makes Christianity more robust and durable (250). And indeed, his account of postcolonial African Christianity shows no preference for traditional orthodoxy, as he discusses the various prophetic movements centered on charismatic preachers in a positive light.

This account of Christianity's essential translatability is difficult to dispute, as Sanneh amply documents his contention that Christianity thrives where it stays true to its translatability and remains marginal at best when it refuses it. Yet throughout his argument there is a pervasive vagueness about what exactly Christianity "is," or better, what Christianity is a translation "of." Sanneh clearly rejects the notion that Christianity is a translation of Judaism. At the risk of oversimplifying, for Sanneh it seems as though Jewish culture just happens to be where it arose, and indeed there is a very real question as to whether Christianity was even properly itself before its translation into a Gentile religion. Sanneh privileges the New Testament as the "Christian Scripture," which "is always translated Scripture"—referring primarily to the "translation" of Jesus's words out of his original Aramaic into the Greek of the canonical gospels, rather than to the Greek Septuagint. The first sentence of Sanneh's introduction is revealing here, as he claims that "from its origins, Christianity identified itself with the need to translate out of Aramaic and Hebrew" (1)—putting the language of the historical Jesus before the language of the only Scriptures the earliest Christians regarded as such.

More broadly, Sanneh consistently characterizes Judaism in very stereotyped ways, as a static and inflexible religion from which Christianity had to escape in order to achieve its true universality. At the same time, he claims that the Gentile mission was meant to uplift a pagan culture that, strangely, his first chapter repeatedly characterizes as having an inferiority complex in the face of the Jewish minority's culture. Here his true target seems to be European Christianity, which serves as the self-enclosed and arrogant Judaism to Africa's contemporary Gentiles. The critique of European Christianity is fair, but one wishes he had found a way to express it that did not reproduce the toxic logic of Christian supersessionism.

Sanneh's true foil, however, is neither Judaism nor European Christianity but Islam, which he portrays as absolutely *refusing* translation. Referring to the Islamic doctrine of the untranslatability of the Qur'an, he claims that "Islamic mission appears to require the disfranchising of the vernacular" (219). Indeed, prospects for Christian and Muslim mission are in his account equally dependent on linguistic factors, but in inverse proportions: "Wherever the mother tongue is depreciated we can predict diminishing prospects for Christian renewal. . . . By contrast, Muslim strength is almost proportionate to the weakening of the vernacular" (224). This creates the puzzle of how Islam could enjoy such worldwide success, which Sanneh attributes to the fact that "understanding the sacred text seems subordinate to venerating it, and that religious impulse Islam has stirred successfully" (254). Here the Qur'an is presented as essentially an idol, which exerts power through obfuscation. Indeed, in a moment of apparent self-contradiction, Sanneh claims, "The very strangeness of Qur'anic Arabic adds to its religious authority and to its appeal as the blueprint for a righteous social order, the more attractive for enjoining religious rules and ideals" (267). Yet how do Muslim converts ever learn of those attractive teachings if they can only ever be expressed in a language they do not understand?

In his *Secular Translations*, Talal Asad has critiqued Sanneh's reading of Islam and specifically of the doctrine of the untranslatability of the Qur'an. As Asad points out, "It is not the Arabic language as such that is attributed to divinity for Muslims, but Qur'anic enunciation—especially in the context of ritual prayer."[8] Relative to everyday Arabic—both today and in the context of the Qur'an's original revelation—the Qur'an's language is strikingly unique, a feature that contributes to the theological belief in its inimitability.[9] To that extent, then, the very untranslatability of the Qur'an calls forth Islamic discourse "through the medium of vernaculars—including demotic Arabic—although then it is, of course, no longer the Qur'an."[10] Sanneh cautions Christian fundamentalists that their attitude "evokes Muslim sentiments about the Qur'an in its original Arabic as infallible for all time" (203), but Asad counters that "the nontranslatability of the Qur'an in a liturgical context makes it difficult for political as well as ecclesiastical authority to control Qur'anic meaning." In contrast to many Christian settings—as among US evangelicals, who often fail to understand that the Bible was not originally written in English—in Islam, "the original is always present, generating unlimited possibilities of meaning."[11]

Ultimately, Asad characterizes Sanneh's one-sided polemic against Islam as a move in a contemporary African culture war: "Sanneh's formulation is of course a way of saying that one cannot be authentically an African if one is also a Muslim, but that one can be African *and* Christian because Christian scriptures and liturgies have been translated into African languages and are thus made at home in African cultures."[12] To the extent that Asad's charge is fair (and I think it is), Sanneh's reductive approach to Islam calls into question whether his infinitely translatable Christianity is really free of the taint of colonialism—an accusation that he seemingly attempts to preempt through his repeated references to Islam's warlike and oppressive nature. While the Crusades (and, implicitly, modern imperialism itself) were a betrayal of true Christianity, he claims, "Islam is not a pacifist religion or a creed for the fainthearted"—war and violence are intrinsic features (48). Such rhetoric, which would not be out of place in apologetics for the so-called "War on Terror," is certainly jarring in a text that so resolutely distances authentic Christianity from imperialism.

Monotheism as Hospitality

The two primary critiques I have leveled against Sanneh—his recapitulation of Christian supersessionism and of Western anti-Islam rhetoric—do not, in my view, represent contingent shortcomings or instances of hypocrisy. Instead, as I hope to show through a translation of his argument into the terms of Jacques Derrida's account of hospitality, they reflect perennial temptations of any attempt to reclaim the Christian legacy. What makes Derrida's discussion of hospitality particularly fruitful for the present discussion is the way he links hospitality, which most Christians likely would not view as a distinctively "religious" theme, with religion and specifically with what he calls the three "Abrahamic" religions: Judaism, Christianity, and Islam. Following Massignon, Derrida finds in Abraham a "saint of hospitality,"[13] which suggests that hospitality could serve as a kind of interpretative key for all the religions that claim Abraham as their father. Both thinkers, then, are trying to define Christianity in terms of an initially counterintuitive trait.

Since it is the most straightforward connection, I begin with Derrida's description of the missionary career of Louis Massignon, a scholar of Islam who gradually developed a call to serve Islamic peoples. This shift from expertise to sympathy fits well with Sanneh's many accounts of missionaries who, often despite themselves, came to identify more strongly with their local hosts than with the country that sent them. Further, Massignon follows Sanneh's pattern whereby Christian mission reinforces what is best in the local culture, though in Massignon's case the process is perhaps more conscious than usual insofar as he sets out specifically to reclaim Islam as "a religion, an ethics, and a culture, of hospitality"[14] and thereby present it as "the most faithful heir, the exemplary heir of the Abrahamic tradition."[15] Indeed, Massignon takes the missionary submission to the local culture further than Sanneh may be comfortable with. In a section of the manifesto for Massignon's Islamic mission quoted by Derrida, he claims that even Christian self-identification is not strictly necessary, because the missionary can take care of that on the receiver's behalf:

> Thus, counting on the divine grace, these Christians [i.e., members of Massignon's missionary community] want to consecrate themselves to the salvation of their brothers, and in this hope of salvation, to give to Jesus Christ, in the name of their brothers, the faith, the Adoration and the love that, because of their imperfect knowledge of the Gospels, they are prevented from giving him themselves. Salvation does not necessarily mean external conversion. It is already a lot to

obtain that a greater number belong to the soul of the Church, that they live and die in a state of grace.[16]

From a certain perspective, the vision of this manifesto represents a kind of zero-degree of mission, insofar as it has Christians venturing outside the Christian fold to bring others in, with little else being required. Yet that minimalism is paired with a hyperbolic one-sidedness, as the missionary strives to be at once the perfect guest—to understand and appreciate the host culture to the greatest degree possible—and the perfect host—including Muslims in the Christian circle in the most intimate way ("the soul of the Church") while not requiring them to do anything, like the over-attentive host who is continually insisting, "No, let me get that for you."

For Derrida, this overlap between guest and host is anything but coincidental. Guided by a linguistic accident—the fact that his native French uses the same word, *hôte*, to refer to both host and guest—Derrida contends that any serious analysis of hospitality will reveal that the line between guest and host is not as clear as it may seem. First of all, there is the mutual dependency of the two: There is no guest without a host, no host without a guest. Although the dependent situation of the guest is perhaps the more obvious, Derrida, in a way that is characteristic of his ethical thought, pushes the obligation of the host to its utmost limit. If the host were to be as rigorously hospitable as possible, he would give the guest *everything*, thus turning himself into the guest and his guest into his host.[17] This overlap between guest and host is what makes Abraham a "saint of hospitality,"[18] one who leaves his home and becomes a guest, yet welcomes guests in turn—guests who include God himself.

Derrida recognizes that absolute hospitality is impossible in practice and that any actual existing hospitality has to be governed by some kind of norm or expectation—some line that separates legitimately "helping yourself" from stealing, for example. Viewed from the perspective of this conditional brand of hospitality, absolute hospitality, even if someone could find a way to achieve it, might even seem to undermine the idea of hospitality altogether and so fail to be hospitality at all. Yet coming from the other direction, which is most often Derrida's own emphasis, conditional hospitality always falls short in the face of the demand of absolute hospitality, so that conditional hospitality also fails to be hospitality at all. Derrida sums up this paradoxical relationship thus: "Between an unconditional law or an absolute desire for hospitality on the one hand and, on the other, a law, a politics, a conditional ethics, there is a distinction, radical heterogeneity, but also indissociability. One calls forth, involves, or prescribes the other."[19]

Thinking through these concepts in light of Sanneh, it seems that this absolute hospitality is akin to the nightmare scenario envisioned by critics who identify mission with colonialism, where the naïve hospitality of the indigenous population leads to a total dispossession that turns them into virtual foreigners in what was once their own country but is now owned by someone else. This comparison to colonialism, it seems to me, challenges both thinkers. On the one hand, it makes it clear how much Derrida's rhetorical strategy is directed at the strong rather than the weak—and how dangerous it can become if the same rhetoric is pointed in the opposite direction. On the other hand, the mutual belonging of absolute and conditional hospitality might call into question the sharp distinction that Sanneh often wants to draw between mission and colonialism—perhaps the "tension" he notes between the two (cf. 4–5, 162) is not the conflict between two parallel and yet separate processes, but rather a tension inherent in the overarching dynamic of hospitality at work in both, the tension between good and bad ways of being a guest.

The Question of Islam and the Trap of Supersessionism

Part of the reason Sanneh may not fully appreciate that tension is that he is so thoroughly identified with the side of the host—namely, the indigenous communities that have welcomed the missionaries into their midst. Though the missionary's visit does bring about change in those communities, the nature and extent of the change are, in Sanneh's account, more or less entirely in the hands of the hosts, who take from their missionary guests what they find most useful. And it is here that we find another parallel between Sanneh and Derrida, insofar as the European thinker, too, is much more focused on the host than the guest. In his case, this imbalance undoubtedly has political motivations, insofar as his entire discourse on hospitality is clearly an intervention into the debate (which has since grown only more urgent) about the place of migrants and refugees in the European Union. Hence in "Hostipitality," he emphasizes that Abraham himself is a migrant and a guest,[20] just as in *Of Hospitality* he can claim that Socrates's purported inexperience in the ways of the judicial system puts him in the position of a foreigner during his trial.[21] In both cases, the rhetorical structure depends on the shock of inversion—generating empathy with migrants and refugees by unexpectedly identifying European culture heroes (Abraham, Socrates) as such. The stability of European identity—which carries with it the assumption that Europe is and will be in a position to choose whether or not to be hospitable in practice—is presupposed even as it is deconstructed.

The very fact that Abraham can be presented precisely as a European culture hero already depends, of course, on the identification of Europe with Christianity. More than that, though, Derrida's "return to Abraham" repeats one of the foundational gestures of Christianity—namely, Paul's attempt to make an end run around the requirements of the Jewish law by positing a direct connection between his community and a more originary faith that we might, following Derrida's terminology, characterize as "Abrahamic." In both cases, the reference to Abraham promises a return to more universal and ethically challenging values that have been forgotten by the purportedly ossified traditions that have claimed Abraham's mantle but betrayed his legacy by embracing arbitrary and exclusionary identities.[22] Admittedly, this observation of the homology between Paul's attempted supersession of Judaism and Derrida's invocation of the Abrahamic may appear counterintuitive or even unfair. In practice, of course, Derrida's unique approach to religion is far from anti-Jewish, and certainly it avoids the conventional clichés about Judaism in which Sanneh unfortunately at times indulges. In fact, Derrida's writings on theology have most often been taken as the inverse or even potentially the remedy to Paul's foundational supersession of Judaism, as when John Caputo uses Derrida's meditations on religion as the occasion to "propose another, demystified, deconstructed—and I would say a slightly de-Paulinized and more Jewish—Christianity."[23] Hence one even might be tempted to read Derrida's reading of Abrahamic hospitality as a kind of corrective to Sanneh's often one-sided and triumphalist account of translatability—until one noticed that one was thereby positioning a secular European thinker as the arbiter of true Abrahamic faith. Even if Sanneh is arguably over-hasty in asserting that the postcolonial translation of Christianity has eliminated the imperialistic accretions introduced by Europeans, surely the answer is not to grant the secular European perspective a line-item veto over Sanneh's creative rearticulation of the Abrahamic tradition for his African context.

Such a move becomes all the more questionable when one realizes how much Derrida's attempt to translate Abrahamic principles into acceptable secular terms leaves out of the biblical narratives. Virtually absent from Derrida's analysis of Abraham's life as a migrant and refugee is the fact that the Promised Land is presented as somehow "really" belonging to Abraham—a theme presupposed, for instance, in the story where he and his relative Lot, both total newcomers to this part of the world, divide the land between them (Genesis 13). One might also think of the repeated motif wherein Abraham refuses to be treated as a guest, as when he rejects any spoil from the seldom-mentioned war in which he participates (14:22–24) and absolutely refuses to accept the gift of a burial site for his wife Sarah (23:3–20), in both cases insisting that he must owe nothing to the inhabitants of the land. It is this underlying presupposition that Abraham is the true owner of the Promised Land that grants the stories of Abraham as a guest a kind of counterintuitive irony similar to that on which Derrida's reappropriation also relies.[24] Arguably even more questionable is Derrida's attempted secularization of the sacrifice of Isaac in *The Gift of Death*, whose main text presents Isaac as a stand-in for the innumerable others that one "sacrifices" every time one attends to any particular other. An essay subsequently added to the text, "Literature in Secret," builds on that reinterpretation by counterintuitively presenting Abraham's silence in the lead-up to the sacrifice as the foundation of the value of free speech that underlies the European institution of "literature." Creative as these readings are, they risk obscuring what is most distinctive in the biblical text in their insistence on extracting an ethical lesson that is legible in secular terms.

If both Derrida and Sanneh are in danger of renewing Christian supersessionism, they are both equally blind to the contributions of an earlier attempt to rework the Abrahamic tradition: namely, Islam. Although Derrida's rhetoric is doubtless more conciliatory and tolerant than Sanneh's, his purportedly greater sympathy for Islam does not translate into a serious firsthand engagement with its primary texts. His only extended discussion of this great Abrahamic tradition is filtered through Massignon's idiosyncratic—and profoundly Christianizing—perspective. And one cannot excuse this lapse by claiming such an investigation would be far afield from Derrida's concerns, because the portrayal of Abraham in the Qur'an or the later Islamic tradition is arguably more compatible with Derrida's ethical project than the biblical account. For instance, the Qur'an repeatedly portrays Abraham trying to reason with his father and broader community to demonstrate that their worship of other gods is illogical (21:51–70, 37:83–98), where the Bible has him abandon his family without a word. Even more dramatic is the Qur'an's reworking of the story of Abraham's sacrifice of his son (Ishmael rather than Isaac, according to most interpreters):

When the boy was old enough to work with his father, Abraham said, "My son, I have seen myself sacrificing you in a dream. What do you think?" He said, "Father, do as you are commanded and, God willing, you will find me steadfast." When they had both submitted to God, and he had laid his son down on the side of his face, We called out to him, "Abraham, you have fulfilled the dream." This is how

We reward those who do good—it was a test to prove [their true characters]—We ransomed his son with a momentous sacrifice, and We let him be praised by succeeding generations. (37:102–109)[25]

Although the basic outline of the story remains the same, Abraham's decision to consult with his son is a far cry from his grim silence—and, as the event approaches, his active deception of Isaac—in the biblical version.

Surely the emphasis on persuasion and consent makes the Qur'anic Abraham more appealing to contemporary secular audiences—yet such an encounter is impossible because Derrida, just as much as Sanneh, treats Islam as irreducibly foreign. Indeed, as Asad points out in his critique of *Translating the Message*, Derrida's attitude toward the Qur'an's supposed untranslatability is virtually indistinguishable from Sanneh's. Responding to a remark of Asad's about "the question of Qur'anic untranslatability as 'fundamental,'" Derrida claimed:

> What you say is fundamental. It is essentially tied to all the fundamentalisms, in particular, in the Islamic areas. Nowhere else is the attachment to the untranslatable letter, the letter of the Qur'an, so inflexible. There is, to be sure, a certain religion of the idiom, everywhere, even within Christianity: French [Catholic] fundamentalism distinguished itself at a certain moment in time through its defense of Latin in the prayer service. But nowhere, it seems to me, does the *fixed* literalness of language, the idiomatic form of the original message, in its very body sanctify itself to the extent it does in the Moslem religion.[26]

There is much that is discouraging in these comments, above all the near-total conflation of Islam with fundamentalism. On a theoretical level as well, it is perhaps surprising to hear such sentiments from the father of deconstruction, who made his name by demonstrating the ultimate inconsistency of every text. Would not his philosophical commitments lead more naturally to a position like Asad's mentioned above, where the Qur'anic letter is a constant provocation that undermines any claim to interpretive closure? Returning to the comparison with Sanneh, we might ask a similar question of him: Why, in Sanneh's terms, can Islam not count as a further translation of the Christian message? Surely it would count as a more radical translation than most, but Sanneh himself does not appear to embrace any principle of orthodoxy that would exclude the possibility of such a reimagining of the biblical tradition. Clearly in Sanneh's case, the emphasis on Islam's untranslatability serves as a rationale for rejecting it as a valid inheritor of the Christian tradition. Can we discern a similar motive operating, even if unconsciously, in Derrida's non-engagement with Islam? Does his failure—beyond a bare verbal acknowledgment—to take seriously the Islamic tradition as an iteration of Abrahamic faith reflect a suspicion that Islam cannot finally be translated into secular terms, meaning that "we" European hosts will always have to deal with "them" as guests?

This missed encounter with Islam is particularly disappointing in that the dynamics of translatability and hospitality potentially provide a fresh perspective on the relation among the three great Abrahamic religions. Derrida's identification of hospitality as an interpretive key for the three Abrahamic religions could expand Sanneh's analysis of Christianity's relationship to Judaism and Islam by adding greater nuance to Sanneh's distinction between a static system and a translatable movement. Viewed in terms of the later dichotomy, Judaism could perhaps appear static, but viewed in terms of hospitality, the continual attempt to maintain Jewish identity in the diaspora can be interpreted as a way of negotiating the inherent tension of being, and *remaining*, a guest—for from the guest's side, the paradox of absolute hospitality entails that being an absolute guest could only mean complete assimilation to the host culture and hence ceasing to be a guest. Coming at the Jewish-Christian encounter from the other side, the emergence of the Christian movement renders Judaism a host, and yet here the guests attempt take over, rejecting and denigrating their hosts—a dynamic Paul is already fighting in his epistle to the Romans—while appropriating the hosts' most precious possession (the Scriptures). Here there is another, less encouraging story to tell about translation. Early Gentile Christians viewed the Greek Septuagint as an inspired Scripture and actually accused the Jews of falsifying the original Hebrew text, above all when the rabbis pointed out that the LXX mistranslated Isaiah 7:14, which Christians took to predict the birth of Christ. The Christian translation becomes a form of appropriation that paradoxically seeks to discredit its original. From this perspective, as Asad suggests, the untranslatability of the Qur'an—which is written and recited in a form of Arabic that has *never* been used for everyday purposes, because even at the time of its revelation its style was highly idiosyncratic—could actually combat the kind of cultural chauvinism that Sanneh is concerned to avoid, by relativizing all cultures and reminding all believers that they are but guests in God's creation.

Unfortunately, neither Christianity nor secularism appears to be fully open to the prospect of learning something from Islam—which is surely the precondition of translation and hospitality alike. The question I would ask in closing is why this should be so. Why should Sanneh's postcolonial translation of Christianity and Derrida's secular translation of the Abrahamic both turn out to be so inhospitable to Islam? The first step to answering this question is to ask what a translation of Christianity is a translation *of*. Sanneh at one point declares: "Solidarity with the poor, the weak, the disabled, and the stigmatized is the sine qua non of Christianity's credibility as a world religion" (11). On this point, Derrida's ethical rearticulation of the Abrahamic tradition appears to be in agreement. Yet in both cases, the supersessionist gesture undercuts those worthy ethical goals. I would suggest that this correspondence is no accident, since both Sanneh's translatability and Derrida's Abrahamic hospitality are at bottom a reiteration of the tradition's foundational supersessionism. That supersessionism is certainly not limited to Christianity. Islam has its own version of it, as does secularism—hence the special rivalry among Christianity, Islam, and secularism perhaps reflects a struggle to be viewed as the most authentic supersession for the modern world. More fundamentally, one can even read the original Abrahamic narratives as supersessionist in relation to the indigenous people and religions of the Promised Land. Hence the project of overcoming supersessionism becomes exceptionally complex, since every attempt to do so seems to echo the logic of the original supersessionist gesture—above all when one claims to have finally purged the tradition of all its destructive elements and arrived at its authentic form. Perhaps the best we can do is resolve to set aside the question of who is the most authentic child of Abraham and focus instead on the ethical practice that is, on both Sanneh and Derrida's account, the goal of the entire Abrahamic enterprise.

Agamben the Theologian

Is Agamben a theologian? He is certainly a prolific commentator *on* Christian theology. Indeed, of all the many contemporary European philosophers who have taken up theological themes—as seen in the so-called religious turn in phenomenology and the more recent studies of the Apostle Paul from a materialist perspective—there is no other single figure who has displayed such an imposing command of the full range of the Christian intellectual heritage, from the New Testament to the great theological debates of the twentieth century, from doctrinal treatises to liturgical texts, from the stakes of the doctrine of the Trinity down to the smallest details of a monk's habit. Although there are always points where one can nitpick (for instance, his tendency to ignore scholarly disputes about the authorship of the Pauline Epistles), Agamben's work on theology is rigorous in a way that goes beyond the basic due diligence of interdisciplinarity. It is creative and at times even paradigm-changing, most notably in *The Kingdom and the Glory*, where he completely reconfigures our understanding of the underlying dynamics of the history of Christian thought and the transition to secular modernity. This tour de force is all the more astonishing when we realize that what would have been a life's work for any other scholar was only one step, albeit a major one, in a much larger project.[1]

When I had the opportunity to meet Agamben in Venice as part of the research for *Agamben's Philosophical Trajectory*, one of my first questions was why he was so drawn to theological materials. His initial answer was to paraphrase Walter Benjamin's famous remark on his own relationship to theology: "My thinking relates to theology like the blotting page to the ink. It is saturated with it. Were one to go by the blotter, however, nothing of what is written would remain."[2] In other words, he would strongly prefer *not* to be compelled to engage so deeply with theology—and a close investigation of his work bears this out. If we compare him with another theologically astute philosopher such as Jean-Luc Marion, we see a clear difference in purpose. Whereas Marion, always a conservative Catholic thinker, has increasingly advanced a confessional theological agenda in his work, Agamben's purpose has been unrelentingly critical and genealogical. Although he does have normative commitments that lead him to privilege certain figures in the history of Christianity—notably Paul and the early Franciscans—and to view later developments as a kind of betrayal, he never advances a doctrine that takes those privileged sources as an authoritative canon. Instead, their successes and failures serve as materials for thinking through our own contemporary dilemmas.

Another way of putting this is that he draws no firm distinction between theological and philosophical materials. He treats both as part of the overall tradition of Western thought (his almost exclusive province), and he takes for granted the existence of debates and developments that proceed indifferently across whatever boundary we may be tempted to draw between the two fields. This procedure has been evident from his very earliest works. Particularly noteworthy here is *Stanzas* (1977),[3] which elaborates on late medieval theories of imagination in a way that shows the same easy communication among poetry, philosophy, theology, and even biology that medieval thought itself displayed, but essentially all the works of Agamben's first two decades as an author include significant engagement with theology.

Agamben therefore lies outside the "religious turn" in two senses. First, he had no need to "turn" to religion, insofar as theology had been a constant point of reference from very early on in his career. Second, and more radically, the very idea of a "turn" toward religion is incoherent in his case, because that "turn" presupposes a clear distinction between theological and philosophical traditions. Not only does such a distinction play no positive role in his thought, but he is always concerned to break it down wherever he finds it. We can see this clearly in his most famous concept—the *homo sacer* or sacred man, who may be killed but not sacrificed, which Agamben claims is the real referent of the modern concept of "the sacredness of human life." I could imagine a secular thinker lamenting that a religious metaphor like sacredness has inappropriately found its way into the political sphere, but for Agamben, the overlap between the political and the religious is a clue that we are dealing with a more primordial phenomenon that precedes the familiar distinction between sacred and profane. In fact, his harshest critique is reserved for theorists of religion who attempt to develop a theory of the sacred based solely on religious experience—leading to an impoverished and, for Agamben, laughably inadequate theory of the "numinous," which attempts to pass off "shivers and goose bumps" as scientific research.[4] By isolating religion into its own separate sphere, the theorists of the numinous do not even get religion right.

We can see the difference between a resolutely secular approach and Agamben's practice of indifference in his engagement with Kantorowicz in both *Homo Sacer* and *State of Exception*.[5] In both cases, he insists that Kantorowicz is wrong to trace the origin of the "king's two bodies" motif—which posits that the monarch possesses, alongside his ordinary human body, a mystical body corresponding to his power as sovereign—back to Christian theology. His objection is not that it would represent an inappropriate mystification of politics with theology. Instead, he argues that recognizing its roots in Roman imperial thought and practice offers a clearer picture of what is actually happening—but again, not because it is a political as opposed to religious origin. What would that distinction mean in the case of a deified emperor? Elsewhere he is quite happy to posit theological origins for ostensibly secular phenomena, most notably in *The Kingdom and the Glory*'s argument for tracing the genealogical roots of modern economic concepts such as the "invisible hand" back to the doctrine of divine providence.

Agamben's practice of indifference toward the distinction between the political and the religious or the philosophical and the theological is rooted in his deepest methodological influences, all of whom systematically break down the religious-secular binary. This is clearest in Walter Benjamin, who is Agamben's intellectual ideal (perhaps even his idol). Benjamin draws on religious and theological materials as a model for political critique and resistance, most famously in the "Critique of Violence" and "Theses on the Philosophy of History." Aby Warburg charts a promiscuous course through all manner of mythological and iconographic traditions—much as Walter Benjamin moves seamlessly from pop culture ephemera to philosophy to mysticism. Martin Heidegger, too, drew indifferently on theological materials, developing some of the core concepts of *Being and Time* through an analysis of the Pauline epistles and devoting considerable attention to theological sources in the "history of Being." For him, Christian theologians are in error not because they are somehow polluting philosophy with religious impurities, but because of the conceptual error of identifying Being with one particular entity (God). Hannah Arendt takes a similar approach, as her critique of Christianity in *The Human Condition* is based on her concern with the distinction between the political and the economic, not the philosophical and the theological.

I have so far emphasized the indifference between the philosophical and the theological in Agamben and his methodological models, largely because I view it as a refreshing alternative to a doctrinaire secularism that either aims to expel religious impurities or—what amounts to the same thing—treats theology with a patronizing "respect" that neutralizes it as a genuine dialogue partner. Yet there *is* a difference between philosophy and theology, and it would be misleading to pretend that this difference does not make a difference. This is not the place to fully elaborate the relation between the two disciplines, which would require demolishing a truly imposing number of clichés—such as the supposed binary of faith and reason, which in its least thoughtful form envisions religious believers as blindly accepting unprovable assertions and robotically executing divine commands. Nevertheless, there is a grain of truth in that distinction, if we take "reason" as a stand-in for the quest for an impersonal and perennial knowledge and "faith" as a form of personal loyalty to certain historical events and institutions. Even if, in Agamben's reading, Plato and Paul have similar critiques of the law, it surely makes a difference that Paul is making his arguments in the context of a personal calling by a particular historical individual whom Paul recognizes as the messiah of a particular nation as predicted in its particular scriptures, whereas Plato is gesturing toward a form of knowledge that is, in principle, available to anyone in any historical setting.

When we speak of a practice of indifference between these two modes of thought, it also makes a difference which side of the divide the indifference is practiced from. A theologian such as John Milbank, for instance, could be said to treat theological and philosophical materials with indifference—but in his case it means that philosophers are read as though they are attempting to be Christian theologians, with the (somewhat predictable) result that secular thinkers turn out to be vile heretics. It is difficult to discern any value to such intentional misreadings, other than to reinforce Christian chauvinism. Agamben and his models could be said to move in the opposite direction, treating theologians as though they are all philosophers—an approach that leads to fewer spurious condemnations, but does produce its own kind of distortion.

Here I would point to Agamben's reading of Paul. In *The Time That Remains*, he declares, "The most insidious misunderstanding of [Paul's] messianic pronouncement does not consist in mistaking it for prophecy, which is turned toward the future, but for apocalypse, which contemplates the end of time," and he criticizes Hans Blumenberg and Karl Löwith for "mistak[ing] messianism for eschatology."[6] This is, from a historical perspective, bizarre—Paul is *obviously* an apocalyptic thinker. Even stranger is Agamben's insistence, in *The Mystery of Evil*,[7] that the narrative of the conflict between the *katechōn* or restrainer and the man of lawlessness in 2 Thessalonians is not in any sense apocalyptic—again, of course it is! In both cases, his exclusion of the apocalyptic element from the messianic leads him to read the Pauline epistles as revealing something like the underlying structure of historical time, a structure that is equally legible in the texts of linguists such as Émile Benveniste and Gustave Guillaume. In other words, to gain this knowledge, we do not need to know about a particular historical Word made flesh, but only to think about our own practice of speech, which is available to anyone at any time. This is not exactly a secularization of the Pauline text, but it certainly seems to miss its historical specificity—not only the particular events that Paul (and whoever wrote 2 Thessalonians) anticipated in the future, but also the particular messianic event to which he pledged his loyalty and gave his life.

Yet there is a further twist here. Using my broad sense of theology as a mode of thought determined by loyalty to particular historical events and institutions, for Agamben virtually *all* of Western thought is "theological." I mean this in the sense that it responds to the historically particular event of anthropogenesis experienced in the West and contributes to building the system of mutually reinforcing destructive institutional forms that Agamben designates as the "Western machine." If he reads Paul in a way that extracts the text from its historical specificity, it is in the service of finding a way out of the self-enclosed tradition that has put itself forward as a spurious universality. For Agamben, authentic philosophy, like authentic messianism, is a critical discourse that contemplates the demolition or immobilization of the "Western machine" in which we are all trapped. Everything else—including, but not limited to, what we would recognize as theology in the conventional sense—is ultimately apologetics for the Western model of "anthropogenesis," which is to say the inhuman way in which Western man became, and keeps becoming, human.

In terms of sheer page count, the most prominent role of theology (as normally defined) in Agamben's thought is in the critical genealogy of the "Western machine" that he undertakes in the *Homo Sacer* series, a multivolume project that culminated in 2014 with *The Use of Bodies*.[8] The second role is to serve as a kind of workshop for what we might call—with all due caution and nuance—the "constructive" side of his thought. Here he is following Walter Benjamin, who couched his most important philosophical and political insights in messianic terms. This "constructive" trend is already visible in 1990's *The Coming Community*,[9] where some of the most memorable and evocative passages of which are meditations on marginal theological themes such as limbo and halos. He continues in a similar vein in the essay "The Glorious Body" in 2009's *Nudities*,[10] where he memorably analyzes the theological conundrums that surround the doctrine of the resurrection of the dead. Will the dead eat, for instance, and if so, will they defecate? Will heaven fill up with their refuse over the course of eternity? And what is the use of the sexual organs when there is no more need for sexual reproduction? In the hands of another thinker, these reflections easily could have been fodder for mockery of Christianity, but Agamben takes these problems seriously as a way of meditating on ways we could reconceptualize the use of our own bodies in the contemporary world. In other words, the apparent irrelevance and unreality of theological speculations about the messianic age are actually points in their favor, as they open up a space for radical new paths of thought.

These two prongs of Agamben's approach to theology come to a head in the two books that together make up the fourth and final "volume" of the Homo Sacer project: *The Highest Poverty* and *The Use of Bodies*.[11] Both include critical genealogies of theology's contributions to the depredations of Western modernity, but both also point out important minority traditions that Agamben tries in some way to reawaken. Hence the theological and juridical debate over Franciscan claims to be incapable of owning property or Leibniz's attempt to rework scholastic ontology to make better sense of Eucharistic transubstantiation can appear no longer as obscure historical trivia, but as pointers toward an alternative history whose potentiality resonates in our present. The same dynamic occurs in an earlier installment in the series, *The Sacrament of Language*, where Jesus and Paul emerge as messianic critics of the regime of the oath, which Agamben views as central to the Western power structure founded on the control of language.[12] Nevertheless, in both *The Use of Bodies* and *The Sacrament of Language*, philosophy takes pride of place over messianism as the discourse that can point us toward a better future. We can see this most clearly in the concluding paragraph of the latter work:

Philosophy is, in this sense, constitutively a critique of the oath: that is, it puts in question the sacramental bond that links the human being with language, without for that reason simply speaking haphazardly, falling into the vanity of speech. In a moment when all the European languages seem condemned to swear in vain and when politics can only assume the form of an *oikonomia*, that is, of a governance of empty speech over bare life, it is once more from philosophy that there can come, in the sober awareness of the extreme situation at which the living human being that has language has arrived in its history, the indication of a line of resistance and change.[13]

In *The Use of Bodies*, the privilege of philosophy is less explicitly stated, but it is clear that the ultimate target of the project is the logic of presupposition, which refers to the repeated pattern of isolating an element within a given field or system and then simultaneously denigrating it and making it foundational to that field or system. The most famous example in Agamben's work is the figure of bare life, which sovereign power at once excludes from the city and establishes as the foundation of its power, but he finds the same dynamic across the linguistic, ontological, and political realms. This great root and motor of the Western machine—the positive *requirement* of some form of abjection within every major area of human experience—can only be deposed or deactivated through taking up a new stance toward the experience of language, which Agamben has long defined as the primary focus of philosophy. Hence we can say that, even if he does not embrace a hard distinction between the two fields, Agamben is positioning himself as "officially" a philosopher and not a theologian.

Yet the more purely philosophical use that Agamben makes of theology in most of his works may not be the last word. After all, during his most productive period, his research was dictated by the demands of his *Homo Sacer* series, whose goals determined the shape even of the many books from the same period (such as *The Time That Remains*) that fall outside its official rubric. In the years since the completion—or, as he puts it, the "abandonment"—of that largely critical project, Agamben has returned repeatedly to theology in new and unexpected ways that seem to stake out a properly "theological" position. This new approach is clearest in 2018's *The Kingdom and the Garden*,[14] a text that, perhaps more than any of his previous works, operates in an almost entirely theological register. To some extent, the argument follows up on another book that appeared shortly after *The Use of Bodies*, namely *Karman* (2017).[15] In that text, whose title is a form of the familiar term "karma," Agamben analyzes the legal and religious roots of modern concepts of moral responsibility. Christianity's role in that genealogy is to enshrine human free will as the seat of the imputability of action and hence of moral accountability, a conception of human action and intention that modern legal codes would ultimately take up. Crucial here is his reading of Augustine, where the great theologian's personal struggle to fully surrender to God's grace turns out to be part of a broader strategy to displace potentiality (the seat of ancient Greek conceptions of moral accountability) with the will. In other words, where the ancient Greeks assessed moral responsibility in terms of what the subject is able to do, starting with Augustine, Christianity fatefully shifts the focus to what the subject intends or wills.

This potentiality-to-will shift fits well when Agamben is recounting Augustine's debate with Pelagius over free will, but when Agamben turns to the *Confessions*, there is something excessive in Augustine's thought that does not seem to fit into the terms of *Karman*'s genealogy—namely, original sin. This strange doctrine, which claims that we are all born in a state of moral failure through no fault of our own, comes in for a thorough critique in *The Kingdom and the Garden*. Agamben's primary argumentative strategy is to demonstrate that Augustine invents this cruel and paradoxical dogma—in which our free will exists only to entrap us in guilt and leave us beholden to the sacramental rites of the institutional church—more or less out of thin air, covering his tracks through tendentious misreadings of biblical and patristic texts and even outright lies.

The level of detail and rigor is astounding, making the chapter on original sin arguably Agamben's greatest contribution to the history of theology thus far—a claim I do not make lightly, as I have already highly praised *The Kingdom and the Glory*. Yet its very thoroughness raises questions about the stakes of the argument. Clearly Agamben objects deeply to the doctrine of original sin, perhaps even more than in the case of previous doctrines he has critiqued such as the *opus operatum* (the idea that the sacrament is effective solely if the priest follows the rite properly, regardless of the priest's moral character or intentions) or the providential economy of salvation (which gives rise to modern systems of economic exploitation and control). But where those two critiques each found their place in a genealogy leading to deleterious consequences in modernity, nothing like that is at play in *The Kingdom and the Garden*. He could easily connect original sin to modern political concepts,[16] but aside from one brief note on "mass politics" as representing the "mass of perdition" from Augustine's doctrine of original sin, he does not. His objection is *theological*, to the extent that I feel comfortable declaring him a Pelagian, at least when it comes to embracing Pelagius's account of human freedom based in potentiality rather than will.

Not only that, but the alternatives he outlines are theological as well—even if he defines their authors as philosophers. The bulk of the text is given over to two representatives of a minority tradition that rejected the doctrine of original sin: namely, John Scotus Eriugena and Dante. In Eriugena, a little-studied early medieval thinker remarkable for his familiarity with Greek sources in an era when that was a rarity in the West, Agamben finds an account of life in which the Aristotelian division between the vegetative, sensible, and intellectual parts of the soul is completely rejected in favor of a radical unity of all living things. In Eriugena's scheme, sin does have damaging effects, but it is unable to corrupt human nature as such. The chapter on Dante focuses on the image of the earthly paradise in the *Purgatorio*, including the mysterious figure of Matelda and Dante's prophetic-apocalyptic vision. Drawing on Dante's political writings, Agamben establishes Dante's earthly paradise as the site of an authentic happiness or beatitude that is available in our present lives, rather than deferred until the hereafter. Agamben is clearly annoyed at the critical consensus that sees Dante as giving a poetic form to preexisting scholastic theology, declaring with exasperation: "As if the mind of Dante (who after all often took care to define himself explicitly as a philosopher) were not, for originality, inventive capacity, and coherence, infinitely superior to that of the scholastic philosophers who were his contemporaries, Aquinas included; and as if *inventio* were not an integral part of poetic practice, which would otherwise be reduced to the futile task of dressing up in rhetorical expedients ideas found by others."[17]

This is not the place to go into further detail on Agamben's analyses of Eriugena and Dante. For present purposes, I would like to take a step back and point out that both figures are presented as philosophers working with theological materials—in a serious, creative, *theological* way. The theological references are not simply illustrations or cultural touchpoints, but materials that the thinkers fully inhabit, taking up their own positions in theological terms. And the position is materially the same as Agamben's own, namely, that the doctrine of original sin is a lie and therefore happiness or beatitude is available in the present life, without the intermediation of any institutional church or sacramental rite. Indeed, the sequence of chapters that dismantle the doctrine of original sin and then treat, in turn, Eriugena and Dante, are bookended by Agamben's own investigation of the notion of the earthly paradise (the Garden of Eden as a place on Earth), which he follows the early patristic tradition in viewing as symbolic of human nature as such. Yet this symbol is never left aside as a "mere" symbol. It is taken seriously (albeit not "literally") on its own terms. Hence, for instance, Agamben is able to reject the Augustinian account in part because it implies that God created the earthly paradise for no reason—a theological objection if ever there was one. And this theological symbol, which never stops being theological and is never "translated" into its "real" secular meaning, is presented as a promising starting point for a new politics.

I have spoken of Benjamin, Warburg, Heidegger, and Arendt as models for Agamben's approach to theological materials, but here I think we can see the influence of another model: Plato. The final major division of *The Use of Bodies* ends with a commentary on the final pages of Plato's *Republic*, which recount the Myth of Er. Agamben approaches this mythical account of the structure of the underworld and the system of reincarnation, wherein each soul has the opportunity to choose the form of life in which it will be reborn, with a similar level of rigor and creativity as he does the image of the earthly paradise. He takes all the details seriously, yet not literally, and he connects them, as Plato does, to an ethical demand to live the philosophical life in the present—yet without reducing the mythical symbolism to a straightforward "message." This approach is in keeping with his understanding of Plato's own method, in which "*mythos* and *logos*, explanation through story and dialectical rigor, are not contradictory but are mutually integrated. . . . The myth is a complex figure, which seems to explain something that *logos* by itself cannot clarify and that therefore demands in its turn an uncommon hermeneutical capacity."[18]

Here theology is arguably still subordinate to philosophy, yet it is irreducibly necessary to the philosophical task. Philosophy reaches its limit and calls upon theology when it comes time to think through the origins of human life as we know it—what Agamben calls anthropogenesis—and thinking through origins always necessarily entails thinking through the potential for transformation, for becoming human in a new way here and now. That is what is at stake, on the individual level, in Plato's Myth of Er, and it is what is at stake, on the collective and therefore political level, in the biblical myth of the earthly paradise. Hence it falls to Agamben, precisely as a philosopher, to declare that in the Garden of Eden (which doesn't exist), the sin of Adam and Eve (which never occurred) did not vitiate human nature and place us in eternal debt to God (who doesn't exist)—not ironically or under erasure, but in all earnestness, indeed with greater honesty and greater theological rigor than St. Augustine himself.

For the most part, Agamben pursues the theological side of philosophy by taking up and reinterpreting the messianic myths of Christianity. Yet recent years have seen him try his hand at writing fresh myths of his own. This more radical approach is perhaps clearest in two striking passages from his 2017 memoir, *Autoritratto nello studio* (Self-portrait in his studio).[19] The first comes amid a discussion of Aristotle's subordination and denigration of vegetable life as compared to sensible and intellectual life, a gesture that Agamben takes to be a prime example of the presuppositional logic of the Western machine. Rejecting Aristotle's view, Agamben declares, "For me plants are a form of life in every sense superior to our own: they live in a perpetual dream, feeding on light."[20] It is a beautiful sentiment that fits perfectly into the style of the memoir by building on some of his past conceptual analyses—in this case the concept of vegetative life, which was an emergent theme in *The Use of Bodies*—in a more poetic and personal mode.

The second passage on plants takes that strategy to the extreme. In *The Use of Bodies*, Agamben had briefly pointed out that Aristotle's analysis of vegetative or nutritive life in *On the Soul* brings it into surprisingly close contact with the intellect and even allows it to partake in some way in divinity.[21] The concluding paragraph of the memoir takes up this insight and expands upon it in a very unexpected way:

> To love, to believe in someone or something does not mean to accept dogmas or doctrines as true. It is, rather, like remaining faithful to the emotion that we felt when looking at the starry sky as children. And certainly in the sense I have believed in the people and things that I am here briefly evoking one by one, have sought not to falsify them, to keep the word I have tacitly given. But if I now had to say in what I have finally put my hopes and my faith, I could only confess in a low voice: not in the heavens—in the grass. In grass—in all its forms . . . [and here he spends several lines listing several varieties of grass, concluding with] the noble acanthus, which covers part of the garden in which I walk every day. Grass, grass is God. In grass—in God—are all those whom I have loved. Through grass and in grass and as grass I have lived and will live.[22]

This declaration is followed by one final image in a book full of them—a photograph of grass, taken by the author himself.

It is difficult, to say the least, to know what to make of this proclamation of the gospel of grass. It feels almost like a momentary flight of fancy or even a fever dream, perhaps a moment of sudden inspiration as Agamben struggled to end a book that, as an attempt to grapple with the relationships and ideas that most deeply shaped him, is intrinsically open-ended. Even granting that difficulty, though, it seems to me that the penultimate paragraph was already a satisfactory ending. There he evokes a sense of the connections between the living and the dead, evoking the resurrection of the dead and seemingly defining God as a place where the dead and the living can meet and recognize each other. He could have left it there—but even if he had, I note that he would still have concluded his memoir with a theological image.

On the theological level, in fact, one could say that the difference between the final two paragraphs of *Autoritratto nello studio* is that between a mild heterodoxy (albeit one that an enterprising theologian could likely square with more traditional formulations) and a wild, untamable theological speculation, a statement of faith that no existing faith tradition could countenance or take on board. What could it possibly mean to view the life of plants as superior to our own, or to revere the most common plant that we daily trample underfoot as the very embodiment of the divine? Yet Agamben's critical-genealogical work shows us that the same perspective that makes it seem obviously ridiculous to divinize the grass beneath our feet also underwrites untold suffering and injustice. If we really are trapped inside a destructive machine that systematically blinds us to other alternatives, then perhaps one way to break with it and truly think through Agamben's demand that we become human in a new and different way would be to think through Agamben's divinization of grass with the seriousness and rigor he brings to the analysis of the Myth of Er or the lifestyle of the resurrected.

I leave it to others to develop Agamben's vegetative theology into a full-blown doctrine. In conclusion, I would like to offer a few initial indications for interpreting this puzzling image. The first is to note that the form of life that Agamben attributes to grass—a passive subsistence, without labor or intellectual reflection—does exist in us in the form of our autonomic body functions. Though it seems foreign to the way we understand human life, grass's form of life is nevertheless absolutely essential to our existence and at the same time unacknowledged. This denigrated, seemingly pointless form of life is what we all share with every other human being who has ever lived as well as with every other living thing of every kind. In contrast with theological systems founded on the absolute qualitative distinction between God and creation, it is precisely this absolutely common, unremarkable life that is designated as divine. Agamben is not asking us to literally become a blade of grass any more than Jesus was asking his followers to become a sparrow or a lily of the field. He is asking us to acknowledge that we already *are* grass and hence—not in our brilliant works of art and philosophy, our scientific discoveries and technological know-how, not even in our works of love, but precisely in the sheer pointless persistence of living—we are already divine.

To find a way to recognize and live into that vision, to be the divine grass we already are, would necessarily entail radically bringing to a halt the machine that operates by dividing us against ourselves. It would bring about the deepest possible transformation by allowing us to become what we have always only been but have somehow never allowed ourselves to be. Such thoughts may seem fanciful or even absurd, and perhaps they are—but as Agamben reminds us, "according to Benjamin, shards of messianic time are present in history in possibly infamous and risible forms."[23]

PART III

Theology and the Genealogy
of the Modern World

The Problem of Evil and the Problem of Legitimacy

The modern discipline of political theology starts from the homology between God and the earthly ruler, but the historical experience that stands at the root of the political theology of the West starts from their radical disjuncture. I am speaking here of the historical experience of the Jewish prophets and intellectuals who attempted to make sense of their special relationship to God in the light of almost inconceivable setbacks and catastrophes: the apostasy of the majority of their fellow Israelites from the divine covenant, the destruction of their kingdom and way of life, and their exile in a foreign land.

These Hebrew thinkers could have been forgiven for turning their backs on their defeated God and bowing down in worship to the foreign gods who had so thoroughly proven their superior power. Instead, they responded to incalculable loss with a bold theological risk. In the face of their God's apparent defeat, they doubled down and claimed that their local God was actually the God of all the earth. Far from being defeated by the pagan empires, the God of Israel had orchestrated their rise—and eventual fall.

The basis for this outlandish claim goes back to the Torah, particularly the Book of Deuteronomy. This book consists primarily of a long speech put into the mouth of Moses, in which he recounts the history of Israel's relationship to God and reiterates the divine commandments on the eve of Israel's entry into the promised land. The story is one of human ingratitude in the face of divine grace and favor. In Moses's account, even after God showed his mighty power by liberating the Israelite slaves from their oppression in Egypt, the people rebelled against his rule, to the point that God condemned the Israelites to wander in the desert for forty years so that the rebellious generation could be superseded by their children. The terms of the covenant are clear: "See, I am setting before you today a blessing and a curse: the blessing, if you obey the commandments of the Lord your God that I am commanding you today; and the curse, if you do not obey the commandments of the Lord your God, but turn from the way that I am commanding you today, to follow other gods that you have not known" (Deuteronomy 11:26–28).[1]

For the intellectuals who collected and consolidated Israelite history and legend, Deuteronomy provided a convenient framework for understanding the political vicissitudes their country had experienced throughout its tumultuous history. The Deuteronomistic paradigm provided them with something like an answer to what we would now call the "problem of evil"—that is to say, the problem of how to reconcile faith in a powerful and beneficent God with the experience of evil and suffering. Their solution preserved faith in God by claiming that the apparent evils they suffered were not truly evils, but were instead well-deserved punishments aimed at putting the people back on track.

This theological paradigm figured God as lawgiver and law enforcer. Yet instead of legitimating an easy parallel between God and the earthly ruler, this theocratic claim rendered every earthly king a potential rival to God's reign. This is not to say that God is necessarily setting up his earthly representatives to fail, for the Book of Deuteronomy itself envisions the possibility of a just king who serves as something like a faithful functionary for the divine ruler, submitting fully to the divine law:

> When he has taken the throne of his kingdom, he shall have a copy of this law written for him in the presence of the levitical priests. It shall remain with him and he shall read in it all the days of his life, so that he may learn to fear the Lord his God, diligently observing all the words of this law and these statutes, neither exalting himself above other members of the community nor turning aside from the commandment, either to the right or to the left, so that he and his descendants may reign long over his kingdom in Israel. (17:18–20)

By contrast, the remainder of the Deuteronomistic history (the segment of the Hebrew Bible made up of Joshua, Judges, 1 and 2 Samuel, and 1 and 2 Kings) is significantly less optimistic about the prospects for an Israelite king. In the famous passage where the Israelites demand that the prophet Samuel appoint a king, Samuel predicts that the king will oppress the people:

These will be the ways of the king who will reign over you: he will take your sons and appoint them to his chariots and to be his horsemen, and to run before his chariots; and he will appoint for himself commanders of thousands and commanders of fifties, and some to plow his ground and to reap his harvest, and to make his implements of war and the equipment of his chariots. He will take your daughters to be perfumers and cooks and bakers. He will take the best of your fields and vineyards and olive orchards and give them to his courtiers. He will take one-tenth of your grain and of your vineyards and give it to his officers and his courtiers. He will take your male and female slaves, and the best of your cattle and donkeys, and put them to his work. He will take one-tenth of your flocks, and you shall be his slaves. And in that day you will cry out because of your king, whom you have chosen for yourselves; but the Lord will not answer you in that day. (1 Samuel 8:11–18)

For his part, God makes the rivalry explicit when he claims that "they have rejected me from being king over them" (8:7). Subsequently, in the view of the Deuteronomistic historian, the fate of Israel hangs on whether the king is a divine functionary within God's rule or a rival to the theocratic ideal.

Earthly rulers thus become a site of intense theological reflection, a trend that is only intensified when successive waves of imperial conquest in the ancient Near East lead to the final defeat of the Israelite kingdoms and the transfer of their intellectual elites to the imperial center. The Hebrew prophets responded to this development with an extension of the Deuteronomistic scheme: They claimed that the pagan kings were actually a tool that God was using to punish and purify the remnant of Israel. When their usefulness to God ran out, however, they would be punished for their own injustice and wickedness. The prophet Jeremiah's account is exemplary here:

Therefore thus says the Lord of hosts: Because you have not obeyed my words, I am going to send for all the tribes of the north, says the Lord, even for King Nebuchadrezzar of Babylon, *my servant*, and I will bring them against this land and its inhabitants, and against all these nations around; I will utterly destroy them, and make them an object of horror and of hissing, and an everlasting disgrace. And I will banish from them the sound of mirth and the sound of gladness, the voice of the bridegroom and the voice of the bride, the sound of the millstones and the light of the lamp. This whole land shall become a ruin and a waste, and these nations shall serve the king of Babylon seventy years. Then after seventy years are completed, I will punish the king of Babylon and that nation, the land of the Chaldeans, for their iniquity, says the Lord, making the land an everlasting waste. I will bring upon that land all the words that I have uttered against it, everything written in this book, which Jeremiah prophesied against all the nations. For many nations and great kings shall make slaves of them also; and I will repay them according to their deeds and the work of their hands. (Jeremiah 25:8–14; emphasis added)

The ambivalence between ruler-as-functionary and ruler-as-rival reappears in an intensified form, insofar as this passage figures Nebuchadrezzar as both "my servant" and as an enemy to be defeated by God. By contrast, other rulers are depicted as more or less entirely positive, most notably Cyrus of Persia, who financed the rebuilding of the Temple in Jerusalem as part of an imperial policy of cultivating local religions destroyed by previous empires. Thus the prophet Isaiah can call Cyrus God's "anointed . . . whose right hand I have grasped to subdue nations before him and strip kings of their robes" (45:1)—a divine role Cyrus can fulfill even though the Word of the Lord, addressing Cyrus, can say, "you do not know me" (45:4).

Within this political-theological scheme, the Jews are encouraged to suspend judgment of the pagan rulers under whom they must live. God will judge in his own due time, and until then, the duty of the Jewish community is to be as faithful as possible to the law and to contribute positively to the surrounding community:

Thus says the Lord of hosts, the God of Israel, to all the exiles whom I have sent into exile from Jerusalem to Babylon: Build houses and live in them; plant gardens and eat what they produce. Take wives and have sons and daughters; take wives for your sons, and give your daughters in marriage, that they may bear sons and daughters; multiply there, and do not decrease. But seek the welfare of the city where I have sent you into exile, and pray to the Lord on its behalf, for in its welfare you will find your welfare. (Jeremiah 29:4–7)

Over the centuries that followed, this prophetic paradigm provided the basic model for the Jewish community's relationship with earthly powers. From this perspective, the model Jew is a figure like Joseph, Daniel, or Esther, who rises to a high government position and yet maintains their Jewish identity, leading the earthly ruler to give glory to the God of Israel.

At times, however, historical conditions became so extreme that this careful balance could no longer be maintained. One such period was the brief but tumultuous reign of the mad king Antiochus Epiphanes in the second century BCE (recounted most vividly in the apocryphal book of 2

Maccabees, widely available in standard translations). The ruler of one of the Hellenistic empires that resulted from Alexander's conquest, Antiochus attempted to impose Hellenistic culture and religion on the Jews, defiling their temple and forcing faithful Jews—under threat of torture and death—to violate the Torah by eating pork. Within both the Deuteronomistic and prophetic paradigms, this turn of events was incomprehensible: They were brutally persecuted, tortured, and even killed precisely *for* being faithful to God's law. Hence the king is no longer God's unwitting servant, but his conscious and willful enemy. Yet though it stretches the Deuteronomistic-prophetic paradigm nearly to the breaking point, this newly emerging apocalyptic paradigm does not depart from it entirely. Even the king conceived as demonic plays a necessary role in God's plan, serving as God's final enemy, whose defeat will usher in the messianic age.

The radical evil of the earthly ruler in the apocalyptic scheme thus paradoxically leads to a more elevated cosmological status. If he is to be a rival to God, he must operate not only on the earthly political plane, but on the spiritual plane as well. Hence the rich imagery of apocalyptic literature, which produces a kind of spiritual overlay for geopolitics—above all in Daniel, whose apocalyptic later chapters narrate the history of world empires up to the time of Antiochus (the "little horn" of the vision). Here we are as far as possible from Schmitt's homology between the divine and earthly ruler. The most relevant theological homology from the perspective of apocalyptic thought is, rather, that between the earthly ruler and God's demonic enemy.

From this perspective, we can see that it is not accidental that the leaders of the Maccabean revolt against Antiochus belonged precisely to the priestly class rather than to the remnants of the ruling dynasty. Within the apocalyptic worldview, at least at this stage of its development, the prospect of a "good king" is no more acceptable than the rule of a "good emperor" on the model of Cyrus. A return to the theocratic ideal is the only legitimate option once the earthly ruler becomes God's cosmic rival.

This is the context within which we must understand the New Testament's calls for the coming of the "Kingdom of God" or the "Kingdom of Heaven"—as well as its straightforward portrayal of Satan as the ruler of this world. This latter point is clear above all in the temptation of Christ, where Satan's offer of worldly power makes no sense unless he really has worldly power to give. More dramatically, the author of Revelation associates contemporary Roman rulers with demonic forces and appears to anticipate a direct take-over by Satan in the near future. And throughout the Pauline epistles, there are references to expelling someone out of the community to make their way through the world as "handing that person over to Satan." For the New Testament authors and the early Christian writers known as the Church Fathers, Christ did not come to suffer the punishment due for our individual sins, but to set us free from the demonic powers that rule this world.

What enabled the Hebrew prophets to make their bold, counterintuitive gesture? Why double down on their apparently defeated God instead of setting him aside? It is likely impossible to know for sure, but we can trace elements in the Hebrew theological tradition that made their daring gambit plausible. First, the God of the Hebrew Bible is not only a god of power, but a God of law and justice. Second, already in the Torah God cannot be limited to a merely local relationship to the Israelites, because he is portrayed as using the Israelites themselves to carry out his judgment against the injustice of the land of Canaan. Nor indeed can he be limited by any created image:

> Then the Lord spoke to you out of the fire. You heard the sounds of the words but saw no form; there was only a voice. . . . Since you saw no form when the Lord spoke to you at Horeb out of the fire, take care and watch yourselves closely, so that you do not act corruptly by making an idol for yourselves, in the form of any figure—the likeness of male or female, the likeness of any animal that is on the earth, the likeness of any bird that flies in the air, the likeness of anything that creeps on the ground, the likeness of any fish that is in the water under the sea. (Deuteronomy 4:12, 15–18)

Hence the prophets can envision God's demand for justice as transcending even the written Torah itself, as when Jeremiah declares that God will make a "new covenant" that will transcend the old insofar as "I will put my law within them, and I will write it on their hearts" (31:33).

This God of justice stands in stark contrast to the Greek and Roman mythological tradition, where the gods are often forces of chaos and destruction. Though the Greco-Roman gods have some inchoate relationship with certain unwritten laws surrounding hospitality and burial rites, it is difficult to come away from a reading of Ovid's *Metamorphoses*, for instance, with a view that the gods are systematically committed to law and justice in general. It is this moral and political difference—and not, as an anachronistic liberalism would have it, simple intolerance—that underwrites the prophetic critique of pagan idolatry. A false idol is a god who is hungry for glory and power, whereas the God of Israel can say, "I desire steadfast love and not sacrifice, the knowledge of God rather than burnt offerings" (Hosea 6:6). Indeed, this conviction that the gods of the other nations were power-mad tyrants provided a crucial background to the apocalyptic diagnosis that the world is ruled by demonic forces opposed to divine justice.

Apocalyptic and Political Theology

Students of contemporary debates in political theology could be forgiven for being unfamiliar with much of this history. This context is completely absent from Badiou, Agamben, and Žižek's studies of the Pauline epistles, for instance. As a result, even though Badiou claims to have utterly no interest in the traditional reception of Paul's thought, he winds up reproducing many of its most toxic elements—most notably its strident anti-Judaism. Žižek offers a more pro-Jewish reading, claiming that Paul offers to Gentiles the same "unplugged" stance toward the law enjoyed by Jews, but his reading is ahistorical and anachronistic, drawing on Eric Santner's work on the psychodynamics of Judaism and projecting that theory onto the very different situation of the first century.[2] For his part, despite the fact that his scholarly work on Walter Benjamin has given him a deep knowledge of Judaism, Agamben makes very limited reference to the Hebrew Bible or Jewish tradition, preferring to concentrate on Paul's influence on the Western tradition.

Within the emerging mini-canon of contemporary philosophical engagements with Paul, only Jacob Taubes's *Political Theology of Paul* fully situates the Apostle in the context of Jewish political theology, and thus only Taubes is able to present Paul's intervention not as merely analogous to politics (as in Badiou), but as directly and irreducibly political: "the Epistle to the Romans is a political theology, a *political* declaration of war on the Caesar." More than that, Paul and his contemporaries are struggling against the dominant political theology of their age: "Christian literature is a literature of protest against the flourishing cult of the emperor."[3]

The same broad historical perspective, first developed in his pathbreaking study *Occidental Eschatology*, allows him to contextualize Carl Schmitt within the tradition of apocalyptic thought.[4] Putting it in slightly different terms than Taubes does, we can view Schmitt's political theology as a recent outgrowth of a profound reversal that took place within Christian political theology after Constantine. Within the apocalyptic framework, these political developments were tantamount to the devil converting to Christianity.

Once the earthly ruler was no longer God's cosmic rival but his faithful servant, Christianity was able to step back from its apocalyptic outlook and embrace the relative stability of something like the Jewish prophetic model. Yet a total reversion to the prophetic model was impossible within the terms of Christianity insofar as Christ's incarnation, death, and resurrection had already begun the apocalyptic sequence. In conceptualizing this strange new development, Christian theologians drew on an enigmatic passage from the (likely spurious) Pauline epistle of 2 Thessalonians:

> Let no one deceive you in any way; for that day [of Judgment] will not come unless the rebellion comes first and the lawless one is revealed, the one destined for destruction. He opposes and exalts himself above every so-called god or object of worship, so that he takes his seat in the temple of God, declaring himself to be God. Do you not remember that I told you these things when I was still with you? And you know what is now restraining [*katechōn*] him, so that he may be revealed when his time comes. For the mystery of lawlessness is already at work, but only until the one who now restrains [*katechōn*] it is removed. And then the lawless one will be revealed, whom the Lord Jesus will destroy with the breath of his mouth, annihilating him by the manifestation of his coming. (2:3–8)

It is impossible to reconstruct with confidence what the author of the passage originally meant by the *katechōn* or *katechon* (the personal and impersonal grammatical forms, respectively), but post-Constantinian interpreters seized on the ambiguous term to designate the Christian ruler's role in staving off the advent of the Antichrist—and hence delaying the apocalypse.

Schmitt himself emphasizes the importance of this concept in *Nomos of the Earth* when describing the European political theology of the medieval period:

> This Christian empire was not eternal. It always had its own end and that of the present eon in view. Nevertheless, it was capable of being a historical power. The decisive historical concept of this continuity was that of the restrainer: *katechon*. "Empire" in this sense meant the historical power to restrain the appearance of the Antichrist and the end of the present eon; it was a power that withholds (*qui tenet*), as the Apostle Paul said in his Second Letter to the Thessalonians. . . . The empire of the Christian Middle Ages lasted only as long as the idea of the katechon was alive.[5]

Indeed, he explicitly cites the concept as a way of overcoming what in his view was a historical deadlock introduced by Christianity's apocalyptic orientation: "I do not believe that any historical concept other than katechon would have been possible for the original Christian faith. The belief that a restrainer holds back the end of the world provides the only bridge between the notion of an eschatological paralysis of all human events and a tremendous historical monolith like that of the Christian empire."[6] It is on the basis of the *katechon* that Taubes will later describe where his thought deviates from Schmitt's, despite their shared apocalyptic outlook:

> Schmitt had one interest: that the Party, that chaos did not win out, that the state stood firm. At whatever cost. . . . That is what he later called the katechon: the restrainer who holds back the chaos bubbling up from the depths. That is not the way I think about the world, that is not my experience. I can see myself as an apocalyptic: it can all go to hell. I have no spiritual investment in the world as it is. But I understand that another does invest in this world and sees the apocalypse, in whatever shape or form, as the adversary and does everything to subjugate and suppress it, because, from there, forces may be released that we are incapable of mastering.[7]

From this perspective, we can see that the decisive question in political theology is not sovereignty, but apocalyptic. Schmitt's focus on sovereignty, which has so deeply shaped the contemporary field of political theology, actually presupposes a prior answer to the more fundamental question of apocalyptic. And apocalyptic is a *political* theological question because it grows out of a long history of theological developments that closely tied the theological problem of evil to the political problem of the ultimate legitimacy of the earthly rulers. Within the Christian framework, the choice is between the apocalyptic paradigm, in which the earthly rulers are God's illegitimate rivals, or the katechontic paradigm, in which the earthly rulers are God's legitimate, if provisional, servants. Yet since the katechontic paradigm can never fully dispense with the apocalyptic framework if it is to remain Christian, it is constantly threatened with apocalyptic dissolution—a prospect that was welcomed by the avowedly apocalyptic early Christian movement, but that gradually came to be viewed as a terrifying eventuality to be staved off at all costs.

The Schmittian framing of the discipline of political theology thus limits it to a very narrow—and deeply reactionary—corner of the intellectual options that developed in the Jewish and later Christian traditions. It influences political theologians to read early Christian sources anachronistically, through a post-Constantinian katechontic lens that obscures their more radical apocalyptic stance. And it encourages them to ignore contemporary theological movements that renew the apocalyptic protest against the illegitimacy of the earthly powers: Latin American liberation theology, radical Black theology of North America, postcolonial theology, feminist theology, queer theology—movements that, despite the clichés about the supposedly intrinsic narrowness of "identitarian" intellectual approaches, are in a rich and continual dialogue with each other and with more traditional theologians as well. The Schmittian enclosure dooms us— we mostly white, mostly male political theologians—to continually replicate the intellectual construct of "The Christian West," with all its deadlocks and blinders.

The Problem of Providence

At the dawn of modernity amid the wars that followed in the wake of the Reformation, this katechontic vision of Christianity began to lose its hold, as the Christian God seemed to be less the guarantor of justice than a force of chaos akin to his pagan predecessors. Although there were radical apocalyptic protests, by and large the secular state emerged as the only force that could subdue the violence of religious conflict. Even at this historical moment, the memory of the deep association between the earthly powers and the demonic still exerts its influence, as Hobbes could figure the state as the Leviathan, a mythical creature that Christian readers of the Book of Job had traditionally associated with the devil.

This basic continuity is a clue that we are dealing here with a mutation in political theology rather than a radically new beginning. Just as in the more explicitly theological schemes, the ruler is not self-legitimating, but needs some outside principle of legitimation. In the Hobbesian paradigm, free human consent replaces the divine decree—and like the divine decree, this human consent is irrevocable, so that anything the ruler does, whether good or evil, is legitimated by the choice to submit to his rule. And in keeping with the katechontic scheme, anything he does is preferable to the apocalyptic scenario of the war of all against all that his rule staves off.

In *The Kingdom and the Glory*, Agamben has shown that the theology of divine providence stands at the genealogical root of modern concepts of economy—the invisible hand is a secularization of the hand of God. Here again, the principle of legitimation changes from God's will to human free will, as expressed through market mechanisms that aggregate and balance individual choices into a single outcome. And again, even apparently evil results are legitimate and necessary insofar as they reflect the outcome of human freedom.

Agamben begins *The Kingdom and the Glory* with the declaration that there are "two paradigms"—the political theological and the theological economic. He leaves unspecified exactly when and where these paradigms hold and how we should view the relationship between them. From the perspective of the present investigation, I suggest that we should view them as distinctively modern paradigms, which are both legitimated by reference to human freedom and which normally coexist. Under "normal" conditions of liberal democracy, they achieve some form of harmony that allows them to mutually legitimate each other—the state, founded in popular sovereignty, is the custodian of the economy, founded in freely chosen contracts, and the economy founds the strength of the state.

Like the God of the prophetic paradigm, the legitimating principle of human freedom expresses itself only indirectly, and sometimes in apparently counterintuitive ways. The connection with the prophetic paradigm goes deeper, however, insofar as the modern subject is always "in exile." In theoretical discourses, our entry into the spheres of the state and market is often figured as requiring us to leave some logically prior, more "natural" state, and our submission to the laws of state and market is presented as a necessary evil given the impossibility of fully actualizing human freedom in the world. We alienate our political power by electing representatives and alienate our productive power through the regime of wage labor. In short, we are never fully "at home" in the institutions of the state or in the marketplace—and as Agamben points out, the modern secular paradigm cuts off all hope of eschatological fulfillment and thus renders our condition always potentially hellish.[8]

The modern prophetic paradigm of liberal democracy attempts to hold the two powers of state and economy in balance. Under extreme conditions, however, apocalyptic protests emerge that not only threaten to shatter the balance, but attempt to eliminate one power entirely.

Fascism asserts popular sovereignty and seeks to permanently overcome the imbalances introduced by the free play of the economy. This leads to a fixation on "foreign" elements within the body politic, which are symbolically associated with the negative effects of the economy, as in the Nazi campaign against the Jews or contemporary movements opposed to immigrants or Muslims in Western countries. Such movements are often deeply legalistic, desperate to find legal legitimation for their violations of the law. It is distressing to realize that arguably everything the Nazis did in Germany was formally legal. More recently, the Bush administration aggressively deployed "legal tools" to legitimate its extralegal actions in the War on Terror.

By contrast, Communism attempts to destroy the state, conceived as an illegitimate tool of class domination, and aggressively develops the "material conditions for full communism," in the hopes of ushering in a new economic order of unprecedented abundance and freedom, unmarked by the contradictions and injustices of capitalism. Communist regimes often flaunt their defiance of conventional political legitimacy, for instance by stealing elections seemingly on principle, even when they would win easily.

This principled illegitimacy still holds in contemporary China, where the Communist Party is not a legally registered organization and where conventional state institutions "exist" in some sense but are basically ignored. In North Korea as well, there is a formal parliament and even official opposition parties, which exist not so much for show as for open mockery.

If these paradigms have any descriptive power, then they vindicate many elements in Agamben's contemporary attempt to expand the political theological enterprise—for instance, his "two paradigms" in *The Kingdom and the Glory*, his insistence in *Homo Sacer* and elsewhere that liberal democracy and totalitarianism participate in the same deep structure. Yet they also show the limitations of his project, cut off as it is from the deeper political theological roots of the Jewish prophetic and apocalyptic traditions. Once his insights are reconsidered in light of those more foundational paradigms, things fall into place more elegantly.

Beyond Freedom

The question that remains now is whether we are at the threshold of a new political theological configuration. At the very least, it seems indisputable that we are at least living through the exhaustion of the modern secular model legitimated by human freedom. Does anyone seriously believe that liberal democratic institutions provide a workable forum for free and equal citizens to collaboratively develop solutions to serious problems? And in the wake of the financial crisis of 2008, can anyone with any intellectual integrity trust that the economy is a reliable tool for increasing human welfare and expressing human freedom? In theory, there are many plausible plans for using state power to reform the economy and return us to the more promising trajectory experienced in most Western countries in the early postwar era. Yet there is apparently no appetite to attempt such measures in any major developed nation, where political elites are essentially all devoted to the neoliberal project of aggressively deploying state power to exacerbate all of the most destructive aspects of capitalism.

In short, the modern answer to the problem of evil has failed. Popular sovereignty and economic freedom are no longer sufficient to the task of legitimating our world order and explaining away its apparent evils as part of a broader good. Indeed, in contemporary discourse, the function of these principles is limited almost exclusively to blaming everyday citizens for the evils in the world. Why do they keep electing these fools? Why don't they turn up and vote sufficiently often or with sufficient enthusiasm? Why don't they choose environmentally sustainable consumer goods, or healthier food? Why don't they develop the job skills necessary to boost employment and global competitiveness?

These types of complaints should not be surprising, given the role of free will in the Christian theological tradition. We are accustomed to viewing free will as the epitome of human dignity. But for mainstream theologians, its primary purpose was to absolve God of responsibility for the existence of evil, off-loading it instead onto his creatures. Free will is first of all a mechanism for producing blameworthiness—free choice is a trap.

But what would it mean to think beyond the horizon of human freedom? Is it possible to find another principle of legitimacy to make our lives livable without forcing us to deny our experience of evil? Or is our only option an absolute apocalyptic refusal to grant any legitimacy to this world? Taubes teaches us that this latter option historically develops into something like Gnosticism—and here we might think of certain Western Marxists or even the later Schmitt, who persist in the work of uncompromising criticism with no genuine reference to the eschatological hopes that founded their discourse—and ends in total nihilism.[9]

If theology has any future, its task must be to grapple with these questions. This will require us to rethink the nature of theology as an intellectual enterprise, setting aside clichés about "belief in God" or the necessity of faithfulness to some presently existing "religious" community. Instead, we should view theology more broadly as a discourse on "ultimate concerns," on what is most meaningful and meaning-making, and what is more, as a critical and historically invested discourse on ultimate concerns. This will allow us to recognize modern political theory and economics as a theology of human freedom. There is much critical work to be done in this vein, and Goodchild's *Theology of Money* might serve as one productive model.[10]

Yet more urgent is the constructive task of theology, which at its most powerful actually *creates* new and promising visions of what our ultimate concern could be, of what our life together might mean—or, perhaps better, of what meaning we might collectively give to our lives. To have any purchase, these new meanings cannot be completely disconnected from what came before them, nor can their ultimate effects be predicted and accounted for. Like the Hebrew prophets, we must take the creative risk of renewing and transforming our tradition against almost impossible odds.

Modernity's Original Sin
Toward a Theological Genealogy of Race

We often hear that slavery is America's original sin, by which one seems to mean that slavery is a permanent stain that prevents America from achieving racial justice. In this essay, I want to take that cliché perhaps more seriously than it deserves by granting it real theological weight. Modern race thinking, I will claim, along the ideology of slavery that it sought to legitimate, really does have its roots in the Christian doctrine of original sin. My guide here will be Sylvia Wynter's essay "Unsettling the Coloniality of Being/Power/Truth/Freedom,"[1] in which she reiterates and deepens her account of the origins of modernity—in part by elaborating an analogy between the medieval doctrine of original sin and the modern concept of race. My goal here will be to deepen the analogy and to demonstrate that the specific features of the doctrine of original sin continue to operate in the modern concept of race, consigning racialized subjects to a form of inescapable moral dereliction for which they are nonetheless held responsible.

For Wynter, the shape of global modernity has been determined by a series of overlapping models, originating in Europe, of what it means to be human. The first is the medieval Christian worldview, which is gradually displaced by two visions of "Man"—namely Man as the rational subject of the political state (which she calls Man$_1$) and Man as the product of natural selection and economic competition (which she calls Man$_2$). Wynter views the shift from Christianity to Man as an ambiguous one at best. On the one hand, she sees the invention of Man$_1$ by the Renaissance humanists as "the first secular or 'degodded' (if, at the time, still only partly so) mode of being human in the history of the species" (263), and the first step of "a 'Big Bang' process . . . initiat[ing] the first gradual de-supernaturalizing of our modes of being human" (263–264). This secularization had the effect of "making possible the cognitively emancipatory rise and gradual development of the physical sciences (in the wake of the invention of Man_1), and then of the biological sciences (in the wake of the nineteenth-century invention of Man_2)," which provided human beings with the first genuinely transcultural knowledge of the material conditions of their existence (264).

On the other hand, this de-theologization did not provide any corresponding knowledge of the specifically social and cultural dynamics of humanity, in all its variety. Instead, "Man," in both its forms, "overrepresents itself as if it were the human itself," or in other words, presents the European mode of being human as normative for all of humanity (260). This assertion of European superiority sets up a hierarchy like that found in Christianity and other premodern societies. What is unique about the modern hierarchy, though, is that it is based not in divine transcendence but in the supposedly transcultural reality known as "race," which "was therefore to be, in effect, the non-supernatural but no less extrahuman ground (in the reoccupied place of the traditional ancestors/gods, God, ground)" of the Western worldview (264). In place of the Christian hierarchy that defined outsiders "as heretics, or as Enemies-of-Christ infidels and pagan-idolaters (with Jews serving as the boundary-transgressive 'name of what is evil' figures, stigmatized as Christ-killing deicides)," the modern hierarchy used the ostensibly secular standards of rationality (for Man_1) and biological superiority (for Man_2) to define "the peoples of the militarily expropriated New World territories (i.e., Indians)" and "the enslaved peoples of Black Africa (i.e., Negroes)" as intrinsically "other" to European Man (266). Yet in Wynter's view, the "multiple anticolonial social-protest movements and intellectual challenges of the period to which we give the name 'The Sixties'" (262) promise an epistemic revolution on par with the discovery of modern science, which, by giving voice to the ever-expanding category that Frantz Fanon designated as the "damnés," will clear the way for "securing the well-being, and therefore the full cognitive and behavioral autonomy of the human species itself/ourselves" (260).

This hope for the future is Wynter's real focus, and hence it is understandable that she does not dwell on the intricacies of the medieval worldview, choosing instead to present it in fairly abstract terms that anticipate the structures that will arise under the names Man_1 and Man_2. Drawing primarily on Jacques Le Goff's work on the medieval social order, Wynter repeatedly characterizes Latin-Christian Europe as divided between "the

'Redeemed Spirit' (as actualized in the celibate clergy) and the 'Fallen Flesh' enslaved to the negative legacy of Adamic Original Sin, as actualized by laymen and women," who needed the sacraments administered by the clergy to obtain salvation (274). This duality between a valorized category and a denigrated category carries forward in modernity with the development of Man_1 and Man_2, for which irrationality and genetic inferiority, respectively, come to play much the same role that original sin played in the Christian worldview. This type of continuity in discontinuity is to be expected, as Wynter claims that both Man_1 and Man_2 "remain inscribed within the framework of a specific secularizing reformulation of that matrix Judeo-Christian Grand Narrative" (318). Yet it is not clear from Wynter's analysis whether original sin contributed any *content* to the modern concept of race. Instead, its main function in her argument is as a particular instance of the general category of denigrated humans that, in her view, is common to all transcendence-oriented premodern societies.

I believe that the doctrine of original sin is simply too bizarre and paradoxical to play such a purely formal role. In its mature form, the doctrine contends that every single human being is born morally damaged by the sin of our first ancestors, Adam and Eve. This moral damage includes a tendency to commit concrete sinful acts, but it does not count as a mitigating factor in judging our moral choices. Instead, the subject of original sin is morally accountable for the very fact of being morally damaged from birth. The "sin" in original sin is every bit as sinful as any particular immoral act we carry out, meaning that every infant is born deserving to go to hell. Between the waning years of the Roman Empire (when Augustine formulated the doctrine) and the dawn of modernity, European Christians had centuries of practice with the conceptual contortions necessary to hold someone morally accountable for the circumstances of their own birth—and my guiding hypothesis in this essay is that they carried over those same habits of thought when it came time to justify their acts of conquest and enslavement. Again and again, they hit on the notion that the colonized and enslaved were not only intrinsically inferior, but for that very reason morally deserving of their treatment. Fanon parodies the basic stance brilliantly in *Black Skin, White Masks*: "Serves them right; they shouldn't be black."[2]

To demonstrate this connection, I begin by establishing that modern racialization involves an element of moral entrapment similar to that found in the doctrine of original sin. Here I draw on one of Wynter's own examples, Shakespeare's *The Tempest*, as well as Saidiya Hartman's account of American racism in the nineteenth century in *Scenes of Subjection*. I then outline the development of the doctrine of original sin in the history of Christian theology, emphasizing two factors that Wynter leaves aside in her duality of clergy and laity—namely, the crucial role of angels and demons in the medieval Christian worldview and the importance of the Jews as a human group that is subject to a kind of redoubled original sin. These two elements will help us understand both the connection between racialization and slavery and the reason why the burden of racialization falls disproportionately on certain human groups rather than applying universally to all human beings as the classical version of original sin does. After establishing those connections, I conclude by suggesting possible directions for a counter-theology that could combat and displace the toxic modern theology of race.

"A born devil, on whose nature nurture can never stick"

I begin my account of race as moral entrapment with a play that has become a commonplace among anticolonial intellectuals from Aimé Césaire to Silvia Federici: Shakespeare's *The Tempest*.[3] First staged early in the same decade that the first enslaved Africans arrived on the shores of the British colonies of the New World, Shakespeare's *Tempest* at first glance appears to be merely a fanciful tale of wish fulfillment. The action follows the exiled Duke of Milan, Prospero, who is forced from office by his brother and takes refuge, with his young daughter Miranda, on an enchanted island. By entrapping a magical spirit named Ariel and enslaving the island's sole human inhabitant, Caliban, Prospero is able to claim absolute power over the island and turn its magic to his own ends. When a ship conveniently carrying all his enemies from Milan sails by the island, Prospero uses his magic to stage an elaborate plan—beginning with the titular storm and subsequent shipwreck—that allows him to reclaim his throne, reconcile with his brother, and even marry off his daughter.

Long viewed as Shakespeare's reflection on the power of theater, *The Tempest* is now more often read as providing a model in miniature of the early modern world-system. And nowhere are the contradictions and hypocrisies of that system more obvious than in the figure of Caliban. As son of the witch Sycorax, who is banished from Algiers and then gives birth to him on a mysterious uninhabited island, Caliban is at once African and "native," embodying both classes of the racialized "other" at a moment when they had not yet been fully differentiated in the English imaginary. Wynter herself draws this connection in her discussion of the play, which she views as illustrative of the "line of nonhomogeneity" that, within the regime of Man_1, "functioned to validate the sociontological line now drawn between rational, political Man (Prospero, the settler of European descent) and its irrational Human Others (the categories of Caliban [i.e., the subordinated Indians and the enslaved Negroes])" (313–314, brackets in original). Within this scheme, Prospero is "made to actualize the new, transumed formulation [of Man$_1$] and its conception of freedom as having no longer mastery over Original Sin (as well as over those Enemies-of-Christ who as such remain enslaved to it), but rather of mastery over their own sensory, irrational nature," in contrast to Caliban, who is "stigmatized as remaining totally enslaved to" such impulses (290).

It is certainly the case that Prospero continually denigrates Caliban in such terms, as part of his campaign to justify his conduct toward Caliban to anyone who will listen. But the heart of his case is a moral one: Caliban deserves punishment for attempting "to violate / The honor of my child" (1.2.346–347), in other words, to rape Prospero's daughter Miranda. Caliban's slavery would then be a justified punishment for a crime—one that he himself does not deny or even appear to regret. At the same time, both colonists agree that this crime is less a discrete blameworthy act than a reflection of Caliban's fundamental nature. Prospero addresses Caliban in quasi-religious terms as "Thou poisonous slave, got by the devil himself / Upon thy wicked dam" (1.2.319–320)—using religious terminology that highlights the continuity between the Christian and Man$_1$ regimes—and Miranda, describing her efforts to educate Caliban prior to the assault, declares, in a more secular vein, "thy vile race, / Though thou didst learn, had in't which good natures / Could not abide to be with" (1.2.357–359). Yet despite this inherent, seemingly irreparable fault in Caliban, Miranda goes on to claim that his crime "deserved more than a prison" (1.2.361). Much later in the play, as he reflects on how to thwart Caliban's revolution, Prospero describes him as

> A devil, a born devil, on whose nature
> Nurture can never stick; on whom my pains,
> Humanely taken, all, all lost, quite lost;
> And, as with age his body uglier grows,
> So his mind cankers. (4.1.188–192)

When the attempted coup fails, Prospero, already planning to leave the island with his recently shipwrecked European confreres, offers Caliban "pardon" (5.1.293) in exchange for one last act of service—a more generous gesture than Miranda's blanket condemnation, perhaps, but one that still presupposes that Caliban is a morally accountable human being. From a naïve, commonsense position, one is tempted to ask: Which is it? Was Caliban born irredeemably evil, such that he cannot control his destructive impulses, or is he a moral agent who is responsible for his actions? The answer, in the emergent racist imaginary articulated in the play as in the Christian doctrine of original sin, is: both.

Ultimately, of course, the modern racial hierarchy distinguished more clearly between the positions of the indigenous colonized population in general and the enslaved African, which are blended in Caliban. For Wynter, this process occurred in two steps, which correspond to the transition between Man$_1$ (centered on rationality) and Man$_2$ (centered on genetic superiority):

> While [during the Man$_1$ stage] the "Indians" were portrayed as the very acme of the savage, irrational Other, the "Negroes" were assimilated to the former's category, represented as its most extreme form and as the ostensible missing link between rational humans and irrational animals. . . . However, in the wake of the West's second wave of imperial expansion, pari passu with its reinvention of Man now in purely biologized terms [i.e., the Man$_2$ phase], it was to be the peoples of Black African descent who would be constructed as the ultimate referent of the "racially inferior" Human Other, with the range of other colonized dark-skinned peoples, all classified as "natives," now being assimilated to its category. (266)

The shift as she describes it may initially appear subtle, but it is decisive. In the first phase the white position, as the ostensible exemplar of human rationality, was the stable reference point against which the rest of the hierarchy was measured. In the second, the Black position is foundational and other positions in the racial hierarchy are defined by their distance from Blackness—and the enslavability that had become functionally identical to Blackness. In other words, the shift is from a model in which Black Africans were one race among others that just happened to be viewed as inferior to a model in which Blackness defines the order of race overall. It is the second model, and its strange afterlife, that Saidiya Hartman analyzes in *Scenes of Subjection*.[4] By contrast with Wynter's global scope, Hartman's focus is on the nineteenth-century United States, but that serves our purposes well, since the United States was the place where the model of race-based chattel slavery for life was practiced most intensively and defended most tenaciously. Hence the American experience provides a unique window into the deepest tendencies and contradictions of the second model of racialization.

Hartman opens her study by announcing her intention to break with the long tradition of dwelling on the spectacle of torture and suffering. Without denying the central role of almost unimaginable violence in American slavery, her goal is "to illuminate the terror of the mundane and quotidian" (4) in order to demonstrate her counterintuitive thesis that, under slavery, "the recognition of [enslaved persons'] humanity and individuality acted to tether, bind, and oppress" rather than liberate (5). This pattern continued after Emancipation, where the rhetoric of personal responsibility acted to entrap the destitute former slaves in exploitative situations that were tantamount to a continuation of slavery in all but name. As she summarizes her argument: "In most instances the acknowledgement of the slave as subject was a complement to the arrangements of chattel property rather than its remedy; nor did self-possession liberate the former slave from his or her bonds but rather sought to replace the whip with the compulsory contract and the collar with a guilty conscience" (6).

Under slavery, the attribution of agency and responsibility to the slave took two primary forms. On the one hand, the slave was regarded as "socially dead and legally recognized as human only to the degree that he is criminally culpable" (24). On the other hand, slave masters regularly compelled slaves to sing and dance for them, reinforcing the narrative (still common among contemporary racists) that the enslaved were happy and content, "as if born to dance in chains" (47). It was not enough that the slaves should simply obey, but they must appear to grant enthusiastic consent to their condition. Thus the attribution of agency to the enslaved places them in a double bind: Either they are taken as endorsing their own enslavement or, if they take their agency seriously and exercise it on their own behalf, they become criminals and run the risk of even more extreme violence or death. As Hartman puts it, within such a system,

> the agency of the enslaved is only intelligible or recognizable as crime and the designation of personhood [is] burdened with incredible duties and responsibilities that serve to enhance the repressive mechanisms of power, denote the limits of socially tolerable forms of violence, and intensify and legitimate violence in the guise of protection, justice, and the recognition of slave humanity. This official acknowledgement of agency and humanity, rather than challenging or contradicting the object status and absolute subjugation of the enslaved as chattel, reinscribes it in the terms of personhood. (62)

Hartman devotes a chapter to one of the most horrific instantiations of this weaponization of agency and consent: the rape of enslaved women. As Hartman points out, this absolutely pervasive feature of American slavery could not register as a crime against the enslaved woman according to the system's twisted moral and legal logic: "As the enslaved is legally unable to give consent or offer resistance, she is presumed to be always willing" (81). The resistance that would signal a refusal to consent, by contrast, is definitionally a crime against the master—for which enslaved women were sometimes actually put on trial, despite their lack of legal rights (including the right to testify in court against a white person). Such farcical show trials highlight the fact that, under slavery, "the enslaved was either a will-less object or a chastened agent" (80), who "was recognized as a reasoning subject who possessed intent and rationality solely in the context of criminal liability; ironically, the slave's will was acknowledged only as it was prohibited or punished" (82).

After Emancipation, the weaponization of freedom, responsibility, and consent against Black Americans continued in new, more refined terms, marking a profound continuity between the antebellum and postbellum periods. The goals of the white former enslavers in the postbellum period were "the resubordination of the emancipated, the control and domination of the free black population, and the persistent production of blackness as abject, threatening, servile, dangerous, dependent, irrational, and infectious" (116). Within this strategy, "the stipulation of abstract equality" (116) proved to be a powerful tool, putting the emancipated subject in the unenviable position of "being freed from slavery and free of resources" (117). The destitute condition of the formerly enslaved produced another situation of moral entrapment "by the liberty of contract that spawned debt-peonage, the bestowal of right that engendered indebtedness and obligation and licensed naked forms of domination and coercion, and the cultivation of a work ethic that promoted self-discipline and induced internal forms of policing" (120). These debts were not only financial but moral, as the white former enslavers viewed freedom not as an intrinsic right that the enslaved were formerly denied, but as a gift generously bestowed upon them, which "established the indebtedness of the freed through a calculus of blame and responsibility that mandated that the formerly enslaved both repay this investment of faith and prove their worthiness" (131). And the way that the formerly enslaved would demonstrate that worthiness was precisely by obeying their former masters in all things, not under coercion but freely. Such obedience was owed even when the former masters violated the terms of the contract, "not because one was still a slave without choice, but, ironically, in order to exemplify the dutiful and rational behavior of a freeman" (149). The ideal free Black laborer, just like the ideal slave, is one who freely and joyfully obeys.

As under slavery, any form of Black agency that did not perform consent to white superiority was regarded as incipiently criminal and therefore subject to legal sanction—or else to the extralegal sanction of lynching.[5] Here, the formal equality of the two "races," which are treated as natural and legally neutral categories, underwrites subordination and ultimately violence. Both antimiscegenation laws and segregation measures passed Constitutional muster because they were formally "equal" in the sense that both races were equally prohibited from crossing the color line. Yet the clear intent of perpetuating and "naturalizing the major incident of slavery" (191), namely race, was to stigmatize Black people as intrinsically foreign and hence to construct a population of "internal enemies against which the comfort and prosperity of the [white] populace could be defended" (199). The limitless violence vented against Black people under slavery was no longer routine or normative, but it was always held in reserve as an option to enforce the racial hierarchy.

While this is not the place to attempt a full-scale extension of Hartman's analysis to the present day, it is difficult to deny that, despite the unquestioned progress that has occurred since *Plessy* v. *Ferguson* was decided, the dynamics Hartman identifies are still very much at work in contemporary modes of racialization. The rhetoric of personal responsibility still trumps any consideration of the deprivation of material resources that the Black community continues to suffer. Black people continue to be victimized by debts and contracts "freely entered into"—such as the subprime loans that were disproportionately offered to Black borrowers, even those who would have qualified for lower-rate standard loans, in the lead-up to the Global Financial Crisis.[6] There continues to be an expectation that Black people must prove their worthiness for every new level of power and privilege, as when Barack Obama and, more recently, Kamala Harris's American citizenship was called into question when they sought high office. And the threat of spectacular violence persists, this time meted out not by an angry mob but by the police. The slavemaster's demand for abject, joyful obedience finds its modern echo in the demand of George Floyd's murderer that he stop resisting a chokehold—a physical impossibility that amounted to the demand that Floyd consent to his own death.

However much the racial hierarchy has weakened, then, and however much room there is for Black individuals to achieve power and status (including even the presidency), the police can still effectively reduce the Black citizen to the radically vulnerable status of the rebellious slave—for any reason, or for no reason at all.[7] This continued susceptibility of Black people to gratuitous violence underwrites Frank Wilderson's controversial Afropessimist thesis that the Black subject position is always necessarily defined by slavery, on an ontological level.[8] By this he does not mean that every Black person is somehow "still" factually enslaved, only that the threat of that level of victimization remains constitutive of Black identity. And correlatively, Wilderson argues, the existence of a category of human beings ontologically subject to such gratuitous violence is constitutive of white identity, regardless of any individual white person's intentions (or indeed horror and revulsion at the prospect). What Hartman's analysis of modern

American racialization demonstrates is that this gratuitous violence must always be interpreted as the deserved punishment of a responsible human agent—albeit one who, in the fatal encounter, can always only respond wrongly.

Satan, Sin, and Slavery

Having established the constitutive function of moral entrapment for the modern concept of race, I now turn to the task of establishing a genealogical connection between race and original sin. Here I will be charting a somewhat different path from the growing body of literature on premodern critical race studies, which investigates medieval European habits of classifying human subgroups by phenotype or descent on their own terms. This approach is in contrast to that of earlier scholars who took the modern definition of race as normative and, on that basis, declared race to be either present or absent in premodern eras.[9] Although I do not plan to draw extensively on the former body of literature in the context of this short essay, neither do I intend to follow the latter group by claiming that there was simply no such thing as "race" prior to the modern period or else by declaring that the undoubted continuities in European attitudes toward certain groups (above all Black Africans) in the medieval and modern periods mean that medieval people thought of race in the same way moderns do. Instead, I proceed from the assumption that colonial conquest and the rise of race-based chattel slavery for life introduced a qualitative shift in racial thinking, with the guiding hypothesis being that the doctrine of original sin provided the conceptual underpinning for that qualitative shift. It is in this sense that we can say, with Marika Rose, that "Christianity invented race" in the modern sense[10]—to which I add that it invented race precisely *as* a system of distributing moral valuation according to irreparable inborn characteristics.

In many ways, the emergence of the doctrine of original sin was itself a qualitative shift in the theological anthropology of Christianity and in prophetic monotheism more generally. Neither Judaism nor Islam preach any doctrine of inborn moral damage to the human race, and within Christianity itself, it is only the Latin West that has made a supposed intrinsic incapacity of human beings to avoid sin central to its account of salvation. The latter development was itself clearly a contingent one, as it stems from the idiosyncratic theological journey of essentially one man—Augustine of Hippo, whose brilliant and voluminous Latin theological writings laid the foundation for Christian intellectual life in the former western territories of the Roman Empire, where knowledge of the Greek language was essentially lost for centuries. Although the New Testament does arguably contain hints of the familiar ideas of inborn sin (which the post-Augustinian tradition would take up and amplify), few would come up with such a doctrine from reading the earliest Christian documents if they did not already have it in mind, simply because the New Testament itself is much less concerned with such issues than with establishing the new messianic community's relative autonomy with respect to Judaism.

Yet just as I am proposing that medieval attitudes toward different human groups do not represent the only relevant genealogical root of the distinctively modern concept of race, I also claim that direct anticipations of human fallenness in the New Testament are not necessarily the most salient genealogical connection between the New Testament and the later doctrine of original sin. Instead, I want to start from the fact that, as Orlando Patterson has pointed out,[11] both the New Testament and the doctrine of original sin are absolutely saturated with the language of slavery (a point that standard New Testament translations tend to obscure by using the euphemistic term "servant"). In Jesus's declaration that the disciples are no longer slaves but friends in John 15:15, Paul's exhortation to his followers not to "submit again to the yoke of slavery" after enjoying the freedom of Christ in Galatians 5:1, and countless other memorable passages, the New Testament literature repeatedly equates damnation with slavery. At the same time, though, slavery to God can figure alongside freedom as an image of salvation, as when Paul declares himself to be the slave of Jesus in Romans 1:1. This ambivalence about slavery in New Testament theology is perhaps best captured in Romans 6:16: "Do you not know that if you present yourselves to anyone as obedient slaves, you are slaves of the one whom you obey, either of sin, which leads to death, or of obedience, which leads to righteousness?"[12] Here our salvation does depend in some sense on our free choice, but it is a paradoxical choice between two different forms of slavery.

During the early patristic period, this verse from Romans served as a kind of theological social contract theory that stood at the heart of a unique account of how the Incarnation of Christ accomplished our salvation.[13] In place of the familiar contemporary narrative that Jesus died to provide vicarious satisfaction for our sins, the patristic authors portrayed the incarnation, death, and resurrection of Jesus as a covert mission to free the human race from a form of spiritual imperialism. Drawing on the narrative of the Garden of Eden—which was completely absent from the preaching of Jesus and appears in the Pauline epistles in a subordinate role relative to the story of Abraham—these authors claimed that when Adam and Eve took the advice of the devil (disguised as a serpent) rather than obeying the divine commandment, they were effectively choosing Satan as their master or ruler. This state of subjection or slavery to the devil is inherited by all subsequent human beings, not biologically, but, as it were, politically, just as children in most case inherit the citizenship of their parents. In Gregory of Nyssa's classic articulation of the patristic view in *The Great Catechism*, the Incarnation lays a trap for the devil. On the one hand, Jesus is a human being born of a human mother and hence formally under the devil's rule. On the other hand, Jesus is fully God and thus cannot be enslaved by anyone. When the devil asserts his dominance over Jesus—initially through attempted persuasion, but ultimately by arranging for his execution—he oversteps his bounds, fatally undercutting his claim to rule over all of humanity. Now that the demonic regime has been disrupted, human beings have the opportunity to switch their political loyalty to God, which they signal through participation in the sacraments of baptism and communion.

This general view of salvation—so strange and unfamiliar to most modern Christians—prevailed at the time that Augustine made his decisive theological intervention. While he never denied the patristic narrative, Augustine functionally displaced it in favor of a new theory of the inborn sinfulness of each individual human being. Augustine achieved this through a reinterpretation of the Eden narrative, where in place of Gregory of Nyssa's emphasis on humanity's enslavement to the devil, he focuses on the corruption caused by Adam and Eve's sinful disobedience. This corruption was not limited to the two individuals involved, for Augustine declares in *City of God* that "so heinous was their sin that man's nature suffered a change for the worse; and bondage to sin and inevitable death was the legacy handed on to their posterity."[14] This corruption affects the body—particularly the sex organs, which become disobedient to the human mind as a result of human disobedience to God (14.24)—but is primarily a corruption of the soul, and more specifically of the human will, which has become permanently deranged from its original state of innocence. Perhaps having in mind the apparently petty nature of humanity's first act of disobedience (eating a particular piece of fruit), Augustine claims that "the first evil act of will, since it preceded all evil deeds in man, was rather a falling away from the work of God to its own works, rather than any substantive act. And the consequent deeds were evil because they followed the will's own line, not God's" (14.11). Moreover, this fault is irreparable from the human side, because it puts us in a position where we can no longer freely will to obey God: "The choice of the will, then, is genuinely free only when it is not subservient to faults and sins. God gave it that true freedom, and now that it has been lost, through its own fault, it can be restored only by him who had the power to give it at the beginning" (14.11). As in Gregory, this healing is made available by Christ through the sacraments of the church.

In contrast to the earlier patristic view, for Augustine we are slaves not so much to Satan as to our own sinful wills. This alteration to the patristic narrative required reconceiving the role of the devil. We are given no background on the serpent in Genesis or anywhere else in the Bible. It is not even explicitly stated that it represents Satan, though it clearly represents some preexisting impulse of evil, rebellion, or mischief in God's perfect creation. Early Christian theologians seized on the opportunity to fill in this crucial gap in the biblical narrative, gradually elaborating an account wherein the devil began as one of the good angels of God but became jealous of God's plans to become incarnate as a human being—an event that, in the early patristic and later Greek Orthodox views, would have occurred even if humanity had never sinned—and set about attempting to sabotage God's new favorites. Augustine replaces this version of the story with a much more abstract account in which the devil rebels against God from the very first moment of his existence, carrying along with him a minority of his angelic colleagues, who then become demons.

The demons' rebellion is not against any particular commandment, but against God's demand—of which we can hear an echo in that of the slave-master and the police officer—that the newly created angels submit immediately and unconditionally to his will. Staging this dramatic confrontation on the first day of creation, when God first creates light and then separates light from darkness, Augustine writes:

> We think that the two companies of angels are also meant by the terms "Light" and "Darkness." One of these companies enjoys God, the other swells with pride; to one is said, "Adore him, all you angels of his"; while the chief of the other company [Satan] says, "I will give you all these things, if you bow down and worship me." The one company burns with holy love of God; the other smoulders with the foul desire for its own exaltation. (11.33)

Like Adam and Eve, the real sin of the devil and his demons is to seek to exercise their free will outside of the appropriate context of submission to God. And in many ways, this sentence is even more exorbitant than humanity's, because the demons' "rebellion" was a response to an empty, context-free demand to submit to God's will. Unlike humanity, however, they have no opportunity for salvation. Both groups of angels are permanently "locked into" the choice they make at the very moment of the creation. The demons' wills are always incurably oriented away from God, just as their obedient counterparts' wills are unswervingly oriented toward their divine master. And both groups are punished or rewarded, for all eternity, as though the now-unchangeable orientation of their will were a fresh choice made in every instance.

Augustine's revision of the narrative of sin and salvation has vast cosmological consequences. In the earlier version, evil was ultimately an episode in the story of God's creation, an unexpected obstacle to the union of God and humanity that was God's end goal in any case. In Augustine's theology, by contrast, evil becomes foundational. Satan and his demonic colleagues rebel from the very first moment of creation, and it is difficult to escape the conclusion that God set them up to fall *so that* he would have some form of evil to combat and redeem. And in fact, Augustine argues that the advent of evil contributes to the greater glory of God:

> The evil will that refused to keep to the order of its nature did not for that reason escape the laws of God who orders all things well. A picture may be beautiful when it has touches of black in appropriate places; in the same way the universe is beautiful, if one could see it as a whole, even with its sinners, though their ugliness is disgusting when they are viewed in themselves. (11.23)

We cannot, of course, attain the God's-eye view that Augustine evokes here. Yet viewing this system from the outside, one can only conclude that we are dealing with a very strange kind of beauty.

It is only centuries later, in the work of Anselm of Canterbury, that the doctrines of salvation, original sin, and demonology are fully synthesized into a form that is recognizable to modern Western Christians—and at the same time more clearly anticipates the modern discourse on race. Where Augustine claimed that all subsequent human beings were damaged by Adam and Eve's sin because the whole of human nature was at that time present in those two individuals, Anselm provides a more elegant—or at least less Lamarckian—account of the effects of original sin on subsequent generations. Anselm's key gesture is to biologize and, more specifically, to sexualize the transmission of original sin.[15] And this, in turn, allows him to clarify why humanity is eligible for salvation while the demons are not.

The core argument appears in his treatise *On the Virgin Conception and Original Sin*, which follows up on his more famous *Why God Became Man*. In the earlier text, Anselm had established that every human being, like every good slave, owes God a debt of absolute obedience at every instant, a debt that could only be repaid through God himself becoming incarnate as an innocent human being who freely chooses to sacrifice himself. The burden of *On the Virgin Conception* is to show at once why all human beings are in default on their obligations to God and why Christ was able to avoid that fate. In place of Augustine's vague theory that the whole of human nature was corrupted in Adam and Eve, Anselm argues that the very act of sexual intercourse guarantees that each individual human being is in fact born with a distorted will, which is to say, born with a will that is always already in a state of rebellion against God. If Adam had remained in a state of obedience to God, human procreation presumably would have proceeded in a purely rational and voluntary fashion, but in our present state of sinfulness, irrational impulses necessarily distort the sex act, and with it the child that is produced (*On the Virgin Conception* 10). Even though this distortion of the will is not the result of the child's own choice, the result is nonetheless that the child is not fulfilling its slave-like obligation to subject its will to God at all times. Hence "all infants are equally unjust, because they have none of the justice which it is each person's duty to have" (24), which means that they are all subject to damnation as much as if they had committed a concrete sinful act (22).

By contrast, since Christ was conceived without the intervention of a sinful human father, his will is perfectly aligned with the divine will at birth, just as Adam's was at the time of his creation—a status that Christ maintains throughout his life, making his suffering and death purely voluntary and meritorious. Having been born of a human mother, he is part of the human race and thus qualified to act on its behalf (specifically by applying the infinite merits he earned as a sinless God-man to humanity's infinite debt of sin). And once again, this tweak to the narrative of salvation requires a slight shift in our perspective on demonology. Toward the end of *Why God Became Man*, Anselm considers the question of whether the demons could be saved in a similar way. In principle, it initially seems plausible: "Just as man could not be reconciled except by a man-God . . . , likewise the condemned angels cannot be saved except by an angel-God." The problem, however, is that "it is not right that an angel should be saved by another angel, even if he were of the same nature, since angels are not of one race as human beings are. For angels are not all descended from one angel in the same way that human beings are descended from one man" (*Why God Became Man* 2.21), but were instead all created individually without the capacity for reproduction.

It is worth stopping to reflect on the concept of race implicit in Anselm's account of sin and salvation. Moral accountability is inseparable from racial belonging, for good and for ill. On the one hand, belonging to the same race as Adam entails not only inheriting the distorted will that resulted from his disobedience, but being held individually accountable for the ineluctable insubordination of one's will just as much as if it resulted from one's own action. On the other hand, belonging to the same race as Christ opens up the possibility of redemption, as Christ's gratuitous decision to submit to suffering and death as an innocent person creates a fund of righteousness on which every human being can draw. At least in this life, however, the human will remains deranged, even among the redeemed. Human nature as it was originally created—as we see in the original state of Adam and Eve and in the lifelong state of Christ (and, according to most medieval accounts, the Virgin Mary)—was perfectly obedient, but humanity as it actually exists in history is ineluctably rebellious. Christ may make up for the deficiencies of his human kinfolk, but to belong to the human race is to be always already irreparably morally compromised. As in Paul's dictum from Romans 6:16, however, the alternative to being entrapped in the status of a perpetually rebellious slave is not freedom, but the opportunity to rejoin the path of perfect obedience that the angels never departed from—in other words, Christ gives humans the chance to be the good slaves they were created to be. By contrast, to exist outside of any network of kinship, as do the angels and demons, means to exist outside any history, to endlessly reenact one's first and only choice—a choice that has no possible content, context, or meaning, but for which one is held accountable for all eternity.

Secular Demonology

Anselm's theology of slavery, race, and domination brings us to the threshold of the distinctively modern concept of race, but one element is missing: the differential treatment of particular human groups. This development could initially appear contrary to the spirit of Christianity, given its message of universalism. Yet as Amaryah Armstrong reminds us, the Pauline proclamation in Galatians 3:28 "that there is no longer slave or free, male or female, Jew or Greek is both compelling and difficult to see enacted in the historical performance of Christianity"—including in Paul's own teaching in that very same letter, which denigrates the Jewish law as a curse and a mark of slavery.[16] I noted above that the primary task of the New Testament literature was to establish Christianity's relationship to Judaism, which is mostly figured as one of supersession: Judaism was the anticipation, Christianity is the fulfillment; Judaism was the letter, Christianity is the spirit; Judaism was the image, Christianity is the reality; and—most fatefully for our purposes—Judaism is the particular, Christianity is the universal. The gospel message is for all nations universally—except for the anti-universal Jewish nation, which refuses to number itself as simply one nation among others.

Whereas Paul declares that "all Israel will be saved" (Romans 11:26)—albeit by ultimately accepting that Jesus is the promised messiah—the canonical gospels increasingly denigrate and even demonize the Jews, blaming them (completely ahistorically) for the death of Christ and, in the Gospel of John, identifying them repeatedly as children of the devil rather than of Abraham. Later, when the doctrine of original sin is firmly established, the gospel narratives provide the basis for Christianity's first experiments in identifying the Jews as a human subgroup with its own, redoubled case of original sin. According to Matthew, when Pilate washes his hands of the guilt of executing the innocent Jesus, the Jewish "people as a whole answered, 'His blood be on us and on our children'" (27:25), a demand that medieval theologians believed that God fulfilled by cursing all subsequent generations of Jews. And just as Adam and Eve's sexual organs rebelled against them as punishment for their rebellion against God, so too, in the Western medieval imagination, does the blood of the Jews rebel against them as a collective punishment for the guilt of spilling Christ's blood. Joshua Trachtenberg has documented the wide variety of medieval stereotypes about the Jews, many of which are blood-centered—for instance, the blood libel accusation that Jews need to ingest the blood of Christian babies to make up for the deficiencies of their own blood, or that Jewish men also menstruate.[17]

Gil Anidjar has demonstrated the centrality of "blood" in Christian self-identification in the late medieval and early modern period, a biologization of European Christian identity that lays the groundwork for the modern system of racial difference.[18] In contrast to most studies of racism, which focus on other-directed rhetoric, Anidjar highlights the importance of blood for intra-Christian identity formation, particularly the role of Eucharistic piety and the late-medieval papal condemnation of the act of spilling "Christian blood." In both cases, though, he acknowledges that the other-directed implications of Christian self-identity are irreducible. Already in the seventh-century monk Radbertus of Corbie's text *De corpore et sanguine Domini* ("The Lord's Body and Blood"), the first-ever treatise devoted entirely to the Eucharist, a good deal of the content focuses on blood-based miracles that protect the sacrament against Jewish interlopers.[19] The 1449 Statutes on the Purity of Blood, which are so central to Anidjar's argument, are similarly anti-Jewish in intent, aimed at unmasking Spanish converts with Jewish blood, on the assumption that such conversions are definitionally insincere and invalid. At the same time, the identification of the Jews with the demonic that had already begun in the New Testament continues apace. In a way, though, that gesture of explicit demonization is almost redundant, as the Jews had already been assimilated to the condition of demons in their permanent orientation toward evil—an incurable condition which is regarded as a damnable offense.

In a bitter historical irony, then, a religion that claimed to be making God's promises available to all people, regardless of their ancestry, now excludes the original bearers of those promises from any possibility of salvation. Fully documenting the complex process whereby the properties associated with the theological position of Jewishness migrate to the ostensibly secular position of Blackness is beyond the scope of this essay, but I can at least provide some initial indications. On one level, it could appear to result from a combination of historical accident and sheer opportunism, though M. Lindsay Kaplan has shown how a long history of analogies relating Jews to slavery, to Africans (via Paul's reinterpretation of the figure of Hagar in Galatians), and to Arabs (via their supposed descent from Abraham's son Ishmael) prepared early modern Europeans for the encounter with Arab traders selling enslaved Africans.[20] And clearly the role of the supposed "curse of Ham" issued by Noah immediately after the Flood is important here, establishing Black Africans (taken to be descendants of Ham) as a subgroup with their own redoubled version of original sin, parallel to the condition of the Jews.[21]

Black thinkers themselves have emphasized the homology between the Jewish and Black experiences. From a theological perspective, Black Christians have always identified with the biblical narrative of God's liberation of the slaves in Exodus, and Black theologians have highlighted the connections between Christianity's claim to supersede Judaism and modern structures of racism.[22] More radically, James Cone has declared that Jesus "*is* black because he *was* a Jew," insofar as "the significance of his past Jewishness is related dialectically to the significance of his present blackness."[23] From a secular perspective, too, Fanon's *Black Skin, White Masks* makes continual reference to Sartre's analysis of anti-Semitism, and Wilderson draws a parallel between Agamben's analysis of the production of bare life in Auschwitz and the Middle Passage. In these latter examples, however, there is an acknowledgment of a quantitative and even qualitative difference between the modern Jewish experience and anti-Blackness. Fanon dismisses the Shoah as "little family quarrels,"[24] while Wilderson claims, "Agamben is not so much wrong as he is late. Auschwitz is not 'so unprecedented' to one whose frame of reference is the Middle Passage, followed by Native American genocide."[25]

In sum, Black thinkers recognize the continuity between the Jewish and Black positions, but also emphasize the uniqueness of the Black experience of what I am calling demonization. This difference reflects one final development in the modern political theology of race. I have mentioned before that Anselm positions the demons outside of any possibility of salvation by excluding them from any racial belonging or network of kinship. The innovation of modern race thinking is to conceptually separate racial belonging and kinship through race-based chattel slavery for life. In "Mama's Baby, Papa's Maybe," Hortense Spillers highlights the way that the principle of *partus sequitur ventrem* (the condition of the child follows that of the mother) serves to destroy all legitimate kinship networks among the enslaved. Where the infamous Moynihan Report had castigated the Black community for its matriarchal family structures, Spillers emphasizes that, under slavery, the identification of Black families as matriarchal is false because "the female could not, in fact, claim her child, and false, once again, because motherhood is not perceived in the prevailing social climate as a legitimate procedure of cultural inheritance." This results in a situation where "(1) motherhood as female bloodright is outraged, is denied, at the *very same time* that it becomes the founding term of a human and social enactment; (2) a dual fatherhood is set in motion, comprised of the African father's *banished* name and body and the captor father's mocking presence."[26] In other words, the enslaved child is not *even* illegitimate, but is instead completely natally alienated and treated as the property of the master, who is often the biological father as well but can never be named as such. In the enslaved Black individual, the doctrines of original sin and demonology, which I have shown to be mutually interdependent from the very beginning, are perfectly intertwined. Like the medieval demon, each enslaved individual is treated as a radical monad, and like the subject of original sin, each enslaved individual is born damned for being born in the wrong way. What is truly unprecedented, though, is the situation of the enslaved Black woman—identified by Spillers as the truly archetypal enslaved subject—who is forced to bring more damned and demonized subjects into the world for the benefit of her enslavers.

The end of race-based chattel slavery for life created a system where this secular form of demonization was no longer normative for all Black individuals. Emancipation opened the door to restoring and gaining official recognition for networks of kinship among Black people, although Spillers's reference to the Moynihan Report highlights the fact that Black families are still treated as dysfunctional or flawed until proven otherwise. Here, unlike in Anselm's theology of race, racial belonging tends only toward damnation, since redemption is defined—for Black people especially but for all people not recognized as white—as rejecting Blackness to conform to white standards. And whereas white people are always judged individually, Black people's failings are taken to demonstrate and even exacerbate the moral burden of the race, in a way that no individual human being born after Adam could do in the Christian scheme. Hence every police brutality case is presented as an isolated incident that must not affect our view of the entire profession (figured as implicitly white), while the presence of looters in the George Floyd protests was taken to call into question the worthiness of Black people in general for the relief they were demanding. In these as in so many other areas, Black people have been consigned to what Hartman calls "an anomalous condition betwixt and between slavery and freedom" (126) and what we can call, in theological terms, a distinctively modern version of original sin, which always threatens to collapse into the outright demonization of mass incarceration and arbitrary police killings.

This brings us back to the cliché with which I opened this essay—namely, that slavery is "America's original sin." From the new perspective we have gained, that may well be true, if we keep in mind that for the mainstream theological tradition, the only way to escape the consequences of original sin is to die and rise again—in other words, to be radically reconstituted as a new kind of being. But slavery is also America's original sin in another sense, namely that it is America's signature contribution to the development of the modern political theology of race out of the Christian doctrine of original sin. Nowhere else were the conceptual and practical demands of race-based chattel slavery for life so radically carried out, nowhere else did so many fight and die to preserve a society and a way of life founded on that unspeakable violence, and nowhere have so many generations struggled so successfully to prevent the total political and economic transformation that would be necessary to displace the foundational role of anti-Blackness for American society and white identity. If America really is damned by its original sin in the first sense, then its crime is using its doctrine of original sin in the second sense to damn so many to an unprecedentedly hellish existence *for no reason*, while endlessly congratulating itself for punishing its victims' sin of being born in the wrong way.

It is difficult to resist the impulse to combat such a system by insisting that Black people do not *deserve* their treatment, that instead they *deserve* to be treated completely equal to whites. The desire expressed in such sentiments is deeply true, but the formulation plays directly into the hands of the racial-moral system, which can always absorb every fresh demand for moral re-valuation into its own corrupt rubrics. To achieve the "gratuitous freedom" that Wilderson counterposes to the gratuitous violence of anti-Blackness,[27] we need a counter-theology that can replace the racial-moral hierarchy with something equally powerful. The recognition that the modern political theology of race descends from Christianity may tempt us to return to some earlier, supposedly more "authentic" version of Christianity—such as the traditions I discuss above which figure salvation in social-political rather than individualistic terms—for resources to combat its bastard offspring. I value the work that has already been done in that vein. For my part, though, I suspect that the only real alternative will be radically anti-Christian, in the sense of rejecting the framework of moral responsibility that is at the root of this entire development. No one "deserves" freedom, no one "deserves" human flourishing, no one "deserves" full participation in social and political life—because if they did, that would imply that they could fail to. A political theology that can counter the racial-moral hierarchy is one that can envision the sharing of all human goods beyond desert, beyond even unmerited grace, simply *for no reason*.

The Trinitarian Century
God, Governance, and Race

There are many ways to characterize the twentieth century, but few in the field would dispute that for confessional Christian theologians, it was the trinitarian century. Arguably more creative work was done on this rarefied doctrine in orthodox circles in the past hundred years than in all the long centuries since Augustine wrote his *De Trinitate*. This development is in many ways surprising. The Trinity was an important point of reference for many modern intellectuals, particularly those associated with Romanticism (such as Coleridge and Hegel), but in ecclesiastical and academic circles, the doctrine had previously come in for relatively little attention in the modern era. The case of Schleiermacher is exemplary here, and particularly striking given his sympathies with the Romantic movement. Though he does not doubt that something like the doctrine of the Trinity is necessary to do justice to the Christian experience of Christ and the Holy Spirit as truly divine, he is highly critical of the speculation about the inner life of God—a reality of which human beings can have no experience or understanding—that has been prompted by the orthodox creedal affirmations.[1]

By contrast, for Karl Barth, who inaugurated the "trinitarian century" with his decision to begin his *Church Dogmatics* with a forceful defense of the doctrine's necessity,[2] it is precisely the Trinity's irrelevance to our experience that most recommends it. Rejecting Schleiermacher's principle according to which Christian theology should reflect human religious experience, Barth asserts that the criterion of theology is the Word of God,[3] which he defines as "God Himself in His revelation."[4] Defining God first of all as Lord, Barth claims,

> Lordship is present in revelation because its reality and truth are so fully self-grounded, because it does not need any other actualisation or validation than that of its actual occurrence, because it is revelation through itself and not in relation to something else, because it is that self-contained *novum*. Lordship means freedom.[5]

This freedom of God in his self-revelation is "the root of the doctrine of the Trinity,"[6] and hence it is ultimately the doctrine of the Trinity that allows Barth to assert that God does not need to rely on any *Anknüpfungspunkt* or point of contact in human nature in order to reveal himself. This claim is a further radicalization of Barth's rejection of natural theology (the idea that human beings can deduce some authentic knowledge of God apart from God's explicit revelation), a doctrine that he associates with Hitler's claim to be "a source of specific new revelation of God" that must lead to "the transformation of the Christian Church into the temple of the German nature- and history-myth."[7] Erik Peterson, a Roman Catholic convert who was deeply influenced by Barth, deployed the doctrine of the Trinity to similar ends in "Monotheism as a Political Problem." There he famously declares that the incommensurability between the divine Trinity and any earthly reality completely vitiates the Nazi jurist Carl Schmitt's project of political theology, based as it is on the analogy between earthly and divine sovereignty.[8] The trinitarian God, for Barth and Peterson, is one who absolutely transcends the principalities and powers of this world and thus radically calls into question every human pretension to lordship and rule. The doctrine's relevance to politics is thus the entirely negative one of depriving any human form of politics of ultimate legitimacy—a powerful counterpoint, at least in Barth and Peterson's minds, to a politics that sought to develop its own history of salvation grounded in the supposed natural law of race science.

Outside of Barthian circles, most postwar Trinitarians took a very different approach. For these thinkers, what is so interesting about the Trinity is not its affirmation of God's radical otherness, but its ethical and political implications for human practice.[9] Far from being an impenetrable divine mystery that defies our human intuitions about how arithmetic works, according to this voluminous literature—embracing mostly traditionalist figures across all major branches of Christianity in the West, but also including some liberationists from the developing world—the Trinity is the model for human community. In the radical equality and interrelation of the trinitarian persons, theologians find an ideal that will reportedly allow us to overcome Western individualism and move into the reciprocity of a gift economy. So central has the Trinity become for Christian social and political thinking that in her pathbreaking (and satisfyingly deflationary) work *God and Difference*, Linn Tonstad can joke, "One sometimes wonders whether Christian theologians think they have *any* nontrinitarian resources for critiquing accounts of the self that emphasize self-seeking and self-possession over service to others."[10]

In this essay, I want to suggest that more is at stake in the twentieth century's trinitarian renaissance than simply a puzzling trend within an obscure academic discipline. The explosion of interest in the doctrine of the Trinity reflects the deep crises that have repeatedly rocked the global system of governance throughout the twentieth century—a system of governance that is, I will argue, an outgrowth of the Trinity's model of divine governance. In order to demonstrate this claim, I will be taking up and extending Giorgio Agamben's argument in *The Kingdom and the Glory*. There Agamben establishes a genealogical connection between the theological debates about God's governance of the created world via the economy of salvation and modern ideas about the governance of the economy by the invisible hand of the market.[11] In Agamben's investigation, the doctrine of the Trinity is the site where the concept of economy first enters into the field of theological reflection proper (i.e., as a term designating God's own inner life), but the focus quickly shifts to the elaboration of the doctrine of divine providence in medieval scholasticism. As a result, there is relatively little reflection in the text on the doctrine of the Trinity as such, particularly on the question of why God's economy of salvation should make use of not one, but *two* creation-facing agencies—in other words, why the Father needs both the Son *and* the Holy Spirit to carry out his salvific plan.

Answering that question will require placing Agamben's genealogy, which focuses exclusively on Western sources, in the broader context of the Hebrew biblical tradition. In that tradition, the claim that the God of one particular nation actually rules the entire world requires the development of a sophisticated theological apparatus to explain the apparent weakness and defeat of God's Chosen People. In this apparatus, God employs two distinct styles of governance to manage two distinct groups of people—namely, the Chosen People and the other nations. It is this dynamic that Paul takes up and reworks in his narration of salvation history in Romans 9–11, where he attempts to demonstrate that Christ's acceptance by the Gentiles and rejection by the Jews is part of God's long-term plan to include both groups in the promises that had previously been limited to the Chosen People. While Paul's emphasis on the Jew vs. Gentile dyad falls by the wayside, I argue that Romans 9–11 provides the template for subsequent Christian conceptions of God's governance of the world, including both the trinitarian model and the providential one that succeeds it. I further suggest that the transition between these models, which Agamben notes without explaining, has its roots in the epochal shift introduced by Constantine into the Christian conception of history. This more expansive genealogical account—or at least the initial sketch of a full genealogical account to come—will then allow me to show, drawing on the work of Gil Anidjar and Jared Hickman, that the doctrine of the Trinity, as a theological theory of governance, provides the model not only for the invisible hand of the market, but for the modern racial order that is inextricably tied up with it. Hence the task of theology, I will suggest in conclusion, may be less the formulation of a better trinitarian vision for human life than the abandonment of the trinitarian model altogether.

The Prophetic Roots of Trinitarian Thought

The most significant weakness in Agamben's genealogy of theological concepts of governance is that the bulk of his narrative proceeds as though the Hebrew Bible had never been written, as though the New Testament authors were more concerned to respond to Xenophon than to Isaiah or Deuteronomy. Christian theology is treated as an unproblematic outgrowth of ancient Greek thought, with no attention to the distinctiveness of the Hebrew biblical legacy that Christianity was engrafting onto the Greco-Roman intellectual tradition. Ultimately Agamben does turn to Jewish sources in the long final chapter, presenting them as what we might call an "external" alternative to the Christian approach to economy and glory. Aside from a brief discussion of the Septuagint and Vulgate translations, Agamben never takes seriously the idea that Jewish and Christian thought introduced a new dynamic into the Western tradition.

Dialogue between Christian theology and Greek thought was doubtless facilitated by the tendency of many schools of Greek philosophy toward some kind of monotheism, but the monotheism that grows out of the Hebrew biblical tradition is distinctive from that philosophical monotheism in many ways. The first, pointed out by Jan Assmann in *The Price of Monotheism*,[12] is the forceful claim of the biblical God to represent a claim to justice *over against* the rulers of this world (including, ultimately, the rulers of God's own Chosen People). On a material level, this oppositional stance grows out of biblical monotheism's unique status as what I call "minority monotheism"—the claim that what appears to be the local god of a particular people is in fact the only *real* God, who is the creator and ruler

of all the world. As I note in "What Is Theology?," this position differs from a transcendental monotheism like that developed in various forms of ancient philosophy, which was fully compatible with recognizing the existing pantheon as subordinate to and somehow emanating from the one God. Biblical monotheism completely denies the legitimacy of any other gods—indeed, in most forms it outright denies that they exist at all. This means that the one God must take responsibility for all significant earthly events, and more than that, he must—in order to demonstrate that the radical innovation of exclusive monotheism is preferable to its predecessors—do so in a way that is compatible with something recognizable as justice.

How to achieve these goals simultaneously is a difficult problem, and the biblical authors made various attempts to square the various theological requirements that their distinctive version of monotheism imposed upon them. As I argue in *The Prince of This World*,[13] the foundational event of the Exodus from Egypt provides the ultimate model for the biblical understanding of the dynamics of world history. On the human level, this event stages a conflict between the enslaved Israelites and their wicked Egyptian oppressors, and God identifies clearly and unambiguously with the former against the latter. After he rescues the Israelites through a series of undeniable displays of divine power (the Ten Plagues), God then solidifies his relationship with his Chosen People by entering into an explicit covenant with them. If the Israelites obey the various moral, legal, and ritual requirements outlined in the covenant, God promises to bless them and make them prosper, and if they do not, he threatens to chastise them. And finally, after a period of testing and purification in the desert, God brings them to the Promised Land where they will establish their new nation. Overall, God intervenes directly and repeatedly into the life of the Israelites and governs them through a series of explicit standards attached to known rewards and punishments.

If God were only the God of the Israelites, that could be the end of the story. But this God claims simultaneously to be the only God of the entire world. Thus he must in some sense control the evil Egyptians as well. Where a contemporary Christian might expect some embarrassment around this point, the Bible unambiguously asserts God's control over his foes. The Book of Genesis establishes that God empowered Egypt—and indeed converted it into a slave-based society in the first place—through the intervention of the Israelite patriarch Joseph. Throughout the Book of Exodus, God actively manipulates Pharaoh by "hardening his heart" to make him resist the call to release the Hebrew slaves. In the former case, one might suspect that God was attempting to benefit the Egyptians somehow, but Exodus makes it clear that God only built up the Pharaoh's power to make his ultimate victory all the more impressive. Yet this contribution to the greater glory of God does not redound to Pharaoh's favor. Despite the fact that Pharaoh was previously unaware of the existence of a singular God, despite the fact that God never clarified to Pharaoh the moral standards by which he would be judged, and indeed despite the fact that God himself is avowedly tampering with Pharaoh's decision-making, God severely punishes Pharaoh for his oppression of the Israelites—destroying his nation, killing Pharaoh's own firstborn son, and then drowning the arrogant king with his army after goading him one last time to chase after the released Israelites.

Though subsequent history was rarely so clear-cut, the Exodus event provided the framework for interpreting later events by setting up a differential treatment between the two major human groups. On the one hand, there was God's Chosen People (the Israelites or Jews, a small and seemingly marginal group), who were parties to an explicit agreement with a God who rewarded and punished them according to known standards. As a result, they had at least the possibility of achieving righteousness in the eyes of a just God. On the other hand, there were the other nations (the Gentiles, a much larger and seemingly more powerful and important group), who were, like disposable pieces on the divine chess board, indirectly manipulated for the sake of a plan that was never really "about" them, and who were, despite these disadvantages, always treated as wicked and, in the long run, worthy of punishment. Or to put it more schematically, the biblical model of divine governance is based on three main binary oppositions that tend to correlate with each other: between the Chosen People and the miscellaneous others, between direct rule and indirect manipulation or management, and between righteousness and wickedness.

This model of minority monotheism came under considerable pressure when the Israelite kingdoms were destroyed by major imperial powers and the Jews became a diasporic people. To account for the apparent triumph of nations that do not recognize God or practice justice and for the Jewish community's corresponding marginality and lack of political autonomy, the biblical prophets claimed that God was indirectly using the wickedness of the nations to test and purify his Chosen People. Ultimately, the Jews will be restored to the Promised Land and the nations, like Pharaoh before them, will be punished for the deeds that, while indirectly serving God's purposes, were nonetheless objectively evil. In the meantime, however, faithful Jews should follow the Torah the best they can under difficult circumstances and otherwise live as good citizens in the land of their sojourn. This prophetic paradigm has been the normative political-theological scheme for the Jewish diaspora for most of its history, and it is easy to see why, as it creates an incentive for maintaining Jewish identity and piety while avoiding any action that would unnecessarily antagonize the powers that be.

However durable the prophetic paradigm has proven, though, it conceives of itself as a temporary state that will culminate in a more direct assertion of God's favor toward his Chosen People. Although some texts of a more apocalyptic bent, such as the final chapters of Daniel, figure this restoration of Israel's fortunes as a conflict between spiritual powers, most prophetic visions seem to envision a more conventional military victory, under the leadership of a righteous king anointed by God—that is, the messiah, for which the equivalent Greek term is of course the Christ. Some readers, however, anticipated an initial apparent defeat of the messianic figure, a minority tradition that the apostle Paul took up in his bold attempt to parlay the shameful execution of Jesus of Nazareth into a necessary step toward an unforeseen divine victory.[14] In Paul's view, the execution of the messiah—at the hands of the Roman Empire (taken as representative for the Gentile nations as a whole), with the complicity of Jewish leaders—created the conditions for a largely unexpected step in God's plan: the extension of God's mercy and grace to the Gentile nations alongside his original Chosen people.

Crucial to Paul's reasoning here is a phenomenon that, like the crucifixion itself, could easily be taken as a defeat but that Paul views as a victory: namely, Paul's own experience that Gentile audiences were much more receptive to his messianic message than Jewish ones. Rather than taking the more straightforward position that this rejection of Jesus by most Jews as evidence that he is not in fact the Jewish messiah, Paul reads it as a signal that God is allowing Gentiles to participate in his promises *as* Gentiles, that is, without any religious or cultural conversion. Indeed, Paul claims in the Letter to the Galatians—by some accounts, the very earliest surviving Christian document—that any attempt to convert to Judaism on the part of Gentile Jesus-followers would represent a rejection of the grace that has been extended to them. As evidence for this somewhat counterintuitive claim, Paul introduces a strange reinterpretation of the biblical story of Abraham, who "had two sons, one by a slave woman and the other by a free woman"—namely, Ishmael and Isaac, respectively (Galatians 3:22).[15] While in the literal narrative, Isaac is an ancestor of the Jewish people and Ishmael gives rise to the Arabs, Paul reverses this identification, claiming that Hagar, the mother of Ishmael, represents "Mount Sinai in Arabia and corresponds to the present Jerusalem, for she is in slavery with her children. But the other woman corresponds to the Jerusalem above; she is free, and she is our mother" (3:25–26).

There is much that could be written about this bizarre passage.[16] For our immediate purposes, though, I would note that Paul's reading of the Genesis narrative is a profound inversion of the Hebrew biblical tradition's moral evaluation of Jews and Gentiles, as Paul presents the most profound sign of the Jews' favor before God—their possession of the divine teaching of the Torah—as a mark of slavery and degradation, while he claims that his Gentile congregation, whom he positively *commands* to avoid all observance of Jewish ritual practice, is made up of "children of the promise, like Isaac" (3:28). More than that, the two groups' respective governance styles are reversed. While the Gentile believers are ostensibly responding freely to God's promises, the Jews are presented as slaves, who are used against their will by someone more powerful than them—the very same role that the seemingly powerful Gentile rulers occupied in the prophetic scheme. God's Chosen People are being treated as enemies.

Yet as Paul later clarifies in the Letter to the Romans, this reversal is only a temporary stage in God's plan to shift both Jews and Gentiles to the positive side of the prophetic ledger. In one sense, God achieves this by demonstrating that "there is no distinction between Jew and Greek; the same Lord is Lord of all and is generous to all who call on him" (Romans 10:12). For Jews who might have felt somehow entitled to salvation, God's completely unmerited favor to the Gentile nations, who have never previously known or willingly served him, demonstrates that salvation is not something that anyone can earn or deserve through their own efforts. At the same time, however, it maintains the distinction between the two groups insofar as God's efforts are ultimately oriented toward the Jews, so that the Gentiles appear to be mere means to an end. This is because the Jews' expectation of special treatment on the basis of their long history with God will make them "jealous" (10:14) of the favor the Gentiles are now enjoying simply because of their faith in Christ, enticing the Jews to embrace Christ as well. Here Paul can even draw a radically counterintuitive parallel between the supposed stubbornness of the Jews and the hardening of Pharaoh's heart (9:17)—but in this case, God's tampering is meant to increase his glory through creating the conditions for extravagant generosity rather than horrific destruction. Having been made aware of God's plan, Gentile believers should not lord it over the Chosen People, whose bond with God is unbreakable: "As regards the gospel they are enemies[17] for your sake; but as regards the election they are beloved, for the sake of their ancestors; for the gifts and calling of God are irrevocable" (11:28–29). The result is a strange hybrid, a kind of universalism that nonetheless attempts to meet the demands of minority monotheism. All nations will enjoy God's mercy, but only as a way to ensure that "all Israel will be saved" (11:26).

Constantine and the Emergence of the Providential Model

Both the prophetic and Pauline paradigms depict God as a clever behind-the-scenes manipulator, easily able to turn short-term apparent defeats into long-term victories by subtly nudging the actions of his creatures toward his own desired ends. This biblical legacy, much more than the pre-Christian Greek sources that Agamben analyzes in *The Kingdom and the Glory*, surely explains why the concept of *oikonomia*—denoting a flexible, semi-improvisational style of managing competing demands—found a welcome home in Christian theological reflection on the divine governance of the world. That same legacy also helps to account for an aspect of the economy of salvation that Agamben does not explicitly interrogate, namely the fact that it operates by means of *two* distinct agencies, the Son and the Holy Spirit.

From the perspective of the prophetic paradigm and its subsequent apocalyptic elaborations, the pairing of the Son and Spirit is easy to explain. It reflects the fact that God's management of world history is ultimately the management of two distinct groups of people, Jews and Gentiles. Already in the apocalyptic visions of Daniel, those two groups each have their spiritual or angelic representatives, namely the Archangel Michael for Israel and the oddly anthropomorphized "little horn" (symbolizing the mad king Antiochus Epiphanes) for the Gentile nations. In *The Prince of This World*, I have argued that this spiritualization of God's earthly opponent is the final step in the elaboration of the figure of Satan, God's eternal rival, a genealogy that I ultimately trace back to the confrontation between God and Pharaoh.

This spiritualization of God's foe is an important step toward the doctrine of the Trinity, and to a certain extent it is an organic development of the prophetic paradigm. Given how perennial this dynamic of indirectly productive yet intrinsically blameworthy rebellion is in God's management of world events, it makes sense to elevate its symbolic representative to the status of an immortal spiritual figure, alongside the Archangel Michael as the representative of God's direct work through his obedient servants. It even makes sense to say that the two opposed figures will in some sense exist alongside God into the infinite future, one in heaven and the other in hell. Even the idea that these two agencies are somehow *identical* to God, as the doctrine of the Trinity claims, could possibly make sense. Such a claim would assert unequivocally that God *is* who he reveals himself to be in his historical relationship with the Jews, that there is no hidden reserve of God apart from that sacred history. There is only one problem: one of the two agencies is evil and hence incompatible with the justice of God. The final move of identifying the two creation-facing agencies with God only becomes truly comprehensible from the perspective of Paul's reimagining of the history of salvation, in which the two modes of divine governance become increasingly intertwined and both human groups ultimately wind up being redeemed.

This is not to say that Paul is clearly trinitarian in the sense of identifying both the Son and the Holy Spirit as co-equal divine persons. The distinction between the resurrected Christ and the Spirit has not yet fully developed in the Pauline epistles, nor indeed in the earliest of the canonical gospels.[18] Yet when such a distinction does begin to emerge in the New Testament literature, it is fairly clear that the trinitarian "division of labor" corresponds to the division of humanity into Jews and Gentiles. On the one hand, the Son becomes incarnate in Jesus of Nazareth, the Jewish messiah who preaches almost exclusively to Jewish audiences. On the other hand, the Spirit is closely identified with the mission to the Gentiles. This is clear already in the famous story of Pentecost, when the Spirit empowers the apostles to speak in the languages of all nations (Acts 2). It is confirmed perhaps most emphatically when the Spirit falls on uncircumcised and unbaptized Gentiles in Peter's presence (10:44–48), demonstrating that access to this divine power does not require the mediation of any religious rite or identity (even the rites and identity of the emerging messianic movement itself). At the same time, in keeping with Paul's role reversal, the identification of the proto-trinitarian persons with God's mode of agency undergoes a shift, as the Holy Spirit becomes much more directly active and the Son's role in the narrative is the indirect one of serving as a stumbling block to the Jews, whose persecution of Jesus-followers only serves to accelerate the spread of the Gospel message—most notably by providing Paul with free passage to the imperial center itself in the closing chapters of Acts.

Historically speaking, two factors have contributed to obscuring the Pauline—and hence prophetic—roots of the doctrine of the Trinity. The first is the Christian theological assertion that the doctrine of the Trinity reflects the way that God "always was," which has led to a search for biblical prefigurations of the entire Trinity (e.g., Abraham's three visitors in Genesis 18:2) or of the trinitarian persons (e.g., the spirit hovering above the water in Genesis 1:2). The second is the apparently indefinite delay of the conversion of the Jews, which has pushed the fulfillment of Paul's hopes in Romans 9–11 to the distant eschatological future. The idea that the ultimate reconciliation of the Jews is part of the divine plan remains "on the books"—Roman Catholics still pray for the conversion of the Jews in the Good Friday liturgy, for example, and apocalyptically minded American evangelicals support Israel in part due to the eschatological role of the Jews—but it has not been the site of significant theological reflection.

Nevertheless, Paul's narration of salvation history as playing out between two distinct human groups arguably provided the template for subsequent reflections on the church's place in an often hostile world. Here the most salient division was no longer that between Jews and Gentiles, but between Christians and pagans, church and empire. The dynamics of direct and indirect agency again come into play, as the Roman Empire's quest for world domination creates the conditions of law and order (not to mention the infrastructure of roads) necessary for the spread of the gospel. Indeed, even Roman persecution of Christians indirectly contributes to the growth of the church, as Tertullian famously declared. And despite the fact that the Book of Revelation clearly identifies the Roman Empire as the earthly reign of Satan, essentially none of the patristic writers viewed Rome as unredeemable—an understandable position if they were transferring the logic of Paul's account of the salvation of the Jews to the most salient opponents of Christianity in their own historical setting. Hence when the Emperor Constantine embraced Christianity, the theologians now known as the Church Fathers were able to take this objectively shocking and counterintuitive development in stride—or even, as in the infamous case of Eusebius, to interpret it as Christ's ultimate triumph.

From our present perspective, what is most striking about this decisive moment in Christian history, when the place of the church in the world was thrown radically into question, is that it was marked by a theological controversy over the relationship between God the Father and Jesus the Son—in other words, over the question of God's governance of the world via his direct representative. And it was a controversy that the as yet unbaptized emperor helped resolve, not only by convening the Council of Nicea, but by submitting to the bishops the first draft of what would come to be known as the Nicene Creed.[19] Although the Holy Spirit is only briefly mentioned in the initial document, the final article of the creed would subsequently be expanded to something more like its contemporary form, as the assertion of the absolute equality of Father and Son logically entailed a parallel elevation of the Spirit as the Son's partner in salvation history.

Theologically speaking, it is difficult to know whether Constantine understood or even cared about the implications of the statement he presented to the assembled bishops. Politically speaking, though, he needed a unified church—not only on the level of doctrine, but on the level of practice, as much of the discussion at Nicea revolved around more mundane questions like the date of Easter. As a western emperor, he lacked a power base in the eastern half of the empire, and the church helped him fill that gap, with church officials serving not only as ideological allies but as administrators, judges, and tax collectors. In a purely factual sense, then, Constantine created a situation where both the direct representatives of God (the church) and the indirect tools of God (the empire) were ruling over the world as co-equal powers within a broader system. And contrary to Erik Peterson's claim that the trinitarian mystery of undivided rule fully shared among distinct agencies has no earthly analogues, Constantine himself was deeply familiar with such a system. It is well known, for instance, that the early Roman empire saw a series of triumvirates, who (at least in theory) shared governance equally among themselves. More directly relevant is the fact that in the decades prior to Constantine's ascension to the throne, the Roman Empire had operated under various combinations of emperors and co-emperors, "partners in power, each doing what he needs to do to make Rome strong," with "no clear subordination of one to the other."[20] His own father had served as one such co-emperor, and Constantine had himself held a similar role before consolidating power for himself alone.

In an admittedly speculative vein, then, one could perhaps see Constantine's creed—with its vivid claims for the equality of the Son with the Father and cursory mention of the Holy Spirit—as reflecting his sense of a new power structure in which the emperor would be identified with God's direct agency (the Son) and in which the role of the church, newly demoted to identification with the indirect agency (the Spirit), was very much "to be determined." In practice, of course, Constantine's dream of a harmonious, unified political-theological model of governance was shattered almost before it began. On the ecclesiastical side, renegade councils rejected the Nicene settlement, and on the imperial side, subsequent rulers opportunistically shifted back and forth between the Nicene and "heretical" Arian position. This political-theological turmoil rendered the life of Athanasius, one of the greatest champions of the Nicene position, a perpetual cycle of exile and return, depending on whether the Nicene or Arian party held sway at any given moment.

It took centuries for what we now designate as "orthodoxy" to gain hegemony in both the Eastern and Western imperial spheres, and in both cases it corresponded to a political settlement—or stalemate, as the case may be. In the Byzantine East, the empire was firmly established as the head of the church and ecclesiastical and imperial administration became increasingly fused. Political-theological conflicts did arise, as in the iconoclastic and monothelite crises, but they no longer took an explicitly trinitarian turn. After the fall of the Roman Empire in the Latin West, by contrast, the papacy represented the only real source of social and political continuity amid the repeated failed attempts of one or another petty king to claim imperial supremacy. And in that Western setting, where the balance of powers that the Trinity symbolically sought to establish was less firm, there was more open contestation of Trinitarianism, as many subversive movements sought to either reclaim the Trinity (as among the Beguine mystics, who routinely claim to have been invited to join the Trinity)[21] or rehistoricize it (as in Joachim of Fiore's translation of the trinitarian persons into distinct historical eras, allowing for the supersession of the church in the forthcoming Age of the Spirit).

In any case, from a purely theological perspective, the consolidation of the doctrine of the Trinity ironically marks the end of its explanatory power, as every action of each of the co-equal divine persons becomes indistinguishable.[22] In the end, orthodox trinitarianism comes to appear functionally indistinguishable from biblical monotheism. This explains Agamben's finding that the doctrine of the Trinity cedes its place relatively quickly to the doctrine of providence as the primary site for reflection on the divine governance of the world. In this history, Augustine even more than Constantine serves as a hinge figure. As I have already pointed out, Augustine is a major trinitarian thinker, whose book *On the Trinity* arguably represents one last burst of creativity within the orthodox trinitarianism of either East or West. As it moves the dialogue forward, however, his work fleshing out the role of the Holy Spirit is in many ways backward-looking, connecting the Holy Spirit to the mission to the Gentiles in a way that echoes Romans 9–11.[23] Yet even Augustine's brilliant rearticulation of the Trinity did not ultimately hold off the collapse back into functional monotheism, one that Augustine himself arguably contributes to in his extended analogies between the Trinity and the individual human mind.

More influential than his trinitarian thought is the new model of divine governance that Augustine lays out in *City of God*, which famously centers on the interplay between the city of God (made up of God's knowingly obedient servants) and the city of Man (made up of sinners whose evil actions indirectly serve God's purposes). Once again, at the end of a long and complicated historical development, we find a model of divine governance premised on distinct styles of rule (direct and indirect) associated with two distinct groups of people with opposed moral valuations. Like the prophets, Augustine is convinced that the line between the two groups also divides those who are ostensibly part of the new Chosen People, as the church includes both sincere believers and insincere hypocrites. But in a decisive break with the minority strains in the Hebrew biblical tradition represented by the books of Jonah and Ruth, Augustine does not entertain the correlative possibility that some of the heathen outsiders may actually belong to the City of God. Not everyone in the church is saved, but there is definitely no salvation outside the church.

Divine Governance in Modern Racial Colonialism

We can thus distinguish two models of divine governance in the medieval Western tradition. The first is the Pauline-trinitarian model, in which two complementary forms of governance harmoniously converge toward the salvation of all people—or rather, of *both groups* of people, however that duality is conceived (e.g., Jew and Gentile or church and empire). The second is the prophetic-providential model, which recapitulates the prophetic division between the insiders who directly serve God's will and the outsiders who can at best contribute indirectly and unintentionally to the greater glory of God even as they are doomed to damnation. Although only one of these models is explicitly trinitarian, I believe we can risk an analogy between them and the distinction that the Christian tradition has advanced between two perspectives on the Trinity: namely, that between the "immanent" Trinity, which focuses on God's internal trinitarian self-relation (i.e., it is "immanent" in the sense of being immanent *to* the divine sphere, which we would normally designate as transcendent from our viewpoint), and the "economic" Trinity, which emphasizes the agency of the Son and the Spirit within the created sphere. Here the universalist Pauline-trinitarian model, in which God will be all in all, corresponds to the immanent Trinity, where the more dichotomized prophetic-providential model corresponds to the economic Trinity. Yet whereas the tradition claims that the immanent and economic modes of thinking about the Trinity ultimately point to the same underlying reality, the trinitarian and providentialist models never really cohered into a single system in the medieval period. Instead, even if it tended to come early in comprehensive theological treatises, the doctrine of the Trinity was effectively an appendix that did not affect the articulation of the providential dynamics that absorbed the lion's share of attention among orthodox theologians.

Agamben's genealogy of modern economic concepts, as sketched out in the appendices to *The Kingdom and the Glory*, seems to me to point toward the conclusion that the "immanent" or explicitly trinitarian structure provides the model for the contemporary mode of governance within the Western sphere itself. When the perpetual stalemate of medieval politics is overcome by the emergence of the modern secular state, the latter discovers that its direct application of power is perpetually accompanied by a newly discovered indirect agency, namely, the market. As Western thinkers and policymakers tried to grasp the dynamics of this new mode of power, they drew explicitly on theological patterns of thought—as in the concept of the "invisible hand," which Agamben traces back to theological models. Ideally, of course, the state and the market as the two agencies of governance should converge to ensure the peace and prosperity of the realm. But this harmony has often proven elusive, as state and market vie for supremacy. For instance, one might think of the classical liberal or later neoliberal insistence that the market is the true foundation for social life, which the state must cultivate and serve, and the rejoinder of thinkers like Karl Polanyi that it is instead the state that founds the market for its own purposes.[24] Yet these conflicts are ultimately superficial and misleading, as no mainstream economist or political theorist seriously questions the fact that both state and market are necessary parts of a single power structure that operates in two distinctive modes and, at least in principle, works for the common good of the nation—the secular equivalent of redemption, as Sylvia Wynter has argued.[25]

What Agamben cannot account for is the "economic" or providential model that governs the West's relationship with its "outside." I share the critiques of those, including Frank Wilderson and Alexander Weheliye,[26] who have castigated Agamben for his one-sidedly intra-Western perspective and his resulting blindness to the realities of colonialism and race. At the same time, however, it is perhaps unrealistic to expect him to break with those habits in this context, since during the period that is Agamben's primary focus in *The Kingdom and the Glory*, Western Christians' attitude toward the vast City of Man outside the boundaries of Christendom was a largely academic matter. Although the preconceptions and stereotypes developed during this period do influence later developments, for most of the medieval period, Europeans were in no position to do much more than opine about the moral quality and ultimate destiny of outsiders. As Gil Anidjar demonstrates in *Blood*,[27] that began to change in the late medieval period with the emergence of the Crusades, which produced a functional unity of Western Christendom for the first time. Arguably even more important, the Spanish Reconquista that followed laid the groundwork for modern concepts of racial hierarchy, by militarizing and then racializing Christian identity via the novel concept of "Christian blood."

Yet those developments, as unfortunate and destructive as they were, cannot fully explain the shift to the modern model of colonial governance by means of that racial hierarchy. Both the Crusades and the Reconquista were ultimately about "purifying" ostensibly Christian territory of foreign influences—not conquering and then indefinitely ruling over nonbelievers *as* nonbelievers. The shift toward a mandate for Christian rule over unbelievers (other than the Jews) was prompted not by endogenous developments within European Christianity, but by what Jared Hickman characterizes as "an eschatological event: the 'discovery of the Indies.'"[28] Building on the pathbreaking work of Sylvia Wynter, Hickman argues that the encounter with "radically unforeseen human diversity" in the event of 1492 opens up a truly unified global space for the first time (12).

In Hickman's account, this unprecedented event has two contradictory effects. On the one hand, it relativizes all religious claims of transcendence, including those of European Christians. Post-1492, "myth," a term which in Hickman's usage encompasses all religious claims, "operates in an echo chamber of the human without a transcendent 'outside' that could be taken for granted" (12). On the other hand, though, far from inaugurating an era of secular tolerance, the revelation of the immanent sphere of the globe inaugurates an era of profound political-theological conflict, as the representatives of different mythologies struggle for dominance. This development leads to an immanentization of the significance of religious claims:

> The primary and most immediate significance of myths became not what they suggested about whatever otherworldly realities they described but rather what they might be made to reveal about the origins and character and thus portend for the destiny of their human bearers in the new, eschatologically-charged here-and-now of global encounter. (12)

Yet this dynamic does not lead to a *secularization* of religious claims in the sense of "translating" them into a shared, transcultural language. Instead, the struggle among competing mythologies becomes an opportunity for self-divinization—particularly for the European conquerors, who eagerly avail "themselves of the opportunity of becoming-God extended by 1492" (12).

In Hickman's account, the primary category through which this global political-theological struggle proceeds is *race*. Contrary to secular accounts of race, which view it as "an abstract metalanguage that for some reason evidently attaches to and engulfs other social relations," Hickman sees race as "a historically particular metacosmography meant to chart the lived eschatology of global life" (51). Although Hickman agrees that race is not "real" in the sense of corresponding to some biological or genetic fact, he does claim that race "is *ontological* in a historically qualified sense. Race is woven into the global cosmos by virtue of its historical role in mapping—not only retrospectively and descriptively but prospectively and prescriptively—that cosmos" (51).

Translating Hickman's argument into the terms established thus far, then, the event of 1492 prompts an immanentization of the providential logic of divine rule that applies distinct modes of governance to distinct groups of people. The distinction between peoples—which had previously taken the forms of Jew and Gentile, church and empire, City of God and City of Man—is now articulated in terms of the distinctively modern category of race. In an accompanying essay in the present collection, "Modernity's Original Sin," I have already shown how the moral valuation characteristic of the prophetic-providential model is mapped out onto modern racial categories. Here I would like to focus on the interplay of direct and indirect styles of governance across those categories. This will require departing somewhat from Hickman's account—though not from what is original in his argument. To the extent that I am critical of Hickman here, I am primarily urging him to discard some of the baggage that results from his approach of "critically 'reoccupying' Blumenberg's Eurocentric account of modernity" (53), particularly Blumenberg's idiosyncratic approach to Gnosticism.

As is well known, Blumenberg presents Gnosticism as the motive force behind an internal dynamic within Christianity that tends toward secularism. Here he embraces the common view of Gnosticism as a form of radical dualism in which the present world is the product of an evil and/or incompetent God and the only hope for salvation is the action of a good God who exists completely outside the present creation. In a lengthy footnote that cites Karen King's *What Is Gnosticism?* Hickman acknowledges that Blumenberg's notion of Gnosticism is somewhat ahistorical, but concludes, reasonably enough, that "the association of something called 'Gnosticism' with a particular kind of cosmological dualism datable to the first centuries of the Christian era remains serviceable for my purposes."[29] My quarrel is less with the historical accuracy of the term—a question on which I take more or less the same pragmatic position as Hickman—than with the exaggeratedly foundational role that Blumenberg, and hence Hickman, grants to Gnosticism in the development of Christian theology. In my view, Gnosticism is an outgrowth of the biblical model of divine governance, which takes the bipolar character of the prophetic paradigm (two modes of governance for two distinct groups of people with two distinct moral valuations) and exaggerates it to the point of completely dissociating the two poles. In the case of Augustine in particular, who was avowedly once a member of a Gnostic cult known as Manicheanism, it may make sense to claim, as Hickman does, that his theology is a recasting of the

Gnostic narrative into more acceptable Christian terms.[30] But on the grand historical scale, for reasons that will hopefully become clear, I believe it is important to recognize Gnosticism not as the *root* of the trinitarian or providential schemes, but as a *reaction* to them.

In any case, Hickman does make use of providential terminology, for example when he critiques mainstream narratives of secularization as "at least tacitly providentialist" (13). Most relevant for the present argument is his call for an examination of the economic role of race: "What has to be dissected and radically transformed is a *cosmic* status quo in which racialization has motivated, enabled, and justified disparate allotments of resources as though they came from a providential 'invisible hand'" (52). This remark helps clarify the division of the direct and indirect styles of governance between racial groups, a distinction that is not immediately evident given that colonial exploitation and racial enslavement were of course extremely "hands-on" endeavors in practice. What the division between metropolitan and colonial spheres and between white and non-white (particularly Black) populations enables is the production of a space of disavowal, a kind of moral laundering where manifestly unjust and violent actions can be presented as a "necessary evil" that (like the unjust and violent actions of foreign nations, which God permits and "manages" in the prophetic paradigm) produces greater social benefit in the long run—at least for the Chosen People, who are here conveniently identified with God.

We are dealing here not with a Gnostic dualism, but with a providential articulation into a bipolar system. This bipolarity can be replicated within the territory of the metropole itself (most dramatically in the division of North and South in the antebellum United States) or even on the more fine-grained level of class division (ultimately between the owners of capital and the workers). And this articulation of the social space at different levels is not merely a matter of homology, but of the concrete exercise of power on a day-to-day level, in which, as Silvia Federici has thoroughly illustrated, techniques of exploitation and suppression tested out in the colonial sphere come to be redeployed within the metropole.[31] Hence what I have characterized as the analogue of the "economic Trinity" within modernity is quite literally an *economic* Trinity, managing the distribution of economic goods along racial lines. And to the extent that the metropole's economy always necessarily depends on the disavowed or morally laundered exploitation of the racialized other, we can perhaps say that Karl Rahner's famous dictum for trinitarian theology also applies to the racialized Trinity of modern global governance: "The 'economic' Trinity is the 'immanent' Trinity and the 'immanent' Trinity is the 'economic' Trinity."[32] In other words, the "internal" governance of Western countries cannot ultimately be distinguished from the "external" governance of the colonial (or now neocolonial) space.

From Gnosticism to Revolution

This modern articulation of the trinitarian and providential models into a unified system of global governance enjoyed its "golden age" during the so-called Long Nineteenth Century, when peace and prosperity prevailed in the European sphere and colonial exploitation reached the furthest corners of the globe. Beginning in the early twentieth century, however, this model has been rocked by crisis after crisis—the nihilism of the First World War, the emergence of Communism as an alternative political-economic model, the disorderly and often catastrophic collapse of colonial empires, the wholesale slaughter of the Second World War, the challenge of postcolonial nationalism to the existing world order, the lingering threat of nuclear annihilation, and the ongoing acceleration of anthropogenic climate change, to name only the most obvious and well known. The Western world system was able to find a new equilibrium—largely through co-opting or otherwise reabsorbing the rebellious elements—in different ways under the postwar Fordist model and subsequently the neoliberal order. But it has always been under siege and remains so to this day.

It is in this context that we must understand the resurgence of trinitarian reflection among twentieth-century theologians—starting with Barth and Peterson, whose desperate appeal to divine transcendence appears in retrospect as an impotent gesture of denial or disavowal, an attempt to convince themselves that God is somehow still the "Lord" of what Bonhoeffer called "a world come of age."[33] As for the trend of social-political trinitarianism, it has been relatively marginal in the postcolonial world,[34] and in its endless permutations in more traditionalist circles, it has mostly attempted to assert the "radicality" of Christianity's personal and communal demands—in other words, to preserve some critical relevance of Christianity for the modern world. Yet although much contemporary trinitarian theology is creative and doubtless well-intentioned, it is ultimately redundant. We already live a trinitarian world. In fact, the modern model of divine governance is arguably more coherent than its predecessor on a purely theological level, insofar as it is able to integrate the universalist Pauline-trinitarian model and the more punitive prophetic-providential model into a single system. It is of course possible, perhaps even plausible, to view the modern Trinity as a betrayal or distortion of the authentic intent of the doctrine—but any attempt to adapt a new counter-Trinity for today's world must take seriously the fact that that betrayal or distortion could so easily occur. In other words, constructive theologians must first take the path of political-theological genealogy if they want to break with the nostalgic moralism that permeates the field today.

More promising would be an explicitly anti-trinitarian position, such as a contemporary Gnosticism. Although I have quibbled with Hickman's use of Blumenberg's Gnostic terminology to characterize the inner dynamics of the premodern Christian tradition, his reading of anticolonial protest through a Gnostic lens is profoundly illuminating. Drawing on C. L. R. James's account of the rebellion of Boukman, a voodoo priest, in the years preceding the Haitian Revolution,[35] Hickman argues that the oppressed become Gnostics to the extent that they "come to recognize their self-divinizing oppressors not as transcendent Savior-Gods but as the bungling pseudo-gods whose creation—the world of coloniality—is a botch-job, a false reality" (67), and call on some version of the pre-contact gods to save them. In cases where such rebellions prove unsuccessful, it may prompt what appears to be resignation to the triumphant Christian-colonial paradigm, even if that resignation takes the form of a principled refusal of the salvation that that system supposedly offers (65). Yet this absolute refusal of salvation may represent the Gnostic impulse at its most radical, which Anthony Paul Smith has characterized as "a rejection of belief in any authority that will come and save us, rather than enslave us."[36]

This absolute negativity may sound like fatalism. But it may also be the first step toward the construction of a new world, one that does not rely on the institutions and cultural authorities of the colonizer. Such, at least, is the sequence that Frantz Fanon prescribes in *The Wretched of the Earth*.[37] In contrast with what I have described as the colonists' claim to govern the entire world through a bipolar but ultimately unified system, Fanon describes the colonial order as "a compartmentalized world" (3), in which the colonizer and colonized "confront each other, but not in the service of a higher unity" (4). This fundamental disconnect between the two realities means that "challenging the colonial world is not a rational confrontation of viewpoints. It is not a discourse on the universal, but the impassioned claim by the colonized that their world is fundamentally different. The colonial world is a Manichaean world" (6)—or in other words, a Gnostic world. Far from representing a nihilistic fatalism, "the Manichaeanism that first governed colonial society is maintained intact during the period of decolonization. In fact the colonist never ceases to be the enemy, the antagonist, in plain words public enemy number 1" (14).

This absolute rejection of the colonizer underwrites the equally absolute violence that the process of decolonization requires—a violence that goes far beyond mere physical destruction to the eradication of the colonizer's cultural standards and categories. Hence, even if "antiracist racism and the determination to defend one's skin, which is characteristic of the colonized's response to colonial oppression, clearly represent sufficient reasons to join the struggle" (89), a thoroughgoing revolution must ultimately go beyond the gesture of inverting the colonizer's racialized dualism:

> The people who in the early days of the struggle had adopted the primitive Manichaeanism of the colonizer—Black versus White, Arab versus Infidel—realize en route that some blacks can be whiter than the whites, and that the prospect of a national flag or independence does not automatically result in certain segments of the population giving up their privileges and their interests. . . . Some members of the colonialist population prove to be closer, infinitely closer, to the nationalist struggle than certain native sons. The racial and racist dimension is transcended on both sides. (93–95)

The path to this overcoming of racialization does not come from the appeal to an empty universalism, however, but through a radical identification with the denigrated racial position—what James Cone or Frank Wilderson might call becoming Black.[38] The terms of the struggle are no longer mapped strictly along the lines of racialization created by the colonizer, and on the level of culture, Fanon calls for the development of a new national culture generated by the struggle for liberation itself, in opposition to the "racialization of thought" imposed by the colonizer (150). The goal is for the division of humanity that underwrote the Western system of governance to fall away in favor of "the creation of new men" (2), the elaboration of a previously unheard-of form of human existence.

This new form of human life together is one in which governance in the strong sense of the word is abolished. To the extent that something like government or leadership exists, its goal is "to politicize the people" so that it can "govern with the people and for the people" (124). Such a movement will require a party structure, but one that "must be the direct expression of the masses" (130). It will require a program, but if that program "is not explained, enriched, and deepened, if it does not very quickly turn into a social and political consciousness, into humanism, then it leads to a dead end" (144). It will require leadership, but of a very different kind from the political leadership that grows out of the Western system of international competition:

> No leader, whatever his worth, can replace the will of the people, and the national government, before concerning itself with international

prestige, must first restore dignity to all citizens, furnish their minds, fill their eyes with human things and develop a human landscape for the sake of its enlightened and sovereign inhabitants. (144)

To the extent that the party leadership exercises something like sovereignty, then, it would have to be what Ted Jennings—thinking at once of Jesus of Nazareth and of the South African anti-apartheid leader Steve Biko— called "contagious sovereignty."[39] The reference to Jesus is perhaps not out of place, insofar as Fanon can say that in the decolonizing struggle, "The minimum demand is that the last become the first" (10). But any vision of Jesus that would be useful to this insurgent nationalism cannot be the ready-made Jesus of colonial Christianity. Instead, it must respond to the implicit theology of a new form of human existence and political community in which "the meeting of the local cell or the committee meeting is a liturgical act" (136). The theology of the future will be the theology that, without presuming to dictate terms to this new creation, prepares us to greet it when it comes.

Acknowledgments

This collection has benefited from the critical eye and constructive suggestions of many friends and colleagues, including Amaryah Armstrong, Colby Dickinson, Jared Hickman, Joshua Ralston, Marika Rose, Bruce Rosenstock, Anthony Paul Smith, Philippe Theophandis (along with the members of his Agamben reading group in Toronto), and Linn Tonstad. I thank all of them for taking time out, amid multiple overlapping world-historical crises, to engage with my work and push me to think further than I could have done on my own. I would also like to thank Jack Caputo and Tom Lay for finding a place for this project in this series, my peer reviewers for their invaluable critiques and suggestions, and the entire editorial staff at Fordham University Press for helping to polish and finalize the book. I also must thank Natalie Scoles for her patience and support as we shared a one-bedroom "home office" for all those many months.

Several of the essays in this volume have appeared elsewhere, in a slightly different form. "Bonhoeffer on Continuity and Crisis: From Objective Spirit to Religionless Christianity" was originally published as "Objective Spirit and Continuity in the Theology of Dietrich Bonhoeffer" in *Philosophy and Theology* 17, no. 1–2 (2005): 17–31; "Resurrection without Religion" as "The Resurrection of the Dead: A Religionless Interpretation" in *Princeton Theological Review* 26, no. 1 (2011): 37–48; "Toward a Materialist Theology: Slavoj Žižek on Thinking God beyond the Master Signifier" as "On Materialist Theology: Thinking God Beyond the Master Signifier" in *Revue Internationale de Philosophie* 66, no. 3 (2012): 347–357; "The

Failed Divine Performative: Reading Judith Butler's Critique of Theology with Anselm's *On the Fall of the Devil*" under the same title in *Journal of Religion* 88, no. 2 (2008): 209–225; and "The Problem of Evil and the Problem of Legitimacy," with the added subtitle "On the Roots and Future of Political Theology," in *Crisis and Critique* 2, no. 1 (2015): 284–299. I am grateful to all the editors and peer reviewers of those publications for their contribution to these essays. In addition, an early version of "The Trinitarian Century" was presented at the conference "Sovereignty, Religion, and Secularism: Interrogating the Foundations of Polity," organized by Robert Yelle and Yvonne Sherwood at Ludwig-Maximilians-Universität München; I thank my hosts and fellow participants for their valuable feedback.

I regret that there is one name that I cannot list among the early readers of this manuscript: Ted Jennings, who died in late March 2020 after a serious stroke. Nonetheless, his influence is present on every page, perhaps even in ways I am no longer conscious of. Ted had a bigger impact on my life than anyone outside my family. He was my *Doktorvater*, but he was also a second father to me, who became one of my closest friends while remaining a valued mentor. In a very real sense, he saved my life. At a time when I was trying to find a way out of a destructive evangelical culture and had a lot of growing up to do, he took me under his wing and helped me to process a huge backlog of anger and shame while constantly challenging me intellectually. I don't know who I would be today without him. As a small token of my gratitude I dedicate this book to his memory.

Notes

Preface

1. Anselm of Canterbury, "Proslogion," trans. M. J. Charlesworth, §1, in *The Major Works*, ed. Brian Davies and G. R. Evans (New York: Oxford University Press, 1998).

2. Theodore W. Jennings Jr., *Introduction to Theology: An Invitation to Reflection upon the Christian Mythos* (Philadelphia: Fortress, 1976), 4.

3. Jennings, *Introduction*, 3.

4. Jennings, *Introduction*, 134.

5. Jennings, *Introduction*, 5.

6. Adam Kotsko, *Agamben's Philosophical Trajectory* (Edinburgh: Edinburgh University Press, 2020), 10.

7. The one exception is "The Failed Divine Imperative," where I found one section so difficult to follow—even as the author!—that I rewrote several paragraphs from scratch, though with the intention of presenting the same basic argumentative steps in a more comprehensible form. See note 47 in that essay.

Introduction: What Is Theology?

1. See Carl Schmitt, *Political Theology: Four Chapters on the Concept of Sovereignty*, trans. George Schwab (Chicago: University of Chicago Press, 2005), and Adam Kotsko, *Neoliberalism's Demons: On the Political Theology of Late Capital* (Stanford: Stanford University Press, 2018), respectively.

2. See, of course, Thomas Kuhn, *The Structure of Scientific Revolutions*, 4th ed. (Chicago: University of Chicago Press, 2012).

3. Mathew Abbott provides a convincing case for applying the term "political ontology" to the work of Martin Heidegger, Jean-Luc Nancy, and Giorgio

Agamben (the latter of whom is normally regarded as a representative of political theology) in *The Figure of This World: Agamben and the Question of Political Ontology* (Edinburgh: Edinburgh University Press, 2014).

4. Plato, *Republic*, trans. Joe Sachs (Newburyport, MA: Focus Publishing, 2007). Subsequent references are given parenthetically in the text.

5. See Giorgio Agamben, *The Use of Bodies*, trans. Adam Kotsko (Stanford: Stanford University Press, 2016), part III, chap. 9, "The Myth of Er."

6. Augustine, *Confessions*, 2nd ed., trans. F. J. Sheed, ed. Michael P. Foley (Indianapolis: Hackett, 2006). Subsequent citations are given parenthetically in the text.

7. Jan Assmann, *The Price of Monotheism*, trans. Robert Savage (Stanford: Stanford University Press, 2010), 18–20. Subsequent references are given parenthetically in the text.

8. See the discussion in "Modernity's Original Sin" below.

9. Here I am indebted to Ted Jennings's pathbreaking commentaries on Mark and Romans—see Theodore W. Jennings Jr., *The Insurrection of the Crucified: The "Gospel of Mark" as Theological Manifesto* (Chicago: Exploration Press, 2003) and *Outlaw Justice: The Messianic Politics of Paul* (Stanford: Stanford University Press, 2013), respectively.

10. Sylvia Wynter, "1492: A New World View," in *Race, Discourse, and the Origin of the Americas: A New World View*, ed. Vera Lawrence Hyatt and Rex Nettleford (Washington, DC: Smithsonian Institution Press, 1995), 17. Subsequent references are given parenthetically in the text; all italics in original.

11. See, for example, Jared Hickman, *Black Prometheus: Race and Radicalism in the Age of Atlantic Slavery* (New York: Oxford University Press, 2017), esp. 35–37, and Denise Ferreira da Silva, "Before *Man*: Sylvia Wynter's Rewriting of the Modern Episteme," in *Sylvia Wynter: On Being Human as Praxis*, ed. Katherine McKittrick (Durham, NC: Duke University Press, 2015), 90–105.

12. For an account of secularism as a quasi-theology that scapegoats religion, see Daniel Colucciello Barber, *On Diaspora: Christianity, Religion, and Secularity* (Eugene, OR: Cascade, 2011).

Bonhoeffer on Continuity and Crisis: From Objective Spirit to Religionless Christianity

1. Ernst Fiel, *The Theology of Dietrich Bonhoeffer*, trans. Martin Rumscheit (Philadelphia: Fortress Press, 1985), 3.

2. Fiel, *Theology*, 4.

3. Dietrich Bonhoeffer, *Letters and Papers from Prison*, ed. Eberhard Bethge, trans. Richard Fuller et al. (New York: Simon & Schuster, 1971), 279.

4. Bonhoeffer, *Letters and Papers*, 275.

5. Bonhoeffer, *Letters and Papers*, 369.

6. Bonhoeffer, *Letters and Papers*, 387.

7. John de Gruchy, ed., *Dietrich Bonhoeffer: Witness to Christ* (Minneapolis: Fortress Press, 1991), 4.

8. Dietrich Bonhoeffer, *Sanctorum Communio: A Theological Study of the Sociology of the Church*, ed. Joachim von Soosten and Clifford Green, trans. Reinhard Krauss and Nancy Lukens (Minneapolis: Fortress Press, 1998), 22.

9. Bonhoeffer, *Sanctorum Communio*, 145.

10. G. W. F. Hegel, *Philosophy of Mind*, trans. by William Wallace and A. V. Miller (Oxford: Clarendon, 1971). This translation renders *Geist* as "mind." Throughout, I alter the translation to "spirit" in order to conform to the usage of Bonhoeffer's translators.

11. Hegel, *Philosophy of Mind*, 241–242.

12. Hegel, *Philosophy of Mind*, 277.

13. Bonhoeffer, *Sanctorum Communio*, 97–98.

14. Bonhoeffer, *Sanctorum Communio*, 48. All italics in quotations from Bonhoeffer's works are in the original.

15. Bonhoeffer, *Sanctorum Communio*, 69.

16. Bonhoeffer, *Sanctorum Communio*, 100.

17. Bonhoeffer, *Sanctorum Communio*, 99.

18. Bonhoeffer, *Sanctorum Communio*, 148.

19. Bonhoeffer, *Sanctorum Communio*, 49.

20. Bonhoeffer, *Sanctorum Communio*, 85.

21. Bonhoeffer, *Sanctorum Communio*, 108.

22. Luca D'Isanto, "Bonhoeffer's Hermeneutical Model of Community," *Union Theological Seminary Quarterly Review* 46, no. 1 (1992): 143.

23. See, e.g., Bonhoeffer, *Sanctorum Communio*, 203 and 214.

24. Bonhoeffer, *Sanctorum Communio*, 77.

25. Bonhoeffer, *Sanctorum Communio*, 208.

26. Bonhoeffer, *Sanctorum Communio*, 214.

27. Bonhoeffer, *Sanctorum Communio*, 215.

28. Bonhoeffer, *Sanctorum Communio*, 234–235.

29. Bonhoeffer, *Sanctorum Communio*, 280–281.

30. Bonhoeffer, *Sanctorum Communio*, 269.

31. Bonhoeffer, *Sanctorum Communio*, 216.

32. Dietrich Bonhoeffer, *Christ the Center*, trans. Edwin Robertson (San Francisco: Harper, 1978), 34.

33. Bonhoeffer, *Christ the Center*, 46.

34. Bonhoeffer, *Christ the Center*, 49–50.

35. Bonhoeffer, *Christ the Center*, 71.

36. Bonhoeffer, *Christ the Center*, 76.

37. Dietrich Bonhoeffer, *The Cost of Discipleship*, trans. R. H. Fuller (New York: Simon & Schuster, 1995), 35.

38. Bonhoeffer, *Letters and Papers*, 369.

39. Bonhoeffer, *Letters and Papers*, 280.

40. Bonhoeffer, *Letters and Papers*, 280.

41. Bonhoeffer, *Letters and Papers*, 282.

42. Bonhoeffer, *Letters and Papers*, 281.

43. Bonhoeffer, *Letters and Papers*, 327.

44. Bonhoeffer, *Sanctorum Communio*, 209.

45. Bonhoeffer, *Letters and Papers*, 381.

46. Bonhoeffer, *Letters and Papers*, 382.

47. See Kenneth Surin, "*Contemptus Mundi* and the Disenchantment of the World: Bonhoeffer's 'Discipline of the Secret' and Adorno's 'Strategy of Hibernation,'" *Journal of the American Academy of Religion* 53, no. 3 (1985): 384–385.

48. Richard Bube, "Man Come of Age: Bonhoeffer's Response to the God-of-the-Gaps," *Journal of the Evangelical Theological Society* 14, no. 4 (1971): 213.

49. Bonhoeffer, *Letters and Papers*, 329 and passim.

50. Bonhoeffer, *Letters and Papers*, 360.

51. Bonhoeffer, *Letters and Papers*, 381–382.

52. Surin, "*Contemptus Mundi*," 397.

53. Barry Harvey, "The Body Politic of Christ: Theology, Social Analysis, and Bonhoeffer's Arcane Discipline," *Modern Theology* 13, no. 3 (1997): 319.

54. Bonhoeffer, *Sanctorum Communio*, 108.

55. Surin, "*Contemptus Mundi*," 397.

56. Bonhoeffer, *Letters and Papers*, 387.

Resurrection without Religion

1. Adam Kotsko, *Politics of Redemption: The Social Logic of Salvation* (New York: T & T Clark, 2010). See in particular chapters 1 and 8.

2. Unless otherwise noted, all biblical translations come from the New Revised Standard Version.

3. In fact, the translators of the NRSV, undoubtedly in deference to the traditional view, misleadingly render "*pneumatikon*" as "physical."

4. Given the uncertain state of the text, it seems the only practical way to proceed here is to follow the tradition and treat the "longer ending" (16:9–20) as a unit together with 16:1–8.

5. In the discussion that follows, I am deeply indebted to Daniel Colucciello Barber's remarks on an earlier draft of this essay.

Toward a Materialist Theology:
Slavoj Žižek on Thinking God beyond the Master Signifier

1. Adam Kotsko, *Žižek and Theology* (New York: Continuum/T & T Clark, 2008).

2. Slavoj Žižek, *The Parallax View* (Cambridge, MA: MIT Press, 2006).

3. Žižek, *Parallax View*, 4–5.

4. Slavoj Žižek, *The Puppet and the Dwarf: The Perverse Core of Christianity* (Cambridge, MA: MIT Press, 2003).

5. Slavoj Žižek, "The Fear of Four Words: A Modest Plea for the Hegelian Reading of Christianity" and "Dialectical Clarity versus the Misty Conceit of

Paradox," in Slavoj Žižek and John Milbank, *The Monstrosity of Christ: Paradox or Dialectic?* ed. Creston Davis (Cambridge, MA: MIT Press, 2009).

6. Žižek, *Parallax View*, 79.

7. Žižek, *Parallax View*, 79.

8. Žižek, *Puppet and the Dwarf*, 171.

9. See Adam Kotsko, "The Christian Experience Continues: On Žižek's Work since *The Parallax View*," *International Journal of Žižek Studies* 4, no. 4 (2010): 1–9.

10. Žižek and Milbank, *Monstrosity*, 29.

11. Augustine, *Confessions*, 2nd ed., trans. F. J. Sheed, ed. Michael P. Foley (Indianapolis: Hackett, 2006), and Pseudo-Dionysius, *The Divine Names*, in *The Complete Works*, trans. Colm Luibheid, ed. Paul Rorem (New York: Paulist, 1987). Further citations from these works will be provided parenthetically in the text, following standard textual divisions.

12. Catherine Keller, *The Face of the Deep: A Theology of Becoming* (New York: Routledge, 2003). See especially 75–77.

13. Though I obviously did not have access to it nearly a decade ago when I originally composed this text, I want to take this opportunity to recommend Marika Rose's *A Theology of Failure: Žižek Against Christian Innocence* (New York: Fordham University Press, 2019), which is framed around a much more thoroughgoing and systematic comparison of Žižek and Pseudo-Dionysius than what I attempt here.

14. See Slavoj Žižek, *The Indivisible Remainder: An Essay on Schelling and Related Matters* (New York: Verso, 1996), particularly chapter 2.

The Failed Divine Performative: Reading Judith Butler's Critique of Theology with Anselm's *On the Fall of the Devil*

1. See, for example, the recent collection *Bodily Citations: Religion and Judith Butler*, ed. Ellen Armour and Susan St. Ville (New York: Columbia University Press, 2006).

2. Anselm of Canterbury, "On the Fall of the Devil," trans. Ralph McInerny, in *The Major Works*, ed. Brian Davies and G. R. Evans (New York: Oxford University Press, 1998), 193–232. The Latin text with facing French translation can be found in Michel Corbin, ed., *L'œuvre de S. Anselme de Cantorbéry*, vol. 2 (Paris: Les Éditions du Cerf, 1986), 251–375.

3. Judith Butler, *Gender Trouble: Feminism and the Subversion of Identity*, 10th anniversary edition (New York: Routledge, 1999).

4. Judith Butler, *Excitable Speech: A Politics of the Performative* (New York: Routledge, 1997), and *The Psychic Life of Power* (Stanford: Stanford University Press, 1997).

5. Louis Althusser, "Ideology and Ideological State Apparatuses," in *Lenin and Philosophy and Other Essays*, trans. Ben Brewster (New York: Monthly Review Press, 1971), 127–186.

6. As one whose understanding of Lacan has primarily been mediated through Žižek and other members of the Slovenian Lacanian school, I was initially baffled by Butler's critiques of Lacan in *Gender Trouble*, as well as the critique of Žižek in *Bodies That Matter: On the Discursive Limits of "Sex"* (New York: Routledge, 1993) and of Dolar in *Psychic Life of Power*. A crucial difference between Butler and the Slovenian school is found not so much directly in their interpretation of Lacan as in their decision of "which" Lacan to privilege as the interpretative key for his widely variegated body of work—for the Slovenians, it is the "late" Lacan of the 1970s and '80s, whereas for Butler it is the "middle" or structuralist Lacan appropriated by American scholars (particularly feminists).

7. Butler, *Gender Trouble*, 38.

8. Butler, *Gender Trouble*, 37.

9. Butler, *Gender Trouble*, 38.

10. Butler, *Gender Trouble*, 71–72.

11. Butler, *Gender Trouble*, 72 (emphasis added).

12. Butler, *Gender Trouble*, 72.

13. Butler, *Gender Trouble*, 72.

14. Butler, *Gender Trouble*, 72.

15. Butler, *Gender Trouble*, 73.

16. Butler, *Excitable Speech*, 31.

17. Butler, *Excitable Speech*, 21.

18. Butler, *Excitable Speech*, 16.

19. Butler, *Excitable Speech*, 102.

20. This reference to the Roman Catholic doctrine whereby the sacramental ritual, simply by virtue of having been performed according to canonical rules, automatically confers God's grace, would be interesting to follow up with reference to Butler's critique of Kripke's theory of "primal baptism" in *Bodies That Matter*, 212–218.

21. Butler, *Excitable Speech*, 50.

22. Butler, *Excitable Speech*, 50–51.

23. Butler, *Excitable Speech*, 50.

24. Butler, *Excitable Speech*, 45.

25. Butler, *Excitable Speech*, 47 (emphasis in original).

26. Butler, *Excitable Speech*, 48.

27. Butler, *Excitable Speech*, 77 (emphasis in original).

28. Butler, *Excitable Speech*, 81.

29. Butler, *Excitable Speech*, 78. For an account of the further mutations of state power in the afterlife of sovereignty, see the chapter "Indefinite Detention" in Judith Butler, *Precarious Life: The Powers of Mourning and Violence* (New York: Verso, 2006).

30. Butler, *Excitable Speech*, 82.

31. Butler, *Excitable Speech*, 101.

32. Butler, *Excitable Speech*, 31, and *Psychic Life of Power*, 110.

33. Butler, *Psychic Life of Power*, 113.

34. Butler, *Psychic Life of Power*, 114.

35. Althusser, "Ideology," 152.

36. Althusser, "Ideology," 177.

37. Althusser, "Ideology," 159, 160, and passim.

38. Butler does refer to "the putative 'eternity' of ideology" in *Psychic Life of Power*, 110, as part of a list of examples from Christianity. It is unclear to me whether this should be taken to refer to the principle in question, but in any case, she never directly quotes it.

39. Butler, *Psychic Life of Power*, 125.

40. Althusser, "Ideology," 161.

41. Althusser, "Ideology," 165.

42. Althusser, "Ideology," 135.

43. Butler, *Psychic Life of Power*, 118.

44. Butler, *Psychic Life of Power*, 130 (emphasis in original).

45. See in particular Butler, *Precarious Life* and *Giving an Account of Oneself* (New York: Fordham University Press, 2005).

46. All references to Anselm's *On the Fall of the Devil* will be given parenthetically in the text and will refer to section numbers, which are consistent across all editions.

47. *Editorial note:* The paragraphs that follow represent by far the most significant changes I have made to a previously published essay in this collection. My original version hewed too closely to Anselm's convoluted argumentative structure, resulting in a summary that even I myself found difficult to follow upon reviewing it. The present revision presents the same basic argument in a hopefully more comprehensible form. I apologize to readers of the original version for any inconvenience.

48. The verb *excuso* has connotations of both "exempting from blame" and the more obvious "excusing." The former connotation, with its "preemptive" quality (for instance, someone could be "excused" from a meeting that has not yet occurred and then be blameless for missing it), is obviously what is desired when the student applies it to God, but the verb is used first of the devil, in which case it would seem to carry connotations of considering mitigating circumstances when assessing a wrong done. The parallelism creates a certain degree of instability: Is the teacher asserting that God had no responsibility to prevent the devil's fall, or is he making excuses for an event God is responsible for? (The translation quoted and altered has "absolves God" for *deum excusat*; I simply restored the parallelism.)

49. Butler, *Psychic Life of Power*, 118.

50. Althusser, "Ideology," 178.

51. Butler, *Psychic Life of Power*, 119.

52. For a more detailed analysis of Nietzsche's account of the Incarnation, see Adam Kotsko, "The Sermon on Mount Moriah: Faith and the Secret in *The Gift of Death*," *Heythrop Journal* 49, no. 1 (2008): 44–61.

53. Butler, *Psychic Life of Power*, 144 (emphasis in original).

Translation, Hospitality, and Supersession:
Lamin Sanneh and Jacques Derrida on the Future of Christianity

1. Homi Bhabha, *The Location of Culture*, 2nd ed. (New York: Routledge, 2004), 34.

2. See, for example, Philip Jenkins, *The Next Christendom: The Coming of Global Christianity*, 2nd ed. (New York: Oxford University Press, 2009).

3. Two examples here are Paul Gifford, *Ghana's New Christianity: Pentecostalism in a Globalizing African Economy* (Bloomington: Indiana University Press, 2004), and Kevin Lewis O'Neill, *City of God: Christian Citizenship in Postwar Guatemala* (Berkeley: University of California Press, 2010).

4. Achille Mbembe, *Critique of Black Reason*, trans. Laurent Dubois (Durham, NC: Duke University Press, 2017), 101–102.

5. Representatives of the phenomenological branch are Jean-Luc Marion, *God without Being: Hors-Texte*, trans. Thomas A. Carlson (Chicago: University of Chicago Press, 1995), and Michel Henry, *I Am the Truth: Toward a Philosophy of Christianity*, trans. Susan Emanuel (Stanford: Stanford University Press, 2002). Marxist studies of St. Paul include Alain Badiou, *Saint Paul: The Foundation of Universalism*, trans. Ray Brassier (Stanford: Stanford University Press, 2003), and Slavoj Žižek, *The Puppet and the Dwarf: The Perverse Core of Christianity* (Cambridge, MA: MIT Press, 2003). And the most prolific representative of the genealogical approach is Giorgio Agamben, perhaps most notably in *The Kingdom and the Glory: For a Theological Genealogy of Economy and Government*, trans. Lorenzo Chiesa and Matteo Mandarini (Stanford: Stanford University Press, 2011).

6. Lamin Sanneh, *Translating the Message: The Missionary Impact on Culture*, 2nd ed. (Maryknoll, NY: Orbis Books, 2009). Subsequent citations are given parenthetically in the text.

7. This attention to the colonial situation contrasts with much of the "religious turn" literature, in particular the approach of Derrida's close associate Jean-Luc Nancy, who in recent years has called for a "deconstruction of Christianity" but who continues to view Christianity as virtually identical to the Western tradition and who claims that the present age is witnessing the complete saturation of the globe by the West. See Jean-Luc Nancy, *Dis-Enclosure: The Deconstruction of Christianity*, trans. Bettina Bergo, Gabriel Malenfant, and Michael B. Smith (New York: Fordham University Press, 2008), and *Adoration: The Deconstruction of Christianity II*, trans. John McKeane (New York: Fordham University Press, 2012).

8. Talal Asad, *Secular Translations: Nation-State, Modern Self, and Calculative Reason* (New York: Columbia University Press, 2018), 56.

9. For a detailed account of the development and implications of this doctrine, see Navid Kermani, *God Is Beautiful: The Aesthetic Experience of the Qur'an*, trans. Tony Crawford (New York: Polity, 2018).

10. Asad, *Secular Translations*, 57.

11. Asad, *Secular Translations*, 61.

12. Asad, *Secular Translations*, 56.

13. Jacques Derrida, "Hostipitality," in *Acts of Religion*, ed. Gil Anidjar (New York: Routledge, 2002), 369.

14. Derrida, "Hostipitality," 365.

15. Derrida, "Hostipitality," 370.

16. Massignon, as quoted in Derrida, "Hostipitality," 379.

17. See particularly Jacques Derrida and Anne Dufourmantelle, *Of Hospitality: Anne Dufourmantelle Invites Jacques Derrida to Respond*, trans. Rachel Bowlby (Stanford: Stanford University Press, 2000), 25–27.

18. Derrida, "Hostipitality," 369.

19. Derrida and Dufourmantelle, *Of Hospitality*, 147.

20. Derrida, "Hostipitality," 369ff.

21. Derrida and Dufourmantelle, *Of Hospitality*, 15–21.

22. Here I build on Jennings's *Reading Derrida/Thinking Paul*, albeit in ways that Jennings himself may have found questionable.

23. John D. Caputo, *The Prayers and Tears of Jacques Derrida: Religion without Religion* (Indianapolis: Indiana University Press, 1997), 222.

24. See Jacques Derrida, *The Gift of Death*, 2nd ed., trans. David Wills (Chicago: University of Chicago Press, 2008).

25. The Qur'an is here quoted in the very readable translation by M. A. S. Abdel Haleem (New York: Oxford University Press, 2016); the reader may also want to consult the many other English translations available for free online.

26. See Asad, *Secular Translations*, 57–58.

Agamben the Theologian

1. Giorgio Agamben, *The Kingdom and the Glory: For a Theological Genealogy of Economy and Government*, trans. Lorenzo Chiesa and Matteo Mandarini (Stanford: Stanford University Press, 2011). See my discussion in *Agamben's Philosophical Trajectory* (Edinburgh: Edinburgh University Press, 2020), chap. 3, for more detail.

2. Walter Benjamin, *The Arcades Project*, ed. Rolf Tiedemann, trans. Howard Eiland and Kevin McLaughlin (Cambridge, MA: Belknap Press of Harvard University Press, 1982), 471 (fragment N7a, 7).

3. Giorgio Agamben, *Stanzas: Word and Phantasm in Western Culture*, trans. Ronald L. Martinez (Minneapolis: University of Minnesota Press, 1993). Publication dates given in the text for Agamben's works always refer to the original Italian publication.

4. Giorgio Agamben, *Homo Sacer: Sovereign Power and Bare Life*, trans. Daniel Heller-Roazen (Stanford: Stanford University Press, 1998), 78.

5. See Agamben, *Homo Sacer*, part 1, chap. 5, and *State of Exception*, trans. Kevin Attell (Chicago: University of Chicago Press, 2005), 83–84.

6. Giorgio Agamben, *The Time That Remains: A Commentary on the Letter to the Romans*, trans. Patricia Dailey (Stanford: Stanford University Press, 2005), 62–63.

7. Giorgio Agamben, *The Mystery of Evil: Benedict XVI and the End of Days*, trans. Adam Kotsko (Stanford: Stanford University Press, 2017).

8. Giorgio Agamben, *The Use of Bodies*, trans. Adam Kotsko (Stanford: Stanford University Press, 2016).

9. Giorgio Agamben, *The Coming Community*, trans. Michael Hardt (Minneapolis: University of Minnesota Press, 1993).

10. Giorgio Agamben, *Nudities*, trans. David Kishik and Stefan Pedatella (Stanford: Stanford University Press, 2011).

11. Giorgio Agamben, *The Highest Poverty: Monastic Rules and Form-of-Life*, trans. Adam Kotsko (Stanford: Stanford University Press, 2013).

12. Giorgio Agamben, *The Sacrament of Language: An Archaeology of the Oath*, trans. Adam Kotsko (Stanford: Stanford University Press, 2011).

13. Agamben, *Sacrament of Language*, 72.

14. Giorgio Agamben, *The Kingdom and the Garden*, trans. Adam Kotsko (Chicago: Seagull Press, 2020).

15. Giorgio Agamben, *Karman: A Brief Treatise on Action, Guilt, and Gesture*, trans. Adam Kotsko (Stanford: Stanford University Press, 2018).

16. I do as much in both *Neoliberalism's Demons* and "Modernity's Original Sin" (in the present volume).

17. Agamben, *Kingdom and the Garden*, 76–77.

18. Agamben, *Use of Bodies*, 255.

19. Giorgio Agamben, *Autoritratto nello studio* (Milan: Nottetempo, 2017). All translations from this text are mine.

20. Agamben, *Autoritratto*, 143.

21. Agamben, *Use of Bodies*, 215.

22. Agamben, *Autoritratto*, 167.

23. Agamben, *Use of Bodies*, 94.

The Problem of Evil and the Problem of Legitimacy

1. All biblical quotations are taken from the New Revised Standard Version.

2. I discuss Badiou and Žižek's readings of Paul at greater length in "Politics and Perversion: Situating Žižek's Paul," *Journal for Cultural and Religious Theory* 9, no. 2 (2008): 43–52.

3. Jacob Taubes, *The Political Theology of Paul*, ed. Aleia Assmann and Jan Assmann, trans. Dana Hollander (Stanford: Stanford University Press, 2004), 16; emphasis in original.

4. See Jacob Taubes, *Occidental Eschatology*, trans. David Ratmoko (Stanford: Stanford University Press 2009), *To Carl Schmitt: Letters and Reflections*, trans. Keith Tribe (New York: Columbia University Press, 2010), and appendices to *Political Theology of Paul*.

5. Carl Schmitt, *The Nomos of the Earth in the International Law of the Jus Publicum Europaeum*, trans. and ed. G. L. Ulmen (New York: Telos, 2003), 59–60.

6. Schmitt, *Nomos*, 60.

7. Taubes, *To Carl Schmitt*, 54.

8. Giorgio Agamben, *The Kingdom and the Glory: For a Theological Genealogy of Economy and Government*, trans. Lorenzo Chiesa and Matteo Mandarini (Stanford: Stanford University Press, 2011), 164.

9. See, for example, Jacob Taubes, *From Cult to Culture: Fragments toward a Critique of Historical Reason*, ed. Charlotte Elisheva Fonrobert and Amir Engel (Stanford: Stanford University Press, 2010), 73.

10. Philip Goodchild, *Theology of Money* (Durham, NC: Duke University Press, 2007).

Modernity's Original Sin: Toward a Theological Genealogy of Race

1. Sylvia Wynter, "Unsettling the Coloniality of Being/Power/Truth/Freedom: Toward the Human, After Man, Its Overrepresentation—An Argument," *CR: The New Centennial Review* 3, no. 3 (2003): 257–337. Subsequent references are given parenthetically in the text. I owe this reference, along with the connection I will later make to Saidiya Hartman's work, to Amaryah Armstrong, who generously commented on an early version of this essay.

2. Frantz Fanon, *Black Skin, White Masks*, trans. Richard Philcox (New York: Grove, 2008), 95.

3. See Aimé Césaire, *A Tempest: Based on Shakespeare's* The Tempest; *Adaptation for a Black Theatre*, trans. Richard Miller (New York: Theater Communications Group, 2002), and Silvia Federici, *Caliban and the Witch: Women, the Body, and Primitive Accumulation*, 2nd ed. (New York: Autonomedia, 2014). All quotations from Shakespeare are taken from *The Tempest: Second Norton Critical Edition*, ed. Peter Hulme and William H. Sherman (New York: Norton, 2019); citations are provided in the text by act, scene, and line.

4. Saidiya Hartman, *Scenes of Subjection: Terror, Slavery, and Self-Making in Nineteenth-Century America* (New York: Oxford University Press, 1997). Subsequent citations are given parenthetically in the text.

5. In keeping with her choice to turn her focus away from spectacular violence, Hartman does not discuss the phenomenon of lynching at any length. For a study connecting this horrific phenomenon to theological themes, see James H. Cone's arguable magnum opus, *The Cross and the Lynching Tree* (Maryknoll, NY: Orbis Books, 2011).

6. See Amaryah Armstrong's discussion of this phenomenon from a theological perspective in "The Spirit and the Subprime: Race, Risk, and Our Common Dispossession," *Anglican Theological Review* 98, no. 1 (2016): 51–69.

7. See also my analysis of the moral entrapment of police shootings in *The Prince of This World* (Stanford: Stanford University Press, 2016), 1–4, and Jared Sexton's much more expansive discussion in *Black Men, Black Feminism: Lucifer's Nocturne* (New York: Palgrave Macmillan, 2018), chap. 1.

8. See Frank B. Wilderson III, *Red, White, and Black: Cinema and the Structure of U.S. Antagonisms* (Durham, NC: Duke University Press, 2010), particularly the introduction and first two chapters.

9. See Dorothy Kim's discussion of both strains of scholarship, including a deservedly harsh critique of the latter, in "Introduction to Literature Compass Special Cluster: Critical Race and the Middle Ages," *Literature Compass* 16, nos. 9–10 (2019): 1–16. I owe this reference to Karl Steel.

10. Marika Rose, "For Our Sins," in *Exploring Complicity: Concepts, Cases and Critique*, edited by Afxentis Afxentiou, Robin Dunford, and Michael Neu (London: Rowman and Littlefield, 2017), 55.

11. See Orlando Patterson, *Slavery and Social Death: A Comparative Study* (Cambridge, MA: Harvard University Press, 1982), 70–72.

12. All biblical quotations are based on the New Revised Standard Version.

13. My discussion of patristic and medieval theology here is necessarily somewhat compressed. Readers seeking more detail can consult my *Politics of Redemption: The Social Logic of Salvation* (New York: T & T Clark, 2010), chaps. 5–6, and *The Prince of This World*, chaps. 2–4.

14. Augustine, *City of God*, trans. Henry Bettenson (New York: Penguin, 1972), 14.1. Subsequent references are given parenthetically in the text.

15. All quotations from Anselm are taken from *The Major Works*, ed. Brian Davies and G. R. Evans (New York: Oxford University Press, 1998), cited by title and standard textual divisions.

16. Amaryah Armstrong, "Of Flesh and Spirit: Race, Reproduction, and Sexual Difference in the Turn to Paul," *Journal of Cultural and Religious Theory* 16, no. 2 (2017): 130. Here she draws on Daniel Boyarin's *A Radical Jew: Paul and the Politics of Identity* (Berkeley: University of California Press, 1994), which also informs my discussion here.

17. Joshua Trachtenberg, *The Devil and the Jews: The Medieval Conception of the Jew and Its Relation to Modern Anti-Semitism* (Philadelphia: Jewish Publication Society, 1983).

18. Gil Anidjar, *Blood: A Critique of Christianity* (New York: Columbia University Press, 2014).

19. This text is available in an abridged English translation as "The Lord's Body and Blood," by Radbertus of Corbie, in *Early Medieval Theology* (The Library of Christian Classics), ed. George E. McCracken (Philadelphia: Westminster, 1957). The full Latin text is available in *Corpus Christianorum, Continuatio Mediaevalis*, vol. 16.

20. See M. Lindsay Kaplan, *Figuring Racism in Medieval Christianity* (New York: Oxford University Press, 2019). I owe this reference to Amaryah Armstrong.

21. See David M. Goldenberg, *The Curse of Ham: Race and Slavery in Early Judaism, Christianity, and Islam* (Princeton, NJ: Princeton University Press, 2005) for a historical overview of this trope, and Sylvester Johnson, *The Myth of Ham in Nineteenth-Century American Christianity: Race, Heathens, and the People of God* (New York: Palgrave Macmillan, 2004) for an account of its role in the American context, including the unexpected efforts of Black Americans to make positive use of the trope. I owe these references to Karl Steel and Amaryah Armstrong, respectively.

22. See, for example, J. Kameron Carter, *Race: A Theological Account* (New York: Oxford University Press, 2008).

23. James H. Cone, *God of the Oppressed*, 2nd ed. (Maryknoll, NY: Orbis Books, 1997), 123; emphasis in original.

24. Fanon, *Black Skin, White Masks*, 115.

25. Wilderson, *Red, White, and Black*, 36.

26. Hortense Spillers, *Black, White, and in Color: Essays on American Literature and Culture* (Chicago: University of Chicago Press, 2003), 228, emphasis in original.

27. Wilderson, *Red, White, and Black*, 23.

The Trinitarian Century: God, Governance, and Race

1. Friedrich Schleiermacher, *The Christian Faith*, ed. H. R. Mackintosh and J. S. Stewart (Edinburgh: T & T Clark, 1999), 738–751.

2. Karl Barth, *Church Dogmatics*, vol. I: *The Doctrine of the Word of God*, pt. 1., trans. G. W. Bromiley, ed. G. W. Bromiley and T. F. Torrance (Edinburgh: T & T Clark, 1975). Subsequent citations are given parenthetically in the text.

3. Barth, *Church Dogmatics* I/1, 47.

4. Barth, *Church Dogmatics* I/1, 295.

5. Barth, *Church Dogmatics* I/1, 306.

6. Barth, *Church Dogmatics* I/1, 307.

7. Karl Barth, *Church Dogmatics*, vol. II: *The Doctrine of God*, pt. 1, trans. T. H. L. Parker, W. B. Johnston, Harold Knight, J. L. M. Haire, ed. G. W. Gromiley and T. F. Torrance (Edinburgh: T & T Clark, 1957).

8. Erik Peterson, "Monotheism as a Political Problem," in *Theological Tractates*, ed. and trans. Michael J. Hollerich (Stanford: Stanford University Press, 2011).

9. For an overview of these trends, see David S. Cunningham, *These Three Are One: The Practice of Trinitarian Theology* (New York: Blackwell, 1998).

10. Linn Marie Tonstad, *God and Difference: The Trinity, Sexuality, and the Transformation of Finitude* (New York: Routledge, 2016), 13. One might relatedly wonder whether Barth or Peterson could have put forward grounds for rejecting Nazism other than the radical transcendence of the trinitarian God.

11. Giorgio Agamben, *The Kingdom and the Glory: For a Theological Genealogy of Economy and Government*, trans. Lorenzo Chiesa and Matteo Mandarini (Stanford: Stanford University Press, 2011).

12. Jan Assmann, *The Price of Monotheism*, trans. Robert Savage (Stanford: Stanford University Press, 2010).

13. See Adam Kotsko, *The Prince of This World* (Stanford: Stanford University Press, 2016), particularly chap. 1.

14. My account of Paul's teaching here relies heavily on Theodore W. Jennings Jr., *Outlaw Justice: The Messianic Politics of Paul* (Stanford: Stanford University Press, 2013).

15. All biblical quotations are drawn from the New Revised Standard Version.

16. See the discussion in the preceding essay, "Modernity's Original Sin."

17. The NRSV gives "enemies *of God*," but the Greek text simply says that they are enemies—perhaps of the Gentile believers themselves or of the Gospel proclamation, but certainly not *of God* in any strong sense, as the remainder of the passage clarifies.

18. See "Resurrection without Religion" in the present volume for more details.

19. My account of Constantine's role at the Council of Nicea is drawn from David Potter, *Constantine the Emperor* (New York: Oxford University Press, 2013), particularly chap. 26.

20. Potter, *Constantine the Emperor*, 35.

21. See, e.g., Mechthild of Magdeburg, *The Flowing Light of the Godhead*, trans. Frank Tobin (Mahwah, NJ: Paulist Press, 1998): "My soul flew to God so swiftly that she literally arose with no effort on her part and snuggled herself into the Holy Trinity, just as a child snuggles into its mother's coat and lays itself right at her breast" (234). I am grateful to Henry Barrett for tracking down this and other references to the Trinity in the Beguine literature as my research assistant (for one blessed semester).

22. This is the primary complaint of Catherine Mowry LaCugna in *God for Us: Trinity and Christian Life* (New York: Harper Collins, 1973), one of the most historically informed texts in the social-political Trinity genre. See chapter 2 in particular for the period under discussion here.

23. See my extended reading of Augustine's doctrine of the Spirit in "Gift and *Communio*: The Holy Spirit in Augustine's *De Trinitate*," *Scottish Journal of Theology* 64, no. 1 (2011): 1–12.

24. See Karl Polanyi, *The Great Transformation: The Political and Economic Origins of Our Time* (Boston: Beacon, 2001), for both sides of this debate.

25. See in particular Sylvia Wynter, "1492: A New World View," in *Race, Discourse, and the Origin of the Americas: A New World View*, ed. Vera Lawrence Hyatt and Rex Nettleford (Washington, DC: Smithsonian Institution Press, 1995), 14.

26. See Frank B. Wilderson III, *Red, White, and Black: Cinema and the Structure of U.S. Antagonisms* (Durham, NC: Duke University Press, 2010), 35–36, and Alexander G. Weheliye, *Habeas Viscus: Racializing Assemblages, Biopolitics, and Black Feminist Theories of the Human* (Durham, NC: Duke University Press, 2014), passim.

27. Gil Anidjar, *Blood: A Critique of Christianity* (New York: Columbia University Press, 2014).

28. Jared Hickman, *Black Prometheus: Race and Radicalism in the Age of Atlantic Slavery* (New York: Oxford University Press, 2017), 11. Subsequent citations are given parenthetically in the text.

29. Hickman, *Black Prometheus*, 400n88. See also Karen L. King, *What Is Gnosticism?* (Cambridge, MA: Belknap Press of Harvard University Press, 2003).

30. As Hickman puts it: "Augustine effectively redeemed Gnosticism's bad Creator-God by sliding him up into the position of the good Savior-God—

through the doctrine of the Trinity—and then slid man up to the position vacated by the bad Creator-God—through his signature doctrine of original sin—thereby leaving Man rather than God to bear the onus of the blighted immanent sphere of creation. The price of exonerating the Creator-God from the world's evil was demonizing but also aggrandizing Man as, in effect, the 'creator' of the fallen world through Adam and Eve's paradigmatic abuse of freedom in Eden. In one sense, the Augustinian reoccupation of Gnosticism thus largely ceded this world to Man in his freedom" (*Black Prometheus*, 56). As should be clear for the reader of "Modernity's Original Sin," I am in broad agreement with Hickman's account of the net effect of Augustine's theological intervention, but I am less sure about his implicit equation of trinitarianism with providentialism.

31. See Silvia Federici, *Caliban and the Witch: Women, the Body, and Primitive Accumulation*, 2nd ed. (New York: Autonomedia, 2014).

32. Karl Rahner, *The Trinity*, trans. Joseph Donceel (New York: Crossroad, 2005), 22; original italics suppressed.

33. Dietrich Bonhoeffer, *Letters and Papers from Prison*, ed. Eberhard Bethge, trans. Richard Fuller et al. (New York: Simon & Schuster, 1971), 329 and passim.

34. See here, for example, the Brazilian theologian Leonardo Boff's *Trinity and Society*, trans. Paul Burns (Maryknoll, NY: Orbis Books, 1988) and the Ghanaian theologian Mercy Oduyoye's *Hearing and Knowing: Theological Reflections on Christianity and Africa* (Eugene, OR: Wipf and Stock, 1986), chap. 11, "Trinity and Community."

35. See C. L. R. James, *The Black Jacobins: Toussaint L'Ouverture and the San Domingo Revolution* (New York: Vintage, 1989), 85–90.

36. Anthony Paul Smith, "Against Tradition to Liberate Tradition: Weaponized Apophaticism and Gnostic Refusal," *Angelaki: Journal of the Theoretical Humanities* 19, no. 2 (2014): 154.

37. Frantz Fanon, *The Wretched of the Earth*, trans. Richard Philcox (New York: Grove, 2004). Subsequent references are given parenthetically in the text.

38. See Wilderson, *Red, White, and Black*, 23, and James H. Cone, *God of the Oppressed*, 2nd ed. (Maryknoll, NY: Orbis Books, 1997), 221.

39. Though this was a frequent refrain in his classroom teaching during my time as his student, I have not been able to find a reference to the concept in Jennings's published writings. A general sense of what he meant by it can be found, however, in Theodore W. Jennings Jr., *The Insurrection of the Crucified: The "Gospel of Mark" as Theological Manifesto* (Chicago: Exploration Press, 2003).

Bibliography

Abbott, Mathew. *The Figure of This World: Agamben and the Question of Political Ontology*. Edinburgh: Edinburgh University Press, 2014.

Agamben, Giorgio. *Autoritratto nello studio*. Milan: Nottetempo, 2017.

Agamben, Giorgio. *The Coming Community*. Translated by Michael Hardt. Minneapolis: University of Minnesota Press, 1993.

Agamben, Giorgio. *The Highest Poverty: Monastic Rules and Form-of-Life*. Translated by Adam Kotsko. Stanford: Stanford University Press, 2013.

Agamben, Giorgio. *Homo Sacer: Sovereign Power and Bare Life*. Translated by Daniel Heller-Roazen. Stanford: Stanford University Press, 1998.

Agamben, Giorgio. *Karman: A Brief Treatise on Action, Guilt, and Gesture*. Translated by Adam Kotsko. Stanford: Stanford University Press, 2018.

Agamben, Giorgio. *The Kingdom and the Garden*. Translated by Adam Kotsko. Chicago: Seagull Press, 2020.

Agamben, Giorgio. *The Kingdom and the Glory: For a Theological Genealogy of Economy and Government*. Translated by Lorenzo Chiesa and Matteo Mandarini. Stanford: Stanford University Press, 2011.

Agamben, Giorgio. *The Mystery of Evil: Benedict XVI and the End of Days*. Translated by Adam Kotsko. Stanford: Stanford University Press, 2017.

Agamben, Giorgio. *Nudities*. Translated by David Kishik and Stefan Pedatella. Stanford: Stanford University Press, 2011.

Agamben, Giorgio. *The Sacrament of Language: An Archaeology of the Oath*. Translated by Adam Kotsko. Stanford: Stanford University Press, 2011.

Agamben, Giorgio. *Stanzas: Word and Phantasm in Western Culture*. Translated by Ronald L. Martinez. Minneapolis: University of Minnesota Press, 1993.

Agamben, Giorgio. *State of Exception*. Translated by Kevin Attell. Chicago: University of Chicago Press, 2005.

Agamben, Giorgio. *The Time That Remains: A Commentary on the Letter to the Romans*. Translated by Patricia Dailey. Stanford: Stanford University Press, 2005.

Agamben, Giorgio. *The Use of Bodies*. Translated by Adam Kotsko. Stanford: Stanford University Press, 2016.

Althusser, Louis. "Ideology and Ideological State Apparatuses." In *Lenin and Philosophy and Other Essays*. Translated by Ben Brewster. New York: Monthly Review Press, 1971.

Anidjar, Gil. *Blood: A Critique of Christianity*. New York: Columbia University Press, 2014.

Anselm of Canterbury. *L'œuvre de S. Anselme de Cantorbéry*. Vol. 2. Edited by Michel Corbin. Paris: Les Éditions du Cerf, 1986.

Anselm of Canterbury. *The Major Works*. Edited by Brian Davies and G. R. Evans. New York: Oxford University Press, 1998.

Armour, Ellen, and Susan St. Ville, eds. *Bodily Citations: Religion and Judith Butler*. New York: Columbia University Press, 2006.

Armstrong, Amaryah. "Of Flesh and Spirit: Race, Reproduction, and Sexual Difference in the Turn to Paul." *Journal of Cultural and Religious Theory* 16, no. 2 (2017): 126–141.

Armstrong, Amaryah. "The Spirit and the Subprime: Race, Risk, and Our Common Dispossession." *Anglican Theological Review* 98, no. 1 (2016): 51–69.

Asad, Talal. *Secular Translations: Nation-State, Modern Self, and Calculative Reason*. New York: Columbia University Press, 2018.

Assmann, Jan. *The Price of Monotheism*. Translated by Robert Savage. Stanford: Stanford University Press, 2010.

Augustine. *City of God*. Translated by Henry Bettenson. New York: Penguin, 1972.

Augustine. *Confessions*. 2nd ed. Translated by F. J. Sheed. Edited by Michael P. Foley. Indianapolis: Hackett, 2006.

Badiou, Alain. *Saint Paul: The Foundation of Universalism*. Translated by Ray Brassier. Stanford: Stanford University Press, 2003.

Barber, Daniel Colucciello. *On Diaspora: Christianity, Religion, and Secularity*. Eugene, OR: Cascade, 2011.

Barth, Karl. *Church Dogmatics*. Vol. I: *The Doctrine of the Word of God*. Pt. 1. Translated by G. W. Bromiley. Edited by G. W. Bromiley and T. F. Torrance. Edinburgh: T & T Clark, 1975.

Barth, Karl. *Church Dogmatics*. Vol. II: *The Doctrine of God*. Pt. 1. Translated by T. H. L. Parker, W. B. Johnston, Harold Knight, and J. L. M. Haire. Edited by G. W. Gromiley and T. F. Torrance. Edinburgh: T & T Clark, 1957.

Benjamin, Walter. *The Arcades Project*. Edited by Rolf Tiedemann. Translated by Howard Eiland and Kevin McLaughlin. Cambridge, MA: Belknap Press of Harvard University Press, 1982.

Bhabha, Homi. *The Location of Culture*. 2nd ed. New York: Routledge, 2004.

Boff, Leonardo. *Trinity and Society*. Translated by Paul Burns. Maryknoll, NY: Orbis Books, 1988.

Bonhoeffer, Dietrich. *The Cost of Discipleship*. Translated by R. H. Fuller. New York: Simon & Schuster, 1995.

Bonhoeffer, Dietrich. *Christ the Center*. Translated by Edwin Robertson. San Francisco: Harper, 1978.

Bonhoeffer, Dietrich. *Sanctorum Communio: A Theological Study of the Sociology of the Church*. Edited by Joachim von Soosten and Clifford Green. Translated by Reinhard Krauss and Nancy Lukens. Minneapolis: Fortress Press, 1998.

Bonhoeffer, Dietrich. *Letters and Papers from Prison*. Edited by Eberhard Bethge. Translated by Richard Fuller et al. New York: Simon & Schuster, 1971.

Boyarin, Daniel. *A Radical Jew: Paul and the Politics of Identity*. Berkeley: University of California Press, 1994.

Bube, Richard. "Man Come of Age: Bonhoeffer's Response to the God-of-the-Gaps." *Journal of the Evangelical Theological Society* 14, no. 4 (1971): 203–220.

Butler, Judith. *Bodies That Matter: On the Discursive Limits of "Sex."* New York: Routledge, 1993.

Butler, Judith. *Excitable Speech: A Politics of the Performative*. New York: Routledge, 1997.

Butler, Judith. *Gender Trouble: Feminism and the Subversion of Identity*. 10th anniversary edition. New York: Routledge, 1999.

Butler, Judith. *Giving an Account of Oneself*. New York: Fordham University Press, 2005.

Butler, Judith. *Precarious Life: The Powers of Mourning and Violence*. New York: Verso, 2006.

Butler, Judith. *The Psychic Life of Power*. Stanford: Stanford University Press, 1997.

Caputo, John D. *The Prayers and Tears of Jacques Derrida: Religion without Religion*. Indianapolis: Indiana University Press, 1997.

Carter, J. Kameron. *Race: A Theological Account*. New York: Oxford University Press, 2008.

Césaire, Aimé. *A Tempest: Based on Shakespeare's* The Tempest; *Adaptation for a Black Theatre*. Translated by Richard Miller. New York: Theater Communications Group, 2002.

Cone, James H. *The Cross and the Lynching Tree*. Maryknoll, NY: Orbis Books, 2011.

Cone, James H. *God of the Oppressed*. 2nd ed. Maryknoll, NY: Orbis Books, 1997.

Cunningham, David S. *These Three Are One: The Practice of Trinitarian Theology*. New York: Blackwell, 1998.

de Gruchy, John, ed. *Dietrich Bonhoeffer: Witness to Christ*. Minneapolis: Fortress Press, 1991.

Derrida, Jacques. *The Gift of Death (and "Literature in Secret")*. 2nd ed. Translated by David Wills. Chicago: University of Chicago Press, 2008.

Derrida, Jacques. "Hostipitality." In *Acts of Religion*. Edited by Gil Anidjar. New York: Routledge, 2002.

Derrida, Jacques, and Anne Dufourmantelle. *Of Hospitality: Anne Dufourmantelle Invites Jacques Derrida to Respond*. Translated by Rachel Bowlby. Stanford: Stanford University Press, 2000.

D'Isanto, Luca. "Bonhoeffer's Hermeneutical Model of Community." *Union Theological Seminary Quarterly Review* 46, no. 1 (1992): 135–148.

Fanon, Frantz. *Black Skin, White Masks*. Translated by Richard Philcox. New York: Grove, 2008.

Fanon, Frantz. *The Wretched of the Earth*. Translated by Richard Philcox. New York: Grove, 2004.

Federici, Silvia. *Caliban and the Witch: Women, the Body, and Primitive Accumulation*. 2nd ed. New York: Autonomedia, 2014.

Ferreira da Silva, Denise. "Before *Man*: Sylvia Wynter's Rewriting of the Modern Episteme." In *Sylvia Wynter: On Being Human as Praxis*, edited by Katherine McKittrick, 90–105. Durham, NC: Duke University Press, 2015.

Fiel, Ernst. *The Theology of Dietrich Bonhoeffer*. Translated by Martin Rumscheit. Philadelphia: Fortress Press, 1985.

Gifford, Paul. *Ghana's New Christianity: Pentecostalism in a Globalizing African Economy*. Bloomington: Indiana University Press, 2004.

Goldenberg, David M. *The Curse of Ham: Race and Slavery in Early Judaism, Christianity, and Islam*. Princeton, NJ: Princeton University Press, 2005.

Goodchild, Philip. *Theology of Money*. Durham, NC: Duke University Press, 2007.

Hartman, Saidiya. *Scenes of Subjection: Terror, Slavery, and Self-Making in Nineteenth-Century America*. New York: Oxford University Press, 1997.

Harvey, Barry. "The Body Politic of Christ: Theology, Social Analysis, and Bonhoeffer's Arcane Discipline." *Modern Theology* 13, no. 3 (1997): 319–346.

Hegel, G. W. F. *Philosophy of Mind*. Translated by by William Wallace and A. V. Miller. Oxford: Clarendon, 1971.

Henry, Michel. *I Am the Truth: Toward a Philosophy of Christianity*. Translated by Susan Emanuel. Stanford: Stanford University Press, 2002.

Hickman, Jared. *Black Prometheus: Race and Radicalism in the Age of Atlantic Slavery*. New York: Oxford University Press, 2017.

James, C. L. R. *The Black Jacobins: Toussaint L'Ouverture and the San Domingo Revolution*. New York: Vintage, 1989.

Jenkins, Philip. *The Next Christendom: The Coming of Global Christianity*. 2nd ed. New York: Oxford University Press, 2009.

Jennings, Theodore W., Jr. *The Insurrection of the Crucified: The "Gospel of Mark" as Theological Manifesto*. Chicago: Exploration Press, 2003.

Jennings, Theodore W., Jr. *Introduction to Theology: An Invitation to Reflection upon the Christian Mythos*. Philadelphia: Fortress, 1976.

Jennings, Theodore W., Jr. *Outlaw Justice: The Messianic Politics of Paul*. Stanford: Stanford University Press, 2013.

Jennings, Theodore W., Jr. *Reading Derrida / Thinking Paul*. Stanford: Stanford University Press, 2006.

Johnson, Sylvester. *The Myth of Ham in Nineteenth-Century American Christianity: Race, Heathens, and the People of God*. New York: Palgrave Macmillan, 2004.

Kaplan, M. Lindsay. *Figuring Racism in Medieval Christianity*. New York: Oxford University Press, 2019.

Keller, Catherine. *The Face of the Deep: A Theology of Becoming*. New York: Routledge, 2003.

Kermani, Navid. *God Is Beautiful: The Aesthetic Experience of the Qur'an*. Translated by Tony Crawford. New York: Polity, 2018.

Kim, Dorothy. "Introduction to Literature Compass Special Cluster: Critical Race and the Middle Ages." *Literature Compass* 16, nos. 9–10 (2019): 1–16.

King, Karen L. *What Is Gnosticism?* Cambridge, MA: Belknap Press of Harvard University Press, 2003.

Kotsko, Adam. *Agamben's Philosophical Trajectory*. Edinburgh: Edinburgh University Press, 2020.

Kotsko, Adam. "The Christian Experience Continues: On Žižek's Work since *The Parallax View*." *International Journal of Žižek Studies* 4, no. 4 (2010): 1–9.

Kotsko, Adam. "Gift and *Communio*: The Holy Spirit in Augustine's *De Trinitate*." *Scottish Journal of Theology* 64, no. 1 (2011): 1–12.

Kotsko, Adam. *Neoliberalism's Demons: On the Political Theology of Late Capital*. Stanford: Stanford University Press, 2018.

Kotsko, Adam. "Politics and Perversion: Situating Žižek's Paul," *Journal for Cultural and Religious Theory* 9, no. 2 (2008): 43–52.

Kotsko, Adam. *Politics of Redemption: The Social Logic of Salvation*. New York: T & T Clark, 2010.

Kotsko, Adam, *The Prince of This World*. Stanford: Stanford University Press, 2016.

Kotsko, Adam. "The Sermon on Mount Moriah: Faith and the Secret in The Gift of Death." *Heythrop Journal* 49, no. 1 (2008): 44–61.

Kotsko, Adam. *Žižek and Theology*. New York: Continuum/T & T Clark, 2008.

Kuhn, Thomas. *The Structure of Scientific Revolutions*. 4th ed. Chicago: University of Chicago Press, 2012.

LaCugna, Catherine Mowry. *God for Us: Trinity and Christian Life*. New York: Harper Collins, 1973.

Marion, Jean-Luc. *God without Being: Hors-Texte*. Translated by Thomas A. Carlson. Chicago: University of Chicago Press, 1995.

Mbembe, Achille. *Critique of Black Reason*. Translated by Laurent Dubois. Durham, NC: Duke University Press, 2017.

Mechthild of Magdeburg. *The Flowing Light of the Godhead*. Translated by Frank Tobin. Mahwah, NJ: Paulist Press, 1998.

Nancy, Jean-Luc. *Adoration: The Deconstruction of Christianity II*. Translated by John McKeane. New York: Fordham University Press, 2012.

Nancy, Jean-Luc. *Dis-Enclosure: The Deconstruction of Christianity*. Translated by Bettina Bergo, Gabriel Malenfant, and Michael B. Smith. New York: Fordham University Press, 2008.

Oduyoye, Mercy. *Hearing and Knowing: Theological Reflections on Christianity and Africa*. Eugene, OR: Wipf and Stock, 1986.

O'Neill, Kevin Lewis. *City of God: Christian Citizenship in Postwar Guatemala*. Berkeley: University of California Press, 2010.

Patterson, Orlando. *Slavery and Social Death: A Comparative Study*. Cambridge, MA: Harvard University Press, 1982.

Peterson, Erik. "Monotheism as a Political Problem." In *Theological Tractates*, edited and translated by Michael J. Hollerich. Stanford: Stanford University Press, 2011.

Plato. *Republic*. Translated by Joe Sachs. Newburyport, MA: Focus Publishing, 2007.

Polanyi, Karl. *The Great Transformation: The Political and Economic Origins of Our Time*. Boston: Beacon, 2001.

Potter, David. *Constantine the Emperor*. New York: Oxford University Press, 2013.

Pseudo-Dionysius. *The Complete Works*. Translated by Colm Luibheid. Edited by Paul Rorem. New York: Paulist, 1987.

The Qur'an. Translated by M. A. S. Abdel Haleem. New York: Oxford University Press, 2016.

Radbertus of Corbie. "The Lord's Body and Blood." In *Early Medieval Theology* (The Library of Christian Classics), edited by George E. McCracken. Philadelphia: Westminster, 1957.

Rahner, Karl. *The Trinity*. Translated by Joseph Donceel. New York: Crossroad, 2005.

Rose, Marika. "For Our Sins." In *Exploring Complicity: Concepts, Cases and Critique*. Edited by Afxentis Afxentiou, Robin Dunford, and Michael Neu. London: Rowman and Littlefield, 2017.

Rose, Marika. *A Theology of Failure: Žižek against Christian Innocence*. New York: Fordham University Press, 2019.

Sanneh, Lamin. *Translating the Message: The Missionary Impact on Culture*. 2nd ed. Maryknoll, NY: Orbis Books, 2009.

Schleiermacher, Friedrich. *The Christian Faith*. Edited by H. R. Mackintosh and J. S. Stewart. Edinburgh: T & T Clark, 1999.

Schmitt, Carl. *The Nomos of the Earth in the International Law of the Jus Publicum Europaeum*. Translated and edited by G. L. Ulmen. New York: Telos, 2003.

Schmitt, Carl. *Political Theology: Four Chapters on the Concept of Sovereignty*. Translated by George Schwab. Chicago: University of Chicago Press, 2005.

Sexton, Jared. *Black Men, Black Feminism: Lucifer's Nocturne*. New York: Palgrave Macmillan, 2018.

Shakespeare, William. *The Tempest: Second Norton Critical Edition*. Edited by Peter Hulme and William H. Sherman. New York: Norton, 2019.

Smith, Anthony Paul. "Against Tradition to Liberate Tradition: Weaponized Apophaticism and Gnostic Refusal." *Angelaki: Journal of the Theoretical Humanities* 19, no. 2 (2014): 145–159.

Spillers, Hortense. *Black, White, and in Color: Essays on American Literature and Culture*. Chicago: University of Chicago Press, 2003.

Surin, Kenneth. "*Contemptus Mundi* and the Disenchantment of the World: Bonhoeffer's 'Discipline of the Secret' and Adorno's 'Strategy of Hibernation.'" *Journal of the American Academy of Religion* 53, no. 3 (1985): 383–410.

Taubes, Jacob. *From Cult to Culture: Fragments toward a Critique of Historical Reason*. Edited by Charlotte Elisheva Fonrobert and Amir Engel. Stanford: Stanford University Press, 2010.

Taubes, Jacob. *Occidental Eschatology*. Translated by David Ratmoko. Stanford: Stanford University Press 2009.

Taubes, Jacob. *The Political Theology of Paul*. Edited by Aleia Assmann and Jan Assmann. Translated by Dana Hollander. Stanford: Stanford University Press, 2004.

Taubes, Jacob. *To Carl Schmitt: Letters and Reflections*. Translated by Keith Tribe. New York: Columbia University Press, 2010.

Tonstad, Linn Marie. *God and Difference: The Trinity, Sexuality, and the Transformation of Finitude*. New York: Routledge, 2016.

Trachtenberg, Joshua. *The Devil and the Jews: The Medieval Conception of the Jew and Its Relation to Modern Anti-Semitism*. Philadelphia: Jewish Publication Society, 1983.

Weheliye, Alexander G. *Habeas Viscus: Racializing Assemblages, Biopolitics, and Black Feminist Theories of the Human*. Durham, NC: Duke University Press, 2014.

Wilderson, Frank B., III. *Red, White, and Black: Cinema and the Structure of U.S. Antagonisms*. Durham, NC: Duke University Press, 2010.

Wynter, Sylvia. "1492: A New World View." In *Race, Discourse, and the Origin of the Americas: A New World View*, edited by Vera Lawrence Hyatt and Rex Nettleford, 5–57. Washington, DC: Smithsonian Institution Press, 1995.

Wynter, Sylvia. "Unsettling the Coloniality of Being/Power/Truth/Freedom: Toward the Human, After Man, Its Overrepresentation—An Argument." *CR: The New Centennial Review* 3, no. 3 (2003): 257–337.

Žižek, Slavoj. *The Indivisible Remainder: An Essay on Schelling and Related Matters*. New York: Verso, 1996.

Žižek, Slavoj. *The Parallax View*. Cambridge, MA: MIT Press, 2006.

Žižek, Slavoj. *The Puppet and the Dwarf: The Perverse Core of Christianity*. Cambridge, MA: MIT Press, 2003.

Žižek, Slavoj, and John Milbank. *The Monstrosity of Christ: Paradox or Dialectic?* Edited by Creston Davis. Cambridge, MA: MIT Press, 2009.

Index

Adam Kotsko teaches in the Shimer Great Books School at North Central College. His most recent books are *Agamben's Philosophical Trajectory* and *Neoliberalism's Demons: On the Political Theology of Late Capital.*

Perspectives in Continental Philosophy
John D. Caputo, series editor

Recent titles:

Kirill Chepurin and Alex Dubilet, eds., *Nothing Absolute: German Idealism and the Question of Political Theology.*

John D. Caputo, *In Search of Radical Theology: Expositions, Explorations, Exhortations.*

Galen A. Johnson, Mauro Carbone, and Emmanuel de Saint Aubert, *Merleau-Ponty's Poetics: Figurations of Literature and Philosophy.*

Ole Jakob Løland, *Pauline Ugliness: Jacob Taubes and the Turn to Paul.*

Marika Rose, *A Theology of Failure: Žižek against Christian Innocence.*

Marc Crépon, *Murderous Consent: On the Accommodation of Violent Death.* Translated by Michael Loriaux and Jacob Levi, Foreword by James Martel.

Emmanuel Falque, *The Guide to Gethsemane: Anxiety, Suffering, and Death.* Translated by George Hughes.

Emmanuel Alloa, *Resistance of the Sensible World: An Introduction to Merleau-Ponty.* Translated by Jane Marie Todd. Foreword by Renaud Barbaras.

Françoise Dastur, *Questions of Phenomenology: Language, Alterity, Temporality, Finitude.* Translated by Robert Vallier.

Jean-Luc Marion, *Believing in Order to See: On the Rationality of Revelation and the Irrationality of Some Believers.* Translated by Christina M. Gschwandtner.

Adam Y. Wells, ed., *Phenomenologies of Scripture.*

An Yountae, *The Decolonial Abyss: Mysticism and Cosmopolitics from the Ruins.*

Jean Wahl, *Transcendence and the Concrete: Selected Writings.* Edited and with an Introduction by Alan D. Schrift and Ian Alexander Moore.

Colby Dickinson, *Words Fail: Theology, Poetry, and the Challenge of Representation.*

Emmanuel Falque, *The Wedding Feast of the Lamb: Eros, the Body, and the Eucharist.* Translated by George Hughes.

Emmanuel Falque, *Crossing the Rubicon: The Borderlands of Philosophy and Theology.* Translated by Reuben Shank. Introduction by Matthew Farley.

Colby Dickinson and Stéphane Symons (eds.), *Walter Benjamin and Theology.*

Don Ihde, *Husserl's Missing Technologies.*

William S. Allen, *Aesthetics of Negativity: Blanchot, Adorno, and Autonomy.*

Jeremy Biles and Kent L. Brintnall, eds., *Georges Bataille and the Study of Religion.*

Tarek R. Dika and W. Chris Hackett, *Quiet Powers of the Possible: Interviews in Contemporary French Phenomenology.* Foreword by Richard Kearney.

Richard Kearney and Brian Treanor, eds., *Carnal Hermeneutics.*

A complete list of titles is available at http://fordhampress.com.